MENU COMMANDS AND KEYBOAR[D]

COMMANDS	KEYBOARD SHORTCUTS	COMMANDS	KEYBOARD SHORTCUTS		
PC DESKTOP (cont.)		**PC DESKTOP** (cont.)			
Controls		Search		Move	
Page layout		Find text in all fields		Telecommunications	
Header/Footer		find Text in sort field		Modem Telecom-	
Tab ruler Edit		Goto record		munications	
Save setup		Controls		File	
Tab ruler display		Page layout		Save	
Overtype mode		Configure autodial		Load	F4
Control char display		Autodial		Edit	
Headlines		Save setup		Edit entry	F6
Expand Current		Window		Create new entry	
Expand All		Change colors		Remove entry	
Show level		†Video size		Actions	
Collapse Current		Switch Active		Dial	F7
Main headline only		Move		Manual	F8
Promote		Resize		Hangup phone	
Demote		Zoom		Setup	
Windows		Appointment Scheduler		Modem setup	
Change colors		File		†Full online screen	
†Video size		Load		Window	
Switch Active		Save		Change colors	
Move		Print		†Video size	
Resize		Autosave		Switch Active	
Zoom		Exit Without Saving		Move	
Databases		Appointment		†Send a Fax	
File		Make new appointment		Actions	
Load form		Delete appointment		Add a new Entry	
Print		Edit appointment		Edit the current Entry	
†Transfer		Find appointment	F5	Delete the current	
†Append		Next appointment	F4	Entry	
†Browse		Find free time	F7	Send files to the	
Edit		Show time usage	F8	selected Entry	
Add new record	F8	Attach note	F6	Check FAX Log	
Delete record		To-Do		Configure	
Undelete records		New to-do entry		FAX Drive	
Pack database		Delete to-do entry		Page Length	
Hide current record		Attach note		Cover Page	
seLect all records		Controls		Time Format	
Edit fields		Appointment settings		Sent From	
Sort database		Holiday settings		Window	
select Records		Delete old entries		Change Colors	
		Wide display		Video size	
		Window		Switch Active	
Version 5.5 only		Change colors		Move	
Version 6.0 only		†Video size		Resize	
		Switch Active		Zoom	

MASTERING
PC TOOLS DELUXE 6

MASTERING
PC TOOLS™ DELUXE 6
Second Edition

PETER DYSON

SYBEX® San Francisco ■ Paris ■ Düsseldorf ■ Soest

Acquisitions Editor: Dianne King
Developmental Editor: Eric Stone
Copy Editor: Kathleen D. Lattinville
Technical Editor: Maryann Brown
Production Editor: Carolina Montilla
Word Processor: Chris Mockel
Layout and Paste-up: Eleanor Ramos
Technical Art: Delia Brown
Screen Graphics: Cuong Le
Typesetter: Winnie Kelly
Proofreader: R. M. Holmes
Indexer: Ted Laux
Cover Designer: Thomas Ingalls + Associates
Cover Photographer: David Bishop

Library of Congress Card Number: 90-70369
ISBN: 0-89588-700-2
Manufactured in the United States of America
10 9 8 7 6 5 4 3 2

To my mother and father

Give us the tools, and we will finish the job

Sir Winston Churchill

ACKNOWLEDGMENTS

Once again I have enjoyed my part in writing this book, but as always, many people have worked on the project, providing technical assistance, advice, and many other services.

I want to thank everyone at SYBEX, particularly Dianne King, acquisitions editor, for her constant encouragement and good spirits. Thanks to editors Vince Leone and Deborah Craig for doing an excellent job on the manuscript. Thanks to technical editor Maryann Brown, word processors Chris Mockel and Deborah Maizels, typesetter Elizabeth Newman, artist Suzanne Albertson, proofreader Lisa Jaffe, and indexer Nancy A. Guenther.

At Central Point Software, Inc. I want to thank Robin Smith and Karen Woodrum of Technical Support for quickly and patiently answering my endless questions.

On a more personal note, I want to thank my wife Nancy for all her encouragement, patience, and support as I worked on this manuscript; fellow Sacramento-based SYBEX author Gene Weisskopf for general advice and good humor; Tom Charlesworth for providing information on data compression techniques; Bob Jungbluth for information on modems and data communications, and Russell McFall for the temporary use of his partition table.

Thanks to Ellen Pfeifer of Central Point Software for providing beta software and documentation for PC Tools Version 6.0, and thanks to Suzanne Seigneur of Intel for providing an Intel Connection CoProcessor PC fax card.

Thanks to the SYBEX people who worked on the second edition: developmental editor Eric Stone; copy editor Kathleen Lattinville; technical editor Maryann Brown; word processor Chris Mockel; typesetter Winnie Kelly; production editor Carolina Montilla; proofreader Rhonda Holmes; artist Eleanor Ramos; and indexer Ted Laux.

CONTENTS AT A GLANCE

TABLE OF CONTENTS

FOREWORD

No matter how you tally the votes—in the press or on the best-seller lists—PC Tools Deluxe has emerged as the clear choice for PC utility software. In fact, no PC is complete without a copy of this timesaving productivity tool.

Now in its sixth major release, PC Tools gives you the five most popular utilities in one integrated package:

- Advanced data recovery

- Fast, reliable hard-disk backup

- A DOS shell with built-in disk and file manager

- A comprehensive desktop organizer

- Programs to enhance your system's performance

When Peter Dyson's *Mastering PC Tools Deluxe* first came to our attention, we were pleased to see a book we could recommend as a companion reference to our product. It is intuitively organized and clearly written, and it contains helpful examples and summary tables that help you get the most from our software.

Mastering PC Tools Deluxe 6 incorporates the same attention to detail as the previous edition. What's more, it helps you get the most from the more than 70 new features and improvements in Version 6. May it speed you along to more productive computing.

Corey Smith
President
Central Point Software, Inc.

INTRODUCTION

There are many reasons for using the programs in PC Tools: They present many essential capabilities in a compact, cost-effective package. They also present alternatives that are easier to use than the equivalent DOS commands, if indeed there are equivalents.

The PC Tools package covers four major areas:

- Preventing and recovering from accidents
- Adding to the capabilities of DOS
- Providing a powerful hard-disk backup capability
- Providing a Desktop Manager containing all the functions you need for efficient management

PREVENTING AND RECOVERING FROM ACCIDENTS

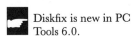 Diskfix is new in PC Tools 6.0.

Problems with hard and floppy disks are both common and avoidable. With PC Shell's Verify Disk and the Compress Surface Scan, you can check your disks for potential problems, and with Diskfix you can fix them before they cost you any data.

Even if your disks are in top condition, you can still lose data by accidentally erasing files or directories that you need. DOS itself does not offer any solution to this problem, but PC Tools does. The Undelete Files command in PC Shell can recover files and directories, including fragmented files. In some cases, you can recover parts of files that have been overwritten by others. You can even use Rebuild to restore the entire contents of your hard disk if you reformat it by mistake.

ADDING TO THE CAPABILITIES OF DOS

All the disk and file management capabilities in PC Shell simplify hard-disk organization and maintenance. You can accomplish tasks previously done from DOS without having to memorize the various forms of numerous DOS commands.

HARD-DISK BACKUP

With PC Backup, you can easily make fast floppy-disk or tape backups of your hard disk. PC Backup also handles the restore process if you ever need to reload your backup disks. The high-speed DMA cuts backup time and minimizes the number of floppy disks needed to contain the backup.

THE DESKTOP MANAGER

The Desktop Manager contains Outlines, Notepads, a Macro Editor, a Communications package with an Autodialer and fax card support, four different calculators, a database system, and an Appointment Scheduler to keep you organized.

WHAT'S NEW IN PC TOOLS VERSION 6.0

Version 6.0 of PC Tools, released in the spring of 1990, adds a considerable number of new features and supported hardware.

- Diskfix is a powerful disk and file repair and maintenance program. It can automatically find and fix many common and uncommon disk problems.

- PC Shell and PC Backup allow you to select your user level from advanced, intermediate, and beginner, so you can tailor your work environment to your own needs.

- PC Backup now supports QIC 40/80 and Irwin tape cartridge backup.

- PC Shell now has fast access to the DOS command line for those users that need it.

- Over 20 new File Viewers have been added to PC Shell so that you can examine files from over 30 different applications programs. File Viewers allow you to look at the file in its native format before you launch the applications program.

- PC Shell also supports an integrated version of LapLink so you can share files between your laptop computer and your regular computer.

- PC-Cache adds write as well as read caching.

- Telecommunications now supports a fax card if you have one in your computer or available to you on your network. Now you can send a fax without leaving your computer.

- The Undelete utility is available from the DOS command line as well as from inside PC Shell.

- A new Programmer's (hex) calculator, based on the Hewlett-Packard HP 16C, has been added.

- New commands, Append and Transfer, have been added to the Database, and now you can look at the data in your database in Browse mode as well as Edit mode.

- Compress allows even more control over where you put your files when unfragmenting your hard disk.

HARDWARE AND SOFTWARE REQUIREMENTS FOR PC TOOLS

PC Tools Deluxe is designed to work with all the IBM PCs, including the PC/XT, PC/AT, all models of the PS/2, and most of the PC-compatible computers. You should have at least 512K of memory (for some of the memory-resident applications, 640K works better) and one or two floppy disks. You should run PC Tools from a hard disk.

PC Tools, with its pull-down menus and dialog boxes, works best with a mouse. If you have a Microsoft mouse, you should be using version 6.14 or higher of the mouse driver. If you have a Dexxa mouse, check that you have version 3.4 or higher of the device driver.

To use the mouse, install its device driver into your CONFIG.SYS file so that the device driver is loaded in the proper sequence each time your computer boots up. Check your mouse documentation for details.

PC Tools runs on DOS 3.0 or higher. To take full advantage of all the features of PC Tools, however, you should use DOS 3.2 or higher. Once installed, PC Tools works with disks formatted with any DOS release.

The figures in this book were all captured in monochrome to provide the clearest illustrations. The default screen positions and sizes were used in most cases. Because you can configure PC Tools in many different ways, do not be concerned about minor differences between the figures in this book and what you see on your computer screen.

HOW TO USE THIS BOOK

This book is organized into 12 chapters, containing both reference and tutorial information. Each chapter describes particular PC Tools and provides examples of how to use them best. At the end of each chapter, a short summary briefly restates the PC Tools functions just covered. Several appendices provide additional information or background to PC Tools.

Chapter 1, "Installing and Using PC Tools Deluxe," introduces PC Tools, describing how you should install them on your hard disk, and introducing ways to use them with the keyboard and the mouse.

Chapter 2, "An Introduction to Disk and Directory Structure," provides a detailed look at disks and their internal organization, and describes how to use PC Shell to explore your disks.

Chapter 3, "Backing Up Your Hard Disk," explains when and how you should back up the files on your hard disk, and introduces PC Backup.

Chapter 4, "Unerasing Files and Data Recovery," explains how to rescue files and directories that you have deleted by mistake, and shows how to recover the contents of your hard disk after it has been accidentally reformatted with the DOS FORMAT command. The disk diagnosis and repair program, Diskfix, is also described here.

Chapter 5, "Organizing Your Hard Disk with PC Shell," describes how you can use PC Shell to your best advantage when organizing your hard disk.

Chapter 6, "Viewing Your System and Improving Performance," looks behind the scenes of your computer, and maps out how you can improve your system's performance.

Chapter 7, "Using the Desktop Manager with Words and Ideas," describes how to use Notepads, Outlines, the Clipboard, and the Macro Editor.

Chapter 8, "Figuring with the Four Calculators," explains the Algebraic calculator, the Financial calculator, the Programmer's (hex) calculator, and the Scientific calculator.

Chapter 9, "Using the Desktop Manager for Appointments," describes how to use the Appointment Scheduler, the Calendar, and the To-Do List to organize your day.

Chapter 10, "Using the Built-In Database," explains how to use the Desktop database and shows you how to design and build your own database from scratch.

Chapter 11, "Telecommunications Made Easy," describes how to use your modem to transfer files from one computer to another. This chapter also shows you how to automate your computer-to-computer communications, and describes how to get the most out of your fax card.

Chapter 12, "Tailoring PC Tools to Your Needs," describes how to set up and save PC Shell configuration information, and how to use LapLink to communicate with your laptop computer.

Appendix A, "Complete Command Reference," contains a brief description of each program, including the program's command syntax and the use of all the available parameters. Use this appendix when you need to remind yourself of how to use the command-line parameters for PC Tools.

Appendix B, "File Types and Computer Numbering Schemes," explains the differences between ASCII and binary files, and describes the different numbering schemes used throughout the book.

Appendix C, "A Note on Data Communications," describes computer-to-computer communications in greater depth, particularly the XMODEM protocol, and provides more background on facsimile machines.

Appendix D, "Memory-Resident Programs," provides more detail on the inner workings of these programs, and describes how to solve conflicts between them.

Although this book is designed to be read from cover to cover, you can begin with a chapter that deals with a particular PC Tool you are working with. In other words, each chapter is fairly self-contained. If you need a refresher course on concepts of disk and file systems, read Chapter 2 before moving on to the other chapters.

MENU COMMANDS IN THE TEXT

When a PC Tools command is given in the text of this book, it is usually spelled out just as it appears on the screen. It is not shown in boldface type. If there is a keystroke shortcut for the command, the shortcut is shown in parentheses immediately after the command. For example, you might see the sentence "select Start Restore (F6) from the Restore pull-down menu."

THE MARGIN NOTES

As you read through this book, you will come across margin notes that are prefaced with a symbol. There are three types of notes:

This symbol indicates a general note about the topic under discussion. I often use it to refer you to other chapters for more information.

This symbol denotes tips or tricks that you may find useful when running PC Tools. They might be shortcuts that I have discovered or just important techniques that need to be emphasized.

Pay close attention when you see this symbol in the margin. It alerts you to potential problems and often gives you methods for avoiding these problems.

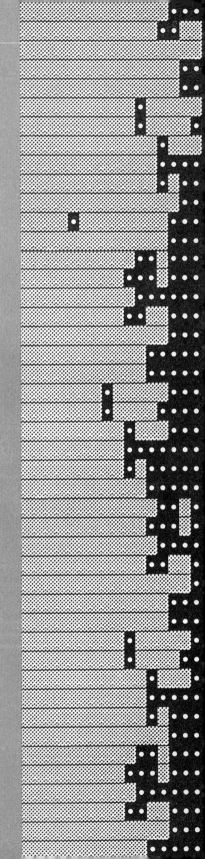

1

Installing
and Using PC
Tools Deluxe

In this chapter, I describe how to install PC Tools onto your hard disk. But first, you should make floppy-disk backup copies of the distribution disks. This protects you in case you accidentally damage the original disks. You will learn two ways of running PC Tools: from the DOS command prompt, and in the full-screen interactive mode using the pull-down menus.

THE DISTRIBUTION PACKAGE

PC Tools 5.5 consists of only four 5¼″ floppy disks or two 3½″ floppy disks.

The PC Tools 6.0 distribution package consists of six 5¼″ floppy disks or three 3½″ floppy disks, and three manuals: *Data Recovery DOS Shell, Hard Disk Backup,* and *Desktop Manager.*

Check to see if there is a README.TXT file on disk 1. Since the README.TXT file contains the latest information about the package—information that may not be in the program manual—you should read it before installing the package. To do this, place disk 1 in drive A, and type

   DIR A:

The DIR command lists all the files on the disk on your computer screen, and you should see one called README.TXT. You can display the contents of the file on your computer screen by typing

   TYPE A:README.TXT

or you can send the file to your printer by typing

   PRINT A:README.TXT

PC TOOLS IN BRIEF

Diskfix, LapLink, Park, and the command line Undelete are new in PC Tools 6.0.

Here is a short description of each of the PC Tools programs. Appendix A gives a complete list of all options for the programs.

- Compress is a disk optimization program that unfragments and reorders the files on your hard disk.

- Diskfix (Version 6.0 only) is a versatile hard disk diagnostic and repair program that can fix disk problems automatically.

- LapLink (Version 6.0 only) connects two computers together for downloading files.

- MI is a memory mapping program run from DOS.

- Mirror saves a copy of the system area of your hard disk—the file allocation table (FAT), the root directory, and the boot record—as a protection against an accidental file deletion or hard-disk reformat.

- Park (Version 6.0 only) is a stand-alone hard-disk head-parking program.

- PC Backup facilitates backing up your hard disk. You can also use it to reload your backup files.

- PC-Cache speeds up hard- and floppy-disk accesses by keeping the most frequently used information in memory.

- PC Desktop is the Desktop Manager containing the Appointment Scheduler, Database, Notepads, Clipboard, Telecommunications, Autodialer, four calculators, the Outlines, and a Macro Editor.

- PC Format is a fast and safe alternative to the DOS FORMAT command.

- PC Secure encrypts, compresses, and hides confidential files on your disk.

- PC Shell contains all the commands you need to manage your computer system easily and effectively.

- Rebuild allows you to recover files and directories on your hard disk after it has been accidentally reformatted with the DOS FORMAT command.

- Undelete (Version 6.0 only) is a DOS command line version of the PC Shell Undelete Files utility.

MAKING FLOPPY-DISK BACKUPS

You should back up any software package immediately after taking it out of the box. Do this even if you plan to install the software on your hard disk. If the original disks are lost, damaged, or destroyed, your backup copy ensures that you can still use the software.

The easiest way to make a floppy-disk copy of the distribution disks is to use the DOS command DISKCOPY. Place the first distribution disk in drive A and a formatted blank disk in drive B, type

    DISKCOPY *.* B:

at the prompt, and press Enter. When the first copy is complete, you will be asked if you want to copy another disk. Answer yes and repeat this procedure with each of the other distribution disks in the package. Label each disk to match the original distribution disk. Store the original disks in a safe place and from now on work with the copies rather than the originals.

Now that you have backed up the original distribution disks, you are ready to install the package on your hard disk.

INSTALLING PC TOOLS ON YOUR HARD DISK

If you bought PC Tools to help you recover an erased file or directory, do not install the programs on your hard disk yet. Instead, use PC Tools from your floppy-disk drive to recover the file, and then continue with this installation procedure. If you install PC Tools without first recovering the file, the installation program may overwrite the area of the disk occupied by the erased file, making its recovery impossible. Chapter 4 describes in detail what actually happens when you delete a file, and it explains how to perform file recovery.

INSTALLING PC TOOLS WITH PC SETUP

Use the installation program PC Setup to install PC Tools. Many files have been compressed to save space and will not run as they are. PC Setup decompresses the files so that they can run properly.

PC Tools includes an installation program, PC Setup, that guides you through the installation procedure step by step, explaining the choices available at each stage. To start PC Setup, insert disk 1 into drive A and type

    PCSETUP

Figure 1.1 shows the opening PC Setup screen.

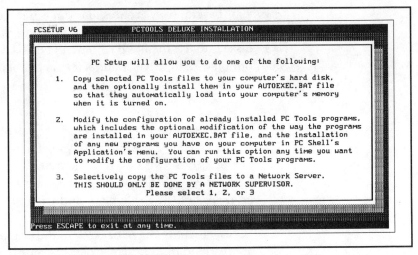

```
┌──────────────────────────────────────────────────────────────┐
│ PCSETUP V6          PCTOOLS DELUXE INSTALLATION                │
│                                                                │
│  ┌──────────────────────────────────────────────────────────┐ │
│  │          PC Setup will allow you to do one of the following: │
│  │                                                            │ │
│  │  1.  Copy selected PC Tools files to your computer's hard disk,│
│  │      and then optionally install them in your AUTOEXEC.BAT file│
│  │      so that they automatically load into your computer's memory│
│  │      when it is turned on.                                 │ │
│  │                                                            │ │
│  │  2.  Modify the configuration of already installed PC Tools programs,│
│  │      which includes the optional modification of the way the programs│
│  │      are installed in your AUTOEXEC.BAT file, and the installation│
│  │      of any new programs you have on your computer in PC Shell's│
│  │      Application's menu.  You can run this option any time you want│
│  │      to modify the configuration of your PC Tools programs.│ │
│  │                                                            │ │
│  │  3.  Selectively copy the PC Tools files to a Network Server.│
│  │      THIS SHOULD ONLY BE DONE BY A NETWORK SUPERVISOR.     │ │
│  │            Please select 1, 2, or 3                        │ │
│  └──────────────────────────────────────────────────────────┘ │
│                                                                │
│ Press ESCAPE to exit at any time.                             │
└──────────────────────────────────────────────────────────────┘
```

Figure 1.1: The opening PC Setup screen

PC Setup allows you to make a choice in your installation, presenting the following three options:

- You can copy certain PC Tools files onto your hard disk, and choose selected programs to be installed as memory-resident programs.

- You can alter an existing installation, making appropriate changes to AUTOEXEC.BAT.

- You can copy certain PC Tools files onto a network server hard disk.

See Chapter 12 for details on installing your programs into PC Shell's application list.

PC Setup for PC Tools 5.5 lists only three main selections: Data Recovery and DOS Utilities, Hard Disk BACKUP and RESTORE, and DESKTOP Organizer.

Choose the first option to install PC Tools on the hard disk and to make selected programs available as memory-resident programs.

The second screen in the PC Tools 6.0 PC Setup serves as a warning not to continue with the installation if you want to recover an erased file. Press Escape to exit, Q to quit, or C to continue with the installation.

After you confirm the type of monitor you have, the next screen asks you to select which of the four major parts of the PC Tools package you want to install on your hard disk. The choices are DOS Shell, Data Recovery Utilities, Hard Disk BACKUP and RESTORE, and DESKTOP Organizer.

If you select DOS Shell, PC Setup scans your disk for popular applications programs like WordStar, WordPerfect, Microsoft Word, Excel, and dBASE. When it finds any such applications, it installs them into PC Shell's Applications menu. (PC Shell is a part of the DOS Shell choice.) Choose all four options, and press C to continue the installation.

The next screen, shown in Figure 1.2, asks in which directory you want to place all the PC Tools programs and data files. This book uses the example directory \PCTOOLS, so go ahead and use this name for the directory.

Next, you specify which disk contains your AUOTEXEC.BAT file. This is usually drive C.

The next few screens ask you how you want to configure the various PC Tools programs on your computer. This is how you customize the programs for your own way of working. If you change your mind in the future, just run PC Setup again and change your selections.

PC Setup will install many of the PC Tools options and parameters into your AUTOEXEC.BAT file for you, or, if you prefer, you can make the changes to AUTOEXEC.BAT yourself.

The next screen asks if you want PC Setup to make these configuration changes for you, or if you just want it to copy the files from the distribution disks onto your hard disk. Select C to have PC Setup copy the files

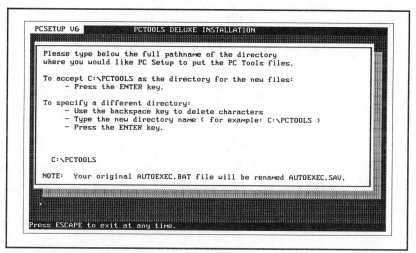

Figure 1.2: PC Setup asks for a directory name

and make the AUTOEXEC.BAT configuration changes, or choose O to copy the files without any changes to AUTOEXEC.BAT.

The next screen asks if you wish to install PC Shell in memory-resident mode or as a shell that you will see each time you start up your computer. Press I to install PC Shell as memory-resident or press S to install it as a shell. Choose C to continue without change.

PC Setup then asks if you want to install the computer-to-laptop link program, LapLink, as a memory-resident program. If you have a laptop computer and plan to download a lot of files, select I to install LapLink memory-resident or C to continue without change.

Next, you are asked if you want to install a small memory-resident program to protect your hard disk against accidental file erasure and reformatting. You should choose I to install the program, as this is a very useful safety feature.

You are then asked if you want PC-Cache or Desktop installed as memory-resident programs. Install both of them and press C to continue.

If you have a modem or a fax card, you can use Desktop's Tele-communications program to upload or download files and to send or receive faxes. If you want to use your modem, you must first choose tone or pulse dial, and then you must specify the serial communications port and the baud rate you want to use.

If you have access to MCI, Easylink, or CompuServe, you can enter your user ID, password, and the phone number of the service here rather than enter it later into Telecommunications.

If you want to use a fax card, you can choose whether you need a network installation or the more usual single-computer installation. Next, PC Setup gives you the opportunity to install the fax controller program ITLFAX as a memory-resident program. Choose I to install ITLFAX if you plan to use your fax card with PC Tools Tele-communications, or C to continue without change.

If you want to use Telecommunications in background mode, you can do so if you install the Backtalk program memory-resident.

In PC Tools 6.0, you can choose a password, as well as configure your user level to suit your needs. You can choose your user level from Beginner, Intermediate, or Advanced. The different user levels are available in PC Shell and in PC Backup only.

PC Setup copies all the files from the floppy disk into the newly created directory on your hard disk, displaying each file name on the

PC Tools 5.5 does not support fax cards.

PC Setup checks that you insert each disk in the correct sequence, so you cannot continue the installation if you have the disks out of order.

screen as it is copied, and prompting you to insert the next disk when it has finished copying the first one. If you are updating from an older version of PC Tools, any user files you have, like configuration files, phone files, and so on, are automatically copied into another directory called OLDPCT so that they are not overwritten by the new files.

PC Setup guides you through the rest of the installation, asking for each disk in turn. It also decompresses several large files that are in compressed form on the distribution disks to save space.

PC Setup searches for the DOS command FORMAT in the root directory and in all other directories on your path, renaming it FORMAT!.COM, and makes a batch file called FORMAT.BAT that actually runs PC Format when you type

```
FORMAT
```

PC Setup also increases the FILES specification in your CONFIG.SYS file to allow for the extra requirements of PC Tools. If you see a DOS error during the installation process, your AUTOEXEC-.BAT, CONFIG.SYS, FORMAT.EXE, or FORMAT.COM files may have the read-only bit set in their attribute byte. Change this with the DOS ATTRIB command.

PC Setup makes any changes to your AUTOEXEC.BAT file required as a result of your choices during the installation process. If changes are necessary, your old AUTOEXEC.BAT file is renamed AUTOEXEC.SAV, and the changes are included in AUTOEXEC.BAT. Reboot your computer to ensure that the new configuration is in effect and the installation of PC Tools is complete.

If you want to change the way PC Tools is installed on your system, you can run PC Setup again and select a different configuration.

RUNNING PC TOOLS

You can run PC Tools from the DOS command line or in interactive full-screen mode.

USING PC TOOLS FROM THE COMMAND LINE

PC Tools is not a single large program, but a set of several powerful utility programs. You can run all the programs in the PC Tools package from the DOS command line, just like any other program or DOS command. You simply type the program name, add optional parameters on the command line after the program name, and press Enter. Appendix A lists all of the optional parameters for all of the PC Tools programs.

You can run some of the programs from inside batch files. Indeed, this is the best way to run some of them.

The following list gives the file name you must type to start the PC Tools programs running.

- COMPRESS
- DESKTOP
- DISKFIX
- KILL
- LLS/LLQ
- MI
- PARK
- PC-CACHE
- PCBACKUP
- PCBDIR
- PCFORMAT
- PCSETUP
- PCSECURE
- PCSHELL
- UNDELETE

USING PC TOOLS' FULL-SCREEN MODE

Most of the PC Tools programs also have a full-screen windowed mode with pull-down menus and function-key shortcuts. To run a program in this mode, just type its name at the DOS prompt. The following programs normally run in full-screen mode:

- COMPRESS

- DISKFIX
- DESKTOP
- PCBACKUP
- PCSECURE
- PCSHELL

You can use the keyboard, or better still, use your mouse to navigate through the pull-down menus in these programs.

PC TOOLS SCREEN LAYOUT All of the PC Tools programs that use a full-screen display share a common user interface designed to make it easy to move from one program to another. I'll use PC Shell to illustrate this user interface. Figure 1.3 shows PC Shell's start-up screen.

PC Shell uses a system of windows and pull-down menus that makes choosing a command quick and easy. In this way, several different things can be shown on the screen at one time: menus, help windows, dialog boxes, and so on.

The screen in Figure 1.3 has the following components:

- The horizontal menu bar runs across the top of the screen and contains the names of the pull-down menus and the

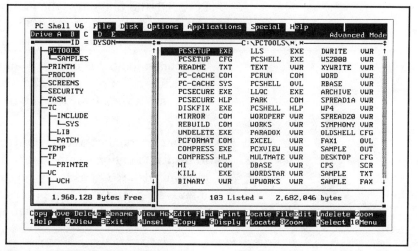

Figure 1.3: PC Shell start-up screen

current time. In PC Shell, the menu bar contains:

PC Shell, the program name.

File, Disk, Options, Applications, Special, and Help commands.

Time, which displays the current computer time.

You select any of these by typing their first letter or clicking on them with the mouse.

- The drive line, the second line in the display, contains the drive letters of all the disk drives PC Shell can find on your system. The current drive is highlighted. You can select from these drives by pressing Ctrl and the drive letter or by clicking on the drive letter with your mouse. In PC Tools 6.0, this line also includes your user level.

- On the left side of the screen is the tree list window, a graphic display of the directories and subdirectories on the current drive. The current directory is highlighted. Vertical scroll bars are located on the right side of the window.

- The file list window on the right side of the screen lists all the files in the current directory. Scroll bars are located on the right side of the window.

- The status line is below the tree list and file list windows. In PC Shell, this line shows the number of files in the directory and their total size in bytes. Other PC Tools programs show different information in the status line.

- The command bar is next, containing commonly used commands from the pull-down menus. Select these commands by typing the highlighted letter, or by clicking on them with the mouse.

- The last line on the screen is sometimes used as a message bar to display additional information and small help messages. Commands are often shown on this line. Select these commands by pressing the appropriate function key from the keyboard, or by clicking on them with the mouse.

You will find these elements (with minor variations depending on the individual application) in all the PC Tools programs that use full-screen displays.

USING THE KEYBOARD   To select a pull-down menu, hold down the Alt key and type the menu's initial letter. For example, to see the File menu, hold down the Alt key and type F; to see the Special menu, type S. Similarly, to select an item from the menu, type the highlighted letter. For example, from the File menu, type C for Copy File, and P for Print File. As each letter can have only one meaning in each menu, the choices may be less than intuitive. You can also use ↑ or ↓ to move up or down the menu items. To close a menu, press Escape.

If a pull-down menu is displayed, press ← or → to display the next menu to the left or right.

Some of the most often used commands have function-key equivalents displayed on the message bar or in the menu itself. To use one of these, just press the appropriate function key. However, the function-key equivalents do not work when their pull-down menus are showing.

To scroll through the tree list or the file list, use ↑ and ↓ to move one line at a time, and the PgUp and PgDn keys to move a whole window at a time. The Home and End keys move to the start and end of the information displayed in the window, respectively. Use the Tab key to move from one window to the other. The active window will be highlighted. To close a window, press Escape.

USING THE MOUSE   PC Tools programs are optimized for the mouse user, and navigating your way through the pull-down menus is easy and fast with a mouse. To select a pull-down menu, click on the command on the menu bar. To select an option from the menu list, just move the mouse and click on the item you want. To remove a pull-down menu from the screen, click in the display area outside the menu sidebars.

Some of the most often used commands have function-key equivalents displayed on the message bar. To use one of these, just click on the word or the function-key name.

To scroll through the tree list or file list window, press the right mouse button and drag the mouse. As it moves, the highlighted bar moves. You can also use the scroll bars. Clicking on the scroll arrows moves the display in the direction of the arrow. Clicking and holding down the mouse button scrolls continuously.

You can use the scroll box to move to a particular part of a display. For example, if you move the scroll box to the middle of the scroll bar, the screen displays the data from the middle section of the list.

Many of the windows have close boxes in the upper-left corner. To close the window, click on the close box with the mouse.

RUNNING PC TOOLS ON A LOCAL AREA NETWORK

You can run PC Tools on a Novell network using Novell Advanced Netware 286 Version 2.15, or on an IBM token ring using IBM PC Local Area Network Program Version 1.20.

Install the PC Tools programs in a write-protected directory on the network server. Then you can run them from any station on the network that has access to the server. Make sure that the server directory is in each user's path, and set an environment variable for each user to specify where PC Tools should keep all the user-specific files such as configuration files. This directory should be specific for each user and the user should have write privileges for it. You can add this environment variable to your station's AUTOEXEC.BAT file with the line

> SET PCTOOLS = *drive:\directory path*

where *drive* is the drive letter and *directory path* is the full path description of the directory where PC Tools should keep the user-specific files.

If you are installing PC Tools on a Novell Netware network, you can make the PC Tools directory path available to all users and use a system login script to define the PC Tools environment variable for all users. For example,

> SET PCTOOLS = *drive:\home\%login__name*

where the directory below *home* has the same name as the user's login name, and the user has write privileges.

PC Setup will not modify a network AUTOEXEC.BAT file, so if any changes are needed, they should be made by the network supervisor.

If you use PC Shell to look at a network file server, PC Shell only lists the directories for which you have at least read privileges, so you will not be overwhelmed by a listing of all the directories on the file server disk.

All of PC Shell's commands are available for use on a network except Rename Volume, Search Disk, Directory Sort, Disk Info, Disk Map, File Map, Undelete, Verify Disk, View/Edit disk, and the Prune and Graft function from Directory Maintenance. Also, Compress will not run on a Novell Network file server or any networked disk.

Finally, note that you need a network or site license to run PC Tools on a local area network. Otherwise, you must purchase a copy of the package for every station on the system.

HOW TO GET HELP

You can get help from some of the PC Tools programs by typing the program name followed by a space, a slash, and a question mark. For example, to get help with PC-Cache, type

    PC-CACHE /?

A short help screen will be displayed, as shown in Figure 1.4.

Help is also available inside all the full-screen programs. You just press the F1 key to open the help window. The help window contains context-specific help about the subject in question. In addition, it allows you to access the help index—a list of topics that you can get help with inside the current application. You can also press F2 to access the help index directly. Then use the arrow keys to make your choice or click on the heading with the mouse. Part of the help index for PC Shell is shown in Figure 1.5.

As you make choices from the pull-down menus throughout the windowed applications in PC Tools, the message bar at the bottom of the screen usually contains a short message describing the use of that menu selection. The message bar may also contain descriptions of the function-key shortcuts available in the current program.

```
                    PC-CACHE, Version 6
           Licensed exclusively to Central Point Software, Inc.
      Copyright 1986, 1989 Multisoft Corporation, All Rights Reserved.
                       Summary of Parameters

      /EXTSTART=xxxxK   Don't use extended memory below xxxxK.
      /FLUSH            Flush cache -- set the cache to empty.
      /Ix               Do not cache drive x.
      /MAX=xx           Read no more than xx sectors ahead.
      /MEASURES         Display measurements.
      /NOBATCH          Don't batch copy to/from the cache.
      /PARAM            Display parameters in effect.
      /SIZE=xxxK        Set up xxxK cache in conventional memory.
      /SIZEXP=xxxxK     Set up xxxxK cache in expanded memory.
      /SIZEXT=xxxxK     Set up xxxxK cache in extended memory.
      /UNLOAD           Un-install the cache.
      /?                Display this information.



C:\PCTOOLS>
```

Figure 1.4: The PC-Cache help screen

Figure 1.5: Part of the help index for PC Shell

SUMMARY

In this chapter, you learned how to back up your PC Tools disks and how to install PC Tools on your hard disk. The PC Tools programs themselves were introduced briefly. You learned how to use them from the DOS command line, as well as in their interactive full-screen mode. Mouse and keyboard use were also described.

In the next chapter, we'll take a closer look at what goes on behind the scenes when you use your hard disk. I'll also show you how to use PC Tools to explore the structure of your disk.

2

An Introduction
to Disk
and Directory
Structure

2

Before learning about file recovery and hard-disk management, you must know in detail many basic aspects of disk organization. This chapter describes floppy- and hard-disk characteristics, and gives a complete picture of the physical and logical framework of floppy and hard disks under DOS. Several PC Shell selections that you can use to explore your disks—including Disk Info and the Disk and File Maps—are covered in depth in the second part of this chapter.

DISK STRUCTURE

The better you understand how the underlying hardware works, the easier it will be to understand what happens when you add or delete a file in DOS, and what procedures you must follow to recover files.

SIDES

The most fundamental characteristic of a floppy disk is that it has two sides. Data can be written to and read from either side.

In early versions of DOS, single-sided disks were common; that is, only one side of the disk was used.

The system considers the first side as side 0, and the second side as side 1. Hard disks, in contrast, may have several recording surfaces, which are called *platters*. Platters are mounted on the same spindle inside the hard disk's sealed enclosure, and each platter has two sides. The numbering scheme is the same as that used for floppy disks: The first side is 0, the next 1, the first side of the second platter is 2, and so on. Each side of a floppy disk and each side of a hard disk's platter has its own read/write head.

TRACKS

Each disk or platter side is divided into concentric circles known as *tracks*. The outermost track on the top of the disk is numbered track 0, side 0, and the first track on the other side of the disk is numbered track 0, side 1. Track numbering increases inwards towards the center of the disk (or platter).

The number of tracks on a disk varies with the media type. 360K floppy disks have 40 tracks per side, 1.2MB floppy disks have 80 tracks per side, and hard disks can have from 300 to 600 tracks per platter side. On a floppy disk, the tracks cover only a small area of the disk, about three-quarters of an inch. A 360K floppy disk is recorded with 48 tracks per inch, and a 1.2MB floppy disk is recorded with 96 tracks per inch. (Tracks per inch is often abbreviated as TPI.)

CYLINDERS

Tracks that are at the same concentric position on the disk (or on platters) are referred to collectively as a *cylinder.* On a floppy disk, a cylinder contains two tracks (for example, track 0, side 0 and track 0, side 1); on a hard disk with four platters, a cylinder contains eight tracks. Figure 2.1 shows cylinders on a hard disk with four platters.

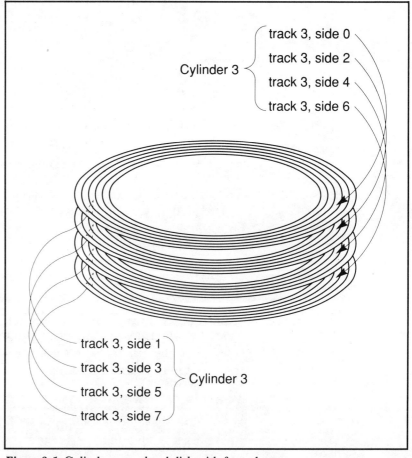

Figure 2.1: Cylinders on a hard disk with four platters

SECTORS AND ABSOLUTE SECTORS

Each track on a disk is in turn divided into *sectors*. Each track on the disk contains the same number of sectors.

When DOS reads or writes data to a disk, it must read or write at least one complete sector.

In all versions of DOS, a sector consists of 512 bytes and is the smallest single area of disk space that DOS can read or write. Each sector has a unique sector address contained in the sector header, and is separated from the next sector by an inter-sector gap. The number of sectors contained in each track on the disk varies according to the media type. A 360K floppy disk has 9 sectors per track, a 1.2MB floppy disk has 15, and most hard disks have 17. Figure 2.2 shows the relationship between tracks and sectors on a 360K floppy disk, which has 40 tracks numbered from 0 to 39, and 9 sectors per track.

In the absolute-sector numbering scheme, the first sector on a disk is identified as side 0, cylinder 0, sector 1.

DOS identifies all the sectors on a disk by numbering them sequentially. On a 360K floppy disk, for example, the sectors are numbered 0-719, and a specific sector might be identified as, say, sector 317. Another way to reference a given sector is to identify it

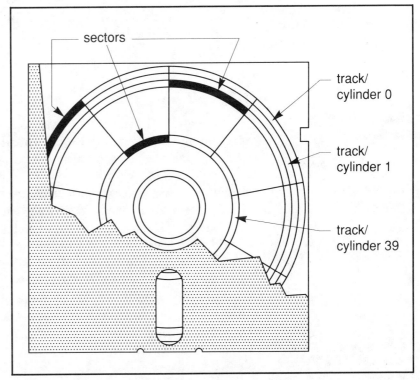

Figure 2.2: Tracks and sectors on a 360K floppy disk

according to its disk side and cylinder and then specify its position in that cylinder. In this case, you might give a sector's location as side 0, cylinder 25, sector 7. When you use this method, you are referring to *absolute sectors*.

THE INTERLEAVE FACTOR

For several reasons, the sectors on a disk are not always numbered sequentially. First, a floppy disk rotates at about 200 RPM inside the disk drive and a hard disk rotates at about 3600 RPM, or one-sixtieth of a second per rotation. DOS reads and writes data in single sectors, but by the time a sector's worth of data is read and stored in memory and the PC is ready to read the next sector, this sector may already have passed under the head. The PC must now wait through a complete disk rotation before it can read the next sector. To minimize this delay, an *interleave factor* is introduced. Interleaving requires that logically sequential sectors are not physically adjacent to each other on the disk but are separated by some number of sectors. In this way, the performance of the disk and the layout of the sectors on the disk can be optimized.

CLUSTERS

The number of sectors per cluster varies depending on the disk media and the DOS version. 360K and 720K floppy disks have 2 sectors per cluster, while 1.2MB and 1.4MB disks have clusters of a single 512-byte sector. Hard disks have clusters of 4, 8, or 16 sectors.

Clusters are called *logical* units. Tracks and sectors are *physical* units.

Although DOS can read and write a single sector, it allocates disk space for files in *clusters*, which consist of one or more sectors. No matter how small a file is, it will always occupy at least one cluster on the disk. A 1-byte file will occupy one cluster, and a 511-byte file on a 1.2MB disk will also occupy one cluster. For example, Figure 2.3 shows a file of 1025 bytes and a cluster size of 1024 bytes, or two sectors. The file data occupy all the first cluster and only 1 byte of the second cluster, yet the area of the second cluster not filled with data is not available for another file. This unused area is called *slack*. The next file must start at the next available cluster. If the first file increases in length, it will occupy more of the second cluster. If the cluster is filled up and more space is needed, the file will continue in the next available cluster.

DOS identifies clusters by numbering them sequentially, with the first cluster labeled cluster 2. Cluster numbering begins in the data area of the disk, so the first cluster on a disk (cluster 2) is actually the

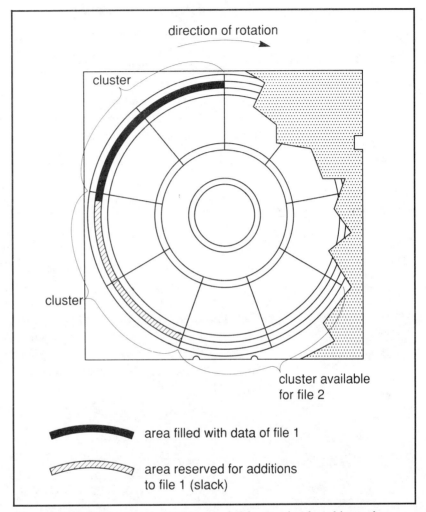

Figure 2.3: A file that needs 1025 bytes of disk space is 1 byte bigger than one cluster and will occupy two complete clusters

first cluster in the data area. This is less confusing when you understand that, unlike tracks and sectors, clusters are not physically demarcated on the disk. DOS merely views groups of sectors as clusters for its own convenience.

Remember that the absolute-sector method for locating sectors locates them according to their physical position on the disk. Because clusters have no physical manifestation, there is no "absolute" method of referencing them.

The efficiency of your hard-disk storage depends in part on the relationship between the cluster size and the most common size of your files. Disk performance becomes a consideration when, to access even the smallest file, DOS has to load a cluster that may contain many empty sectors.

Changing the number of sectors per cluster is a complicated operation that you should only attempt after you have made a complete backup of the hard disk. A detailed description of the process is outside the scope of this book.

EXAMINING THE SYSTEM AREA

You can reference sectors in the system area with the DOS numbering system or the absolute-sector method. You cannot reference clusters in the system area because cluster numbering starts in the data area.

When you format a disk, DOS always reserves the outermost track on side 0 for its own use. This area is called the *system area* and is subdivided into three parts: the *boot record*, the *file allocation table* or FAT (of which there are usually two identical copies), and the root directory. The remaining space on the disk after the system area is called the *data area*. This is the part of the disk where applications programs and data are located. The data area is far larger than the system area. On a 360K floppy disk, the system area occupies 1.6 percent of the whole disk, and on a 20MB hard disk the system area occupies a meager 0.2 percent of the total disk space.

THE BOOT RECORD

The boot record, which is on all formatted disks, contains the BIOS parameter block (BPB). This block holds information about the disk's physical characteristics, which is needed by device drivers. The information contained in the BPB is shown in Table 2.1.

The disk space occupied by the boot record is one sector, which includes the BPB, boot program, and slack.

The boot record also contains the boot program that is used to start the computer after a system reset or after power is applied. When you first turn on your computer, it runs a set of diagnostic routines to ensure that the hardware is in good order. If you have a hard disk or have loaded a floppy disk, the ROM bootstrap program next loads the boot record from disk into the computer's memory.

The bootstrap program checks the disk for the DOS system files (IO.SYS or IBMBIO.COM and MSDOS.SYS or IBMDOS-.COM). If they are present, it loads them into the computer and

Table 2.1: Information Contained in the BIOS Parameter Block (in the boot record)

INFORMATION STORED	NUMBER OF BYTES USED	ADDITIONAL INFORMATION
Version of DOS used to format the disk	8	
Number of bytes per sector	2	
Number of sectors per cluster, per track, and per disk (or hard-disk partition)	1	
Number of reserved sectors used by the system area	2	
Number of FAT copies and sectors used	1	
Number of root directory entries	2	112 entries on 360K floppy or 1024 entries on hard disk
Number of sectors on disk	2	720 sectors for 360K floppy, thousands for hard disk
Media descriptor	1	Indicates the type of disk
Number of sectors per FAT	2	Sectors per FAT vary depending on disk's capacity (FAT references every cluster)
Number of sectors per track	2	360K floppy has 9 sectors per track, 1.2MB floppy has 15, hard disk usually has 17

Table 2.1: Information Contained in the BIOS Parameter Block (in the boot record) (Continued)

INFORMATION STORED	NUMBER OF BYTES USED	ADDITIONAL INFORMATION
Number of heads	2	Floppy-disk drive has 2, hard disk has 4
Number of hidden sectors	2	Hidden sectors are the system area

passes complete system control over to DOS's COMMAND.COM. During this process, the CONFIG.SYS and AUTOEXEC.BAT files are loaded, as are any installable device drivers that a mouse or a RAM disk may need (for example, the device driver VDISK.SYS). Once everything has been loaded and you see the DOS prompt, your computer is ready for use.

However, when the computer can't find the DOS system files on the disk, it displays the error message

> Non-System disk or disk error
> Replace and strike any key when ready

and waits for you to either remove the nonsystem disk from the floppy-disk drive so it can use the hard disk, or place a system disk in your floppy-disk drive.

THE PARTITION TABLE

The DOS FDISK command establishes the partition table after low-level formatting of the disk is complete. You can use it to create or delete a DOS partition, to change the active partition, or to display the current active partition data.

The partition table, present on all hard disks, allows you to divide a hard disk into areas (called *partitions*) that appear to DOS as separate disks. The partition table also allows you to reserve space for other operating systems (which you can then install and use to create their own partitions). For example, DOS and XENIX can run on the same computer. A DOS disk can contain as many as four partitions, but only one of these may be active at any one time.

Floppy disks do not have partition tables and cannot be shared between different operating systems.

The partition table begins with a code called the *master boot record.* This code contains a record of which partition was the active partition—the one used to boot the system. The master boot record also contains the locations of the boot records for the operating system of the active partition (and any other operating system installed on the disk). When the computer is started, it uses this information to boot the active partition's operating system. If you are running DOS and no other operating system, you should make the DOS partition occupy the whole hard disk.

THE FILE ALLOCATION TABLE (FAT)

The next part of a disk's system area is occupied by the file allocation table (FAT), which is also created by the DOS FORMAT command. The FAT is part of the system that DOS uses to keep track of where files are stored on a disk. The FAT is so important that DOS actually creates two copies of it. If the first copy becomes corrupted, DOS uses the second copy. Think of the FAT as a two-column table. In one column is a sequential list of numbers that, from DOS's point of view, are the "addresses" of each of the clusters in the disk's data area. In the other column is a number that gives specific information about that cluster. If the cluster is being used to store file data, the second column contains the "address" of the next cluster in that file. (Remember that the data in a file are not necessarily stored in consecutive clusters.) Otherwise, the second column contains a special number that indicates one of the following:

(0)000H	The cluster is available for storing data
(F)FF7H	The cluster is bad and will not be used for storing data
(F)FF0-(F)FF6H	The cluster is reserved and will not be used for storing data
(F)FF8-(F)FFFH	The cluster is the last cluster in a file

Figure 2.4 illustrates how FAT entries are chained together. Each cluster number entry points to the number of the next cluster in use by the file. A special entry indicates the end of the file. In the figure, for example, file A starts in cluster 2 and then continues in cluster 8. The entry for cluster 8 points to cluster 11. Cluster 11 in turn points to cluster 12 where the file ends. Thus, file A is split between four clusters, three of which are not in sequence. This is called *fragmentation* and is discussed in detail in Chapter 5. File B is less fragmented. It occupies clusters 3, 4, 5, 6, 7, 9, and 10. The entry for cluster 7 points to cluster 9, where the file continues. Cluster 9 points to cluster 10, which contains the end-of-file value.

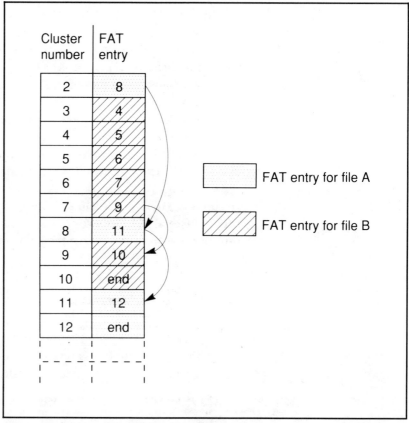

Figure 2.4: FAT entries chained together

THE ROOT DIRECTORY

Directly following the FAT is the root directory, which is the third part of the system area on a formatted disk. The size of the root directory cannot be changed, but it is proportional to the media type. For example, a 360K floppy has space for 112 entries in the root, while a hard disk has space for 512 or 1024 entries.

If the disk is a system disk, the first two files listed in the root directory are always the files containing the MS-DOS BIOS and the DOS kernel. The disk bootstrap program uses these entries when it loads the operating system into memory and starts executing DOS.

Each directory entry is 32 bytes long. The entry may contain information about a file or a subdirectory. The format of a file entry in the root directory is as follows:

On a 360K floppy, the root directory takes up 7 sectors of disk space.

Base name	8 bytes, ASCII
Extension	3 bytes, ASCII
Attribute	1 byte, each bit represents an attribute
	bit 0, file is read-only
	bit 1, file is hidden
	bit 2, file is a system file
	bit 3, entry is a volume label
	bit 4, entry is a subdirectory
	bit 5, archive bit
	bit 6, 7, unused
Reserved	10 bytes, reserved for future use
Time	2 bytes
Date	2 bytes
Starting FAT entry	2 bytes
File size	4 bytes

The file name is an 11-byte entry, divided into an 8-byte base name and a 3-byte extension, which are separated by a period. The period is not stored as a byte, but you must type it between the eighth and the ninth characters to use a file extension.

If the first byte of a file name has a value of 0, the directory entry is unused, and indicates the end of the active directory entries. If the first byte of a file name is a period (that is the . and .. files), the file is reserved by DOS.

If the first byte of a file name is a Greek sigma character (ASCII 299 decimal, E5 hex), the file has been erased. When erasing a file using DEL or ERASE, DOS marks the first character of the file name with the E5 hex character to show that it has been erased and then clears the file's entries from the FAT. As DOS leaves the starting cluster number and the file length in the directory and leaves the data on the disk, the first cluster of a file can be found and recovered quite easily as long as the clusters have not been overwritten by another file.

The attribute byte can have one or more of the attribute bits set at the same time. For example, a system file can also be hidden. An attribute is said to be set if the appropriate attribute bit is set to a value of 1. If the attribute byte has no bits set, or a value of 0, the file is a normal data or program file and may be written to or erased. This probably applies to the majority of your files.

- Read-only files can be used, but you can't make changes to their contents.

- Hidden files do not appear in directory listings made by DIR. You can't duplicate them with COPY or delete them with ERASE or DEL. However, you can copy them with the DOS DISKCOPY command.

- System files are read-only files.

- The volume label is a short piece of text used to identify the disk. You can specify up to 11 characters for it when you label your disk. The label's directory entry looks like a file that has no length.

- Subdirectory names have the same format as file names.

- The archive bit is used when backing up. If a new file is written to disk or an existing file is modified, this bit is set

---

You can use letters, numbers, and any other characters except ."/\[]¦> < +:, = ; in your files' base names and extensions.

Attributes are explained in Chapter 5.

(changed to 1). After the backup program has copied the file, it resets the bit to 0. This way, the backup program knows which files need to be copied.

SUBDIRECTORIES

The root directory has a fixed size and a fixed location on the disk. In contrast, subdirectories can be of any size and can be located anywhere they are needed on the disk. You cannot delete the root directory, but you can create, delete, rename, expand, or contract a subdirectory as needed. Subdirectories are usually just called directories.

EXAMINING THE DATA AREA

The rest of the DOS partition (or unpartitioned hard disk or floppy disk) is the data area and can store files and subdirectories. This is the largest part of the disk and is where all your programs are found, including spreadsheets, word processors, program language compilers, and data files.

Figures 2.5 and 2.6 illustrate disk structure in different ways and draw together many of the concepts presented so far in this chapter. Both figures assume a 360K floppy disk.

EXPLORING YOUR DISK WITH PC SHELL

You can use several of the selections in PC Shell to explore your disks and files: Disk Info in the Disk menu, Disk Map and File Map in the Special menu, and View/Edit Disk in the Disk menu.

USING DISK INFO

Disk Info provides you with a wealth of technical information about your disks that is not normally available without complex programming. From the PC Shell start-up screen, type D for the Disk menu, followed by I for Disk Info. Figure 2.7 shows the resulting data for my hard disk, drive C.

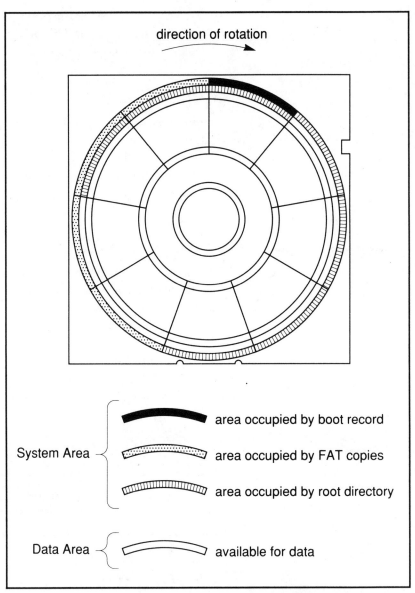

direction of rotation

System Area
- area occupied by boot record
- area occupied by FAT copies
- area occupied by root directory

Data Area
- available for data

Figure 2.5: Locations of system area and data area on a 360K floppy

    The hard disk has 33,450,496 bytes (about 32MB) of disk space in total, of which 2,039,808 bytes (2MB) are available. Hidden files occupy 63,488 bytes of disk space, 2010 user files take up 31,162,368

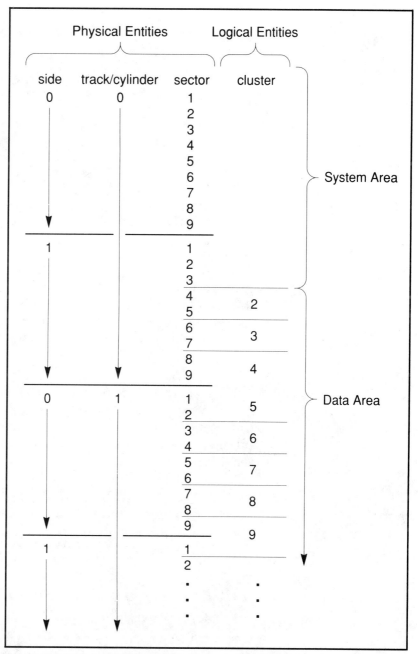

Figure 2.6: Relationships between elements of disk structure on a 360K floppy

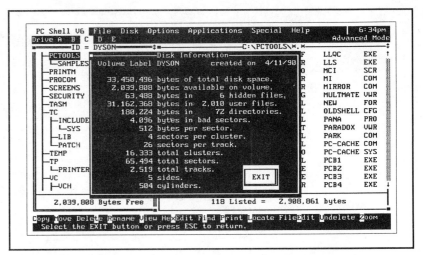

Figure 2.7: Disk Info run for drive C

bytes (about 30MB), and 72 directories occupy 180,224 bytes. 4096 bytes of the disk have been set aside as bad by the formatting program. The disk is divided into 65,494 512-byte sectors organized into 16,333 clusters, with 4 sectors per cluster. There are 2519 tracks, 504 cylinders, and 4 sides or platters.

To run Disk Info on a floppy disk, first press Escape to return to the main PC Shell display and insert a floppy disk into drive A. Make that drive the current drive by pressing Ctrl and the drive letter at the same time; in this case press Ctrl-A. Notice that both the tree and the file lists change to reflect the contents of the floppy disk in drive A. Now type D to open the Disk pull-down menu or click on Disk. Choose Disk Info and you will see a display similar to the one shown in Figure 2.8 if you used a 360K floppy disk.

The differences in the information shown for the floppy-disk drive and the hard-disk drive have to do mostly with storage capacity—the number of sectors and the number of clusters, as you would expect.

LOOKING AT DISKS WITH DISK MAP

From the PC Shell start-up screen, press S for the Special menu and them M for Disk Map, or click the mouse on these two selections. Figure 2.9 shows the Disk Map display for a 20MB hard disk.

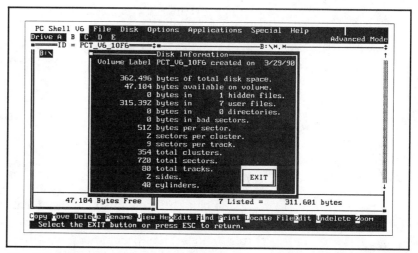

Figure 2.8: Results of Disk Info for a 360K floppy disk in drive A

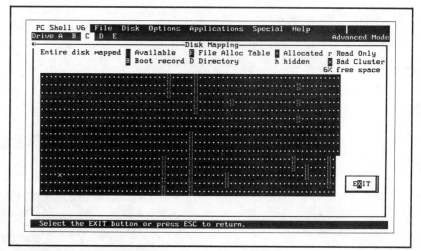

Figure 2.9: Typical Disk Map display for a 20MB hard disk

Each small square indicates several clusters of disk space occupied by your files. The shaded area is the unused space on your disk. In this case, the free space is 6 percent of the whole disk.

Free space is sometimes surrounded by clusters in use. These gaps result when you delete files and the disk space is deallocated from the FAT. The space then becomes available for other files, and will eventually be used again.

The x represents an area of bad sectors. These sectors were found to be damaged when the disk was formatted. A special entry in the FAT denotes that the area is bad and keeps it from being used.

Since the system area on this disk is small compared to the data area, the boot record, FAT, and root directory cannot be shown as individual elements in the display. If you make a disk map of a floppy disk, however, these areas will be explicitly called out in the display, as shown in Figure 2.10.

USING FILE MAP

You can also view this kind of information with File Map. Select the \PCTOOLS directory and the file README.TXT from the tree. Choose the Special menu and then choose File Map. The display for the file README.TXT is shown in Figure 2.11.

In Figure 2.11, the file name is displayed at the top of the screen, along with explanations of the symbols used in the display. Again the FAT, boot record, and root directory are too small to show as individual elements in this display. As you can see, the README.TXT file is recorded on this hard disk in ten noncontiguous areas, starting at cluster 10,306, sector 41,377.

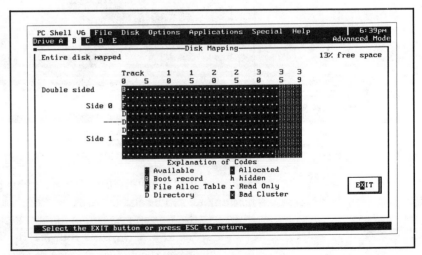

Figure 2.10: Disk map for a 360K floppy disk

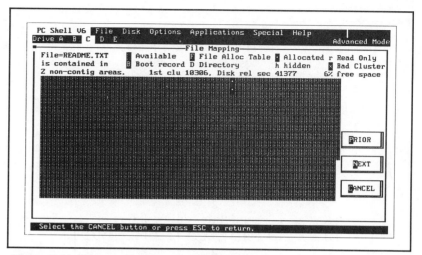

Figure 2.11: File map for the README.TXT file

You can use PRIOR to show details of the previous file in your selection, or NEXT to show details of the next file. This enables you to look at several files without returning to the Special menu level.

Use CANCEL when you are ready to leave File Map.

VIEW/EDIT DISK

View/Edit Disk is a very powerful PC Shell selection that allows you to browse through any area of a disk, viewing and editing data in that area either in ASCII form or in hex notation. You can actually edit this data at the byte level, which can be very dangerous. Make sure that you read all the warnings on the help screen, especially before attempting to edit the FAT or the root directory.

Insert your copy of the first PC Tools distribution disk, disk number 1, into drive A to follow this next example. In PC Shell, press Ctrl and A to select drive A as the current drive and then select View/Edit from the Disk pull-down menu. What you see on your screen is a part of the boot record for the floppy disk. This display is rather difficult to interpret as it is a binary file. For a clearer example, look at the README.TXT file that is sent with the PC Tools package. This file starts at cluster number 141 on distribution disk number 1.

The other choices in this menu allow you to select the boot record, the first sector of the FAT, the first root-directory sector, or the first sector in the data area.

Some of the data may appear unreadable if you View/Edit a program file. This is because those bytes are program code or data statements and were never intended to be read as text.

To display README.TXT, choose S for Change Sector from the message line at the bottom of the Disk View screen. At the next screen, choose Change Cluster # and enter 141 as the cluster number. You could also choose Change Sector # and enter a sector number of 290 to get to the same place on the disk. You will see the first part of the READ-ME.TXT file displayed in Figure 2.12.

The leftmost column of figures shows the decimal locations of the data, in terms of a byte offset count from the beginning of the sector. The next column (in parentheses) contains the hex equivalents of these decimal offsets. Each of the 512 bytes in the sector are numbered from 0 to 511 in decimal, or from 0 to 01FF in hex. The first line of the display shows the first 16 bytes in the sector, bytes 0 to 15, and the next line shows the next 16, bytes 16 to 31, and so on. The central area of the display shows the data in the file as two-digit hex numbers. On the right side of the display, the same 16 bytes are shown in ASCII form.

From the display of the README.TXT file, it is easy to follow the correspondence between the hex part and the ASCII part of the display. For example, starting at byte 0010 hex, 20 hex is a space character, 50 is P, and 43 is C, representing the first part of the text in the file. This correspondence will not be as obvious if you View/Edit

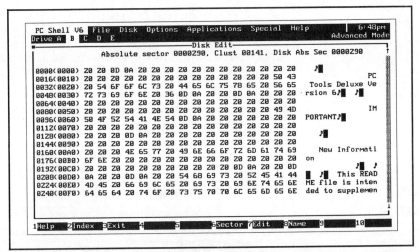

Figure 2.12: View/Edit display showing the \PCTOOLS README.TXT file

See Appendix B for a complete listing of all ASCII characters in decimal and hexadecimal.

a program file. In fact, some of the data may be completely unreadable. This is because a program file is a binary file, not ASCII or text, and contains program statements that were never intended to be read as text.

You can use the PgUp and PgDn keys to move through the data, half a sector at a time, and you can use the Home or End keys to go from one end of the file to the other.

To look at another area of the disk, choose Change Sector. From the Change Sector menu you can display the boot sector, the first FAT sector, the first root directory sector, or the first sector of the data area on the disk. You can also enter a cluster number or a sector number directly. Directories are treated as though they are files and are displayed in the same format.

You can edit the data by choosing Edit. You can use the F8 function key to toggle back and forth between the ASCII display and the hex display. New data that you enter is shown highlighted, and is always entered in the overstrike mode, never in the insert mode. Changes that you enter via the hex window are preserved and shown if you change back to the ASCII window.

When your changes are complete, use the Save option (F5) to save them to disk.

USING HEX EDIT TO LOOK AT A FILE

Using Hex Edit is very similar to using View/Edit from the Disk pull-down menu. In hex mode, the file is displayed in the middle of the screen. The leftmost column of figures shows the decimal locations of the data, in terms of a byte offset count from the beginning of the sector. The next column (the numbers in parentheses), contains the hex equivalents of these decimal offsets. Each of the 512 bytes in the sector are numbered from 0 to 511 in decimal, or from 0 to 01FF in hex. The first line of the display shows the first 16 bytes in the sector, bytes 0 to 15, the next line shows the next 16, bytes 16 to 31, and so on. The central area of the display shows the data in the file as two-digit hex numbers. On the right side of the display, the same 16 bytes are shown in ASCII form.

This time, however, the Change Sector option works slightly differently. It only allows you to enter sector numbers and only lets you explore sectors contained within your chosen file.

ASCII/HEX toggles the cursor between the ASCII and the hex displays. Use Escape to return to the main PC Shell menus. If you use a mouse, click on the close box in the upper-left corner of the display.

USING EDIT FILE

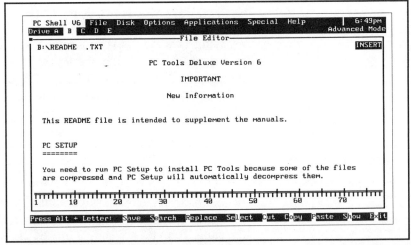

In PC Tools 5.5 Edit File is called File Edit.

Edit File will not load files with the extensions .EXE, .COM, .BAK, or .$$$, as it assumes they are binary files and not text files.

Edit File from the File pull-down menu is really a small word processor or editor. Normally, you would use Notepads in the PC Desktop program for most of your word processing. For a fast file edit, however, you can use Edit File.

As an example, first choose the README.TXT file from the \PCTOOLS directory and then select Edit File from the File pull-down menu. Edit File first asks if you want to edit this file, create another file, or leave Edit File. Choose Edit, and you will see the editing commands displayed on the bottom line of the screen, just below the ruler. Figure 2.13 shows the resulting display. Table 2.2 lists the text-editing keys you can use in Edit File.

To add text to a file, just start typing: The editor handles word wrap at the end of the line. Use the Enter key to end a paragraph.

The editor has four commands to help you work with blocks of text: Select, Cut, Copy, and Paste.

Figure 2.13: Edit File displaying README.TXT from the \PCTOOLS directory

Table 2.2: Editing Keys

KEY	FUNCTION
type the character	Insert a character at the cursor
Tab	Insert a tab at the cursor
Enter	Insert a paragraph break at the cursor
Del	Delete the character at the cursor
Backspace	Delete the character to the left of the cursor
Up Arrow (↑)	Move up one line
Down Arrow (↓)	Move down one line
Left Arrow (←)	Move left one character
Right Arrow (→)	Move right one character
Home	Move to the beginning of the line
End	Move to the end of the line
Home Home	Move to the beginning of the window
End End	Move to the end of the window
Ctrl-Home	Move to the beginning of the file
Ctrl-End	Move to the end of the file
PgUp	Scroll up one window
PgDn	Scroll down one window

To select a block of text, position the cursor at the start of the appropriate block of text and choose the Select command. Use ↑ or ↓ to select lines of text, or → or ← to select single characters. To select a whole page of text, use the PgUp or PgDn keys.

To cut text from the file after you have selected the block, choose the Cut command. This removes the selected text from the screen and puts it into a special Paste buffer for use later.

To paste this text into your file, use the cursor-control keys or the mouse to move to the right place in the file, select the Paste option and the text will appear in the file at that point. The Paste buffer only holds one piece of text at a time. To move two pieces of the file, you must move them one at a time.

To find and change text in the file, you can use the Search and Replace selections.

To search for a specific block of text, choose Search, enter the desired text into the dialog box on the screen, and press Enter. This search is not case sensitive—the difference between upper- and lower-case letters is ignored—so, for instance, PC SHELL and PC Shell are considered to be the same text. Once a match has been found, use Search again to look for other occurrences of the text in the file.

To find and replace text in the file, use the Replace option. You are asked first to enter the text to replace, and then for the text you want to replace it with. Press Enter to start the replace operation. The editor stops at each occurrence of the search string so that you can replace it if you wish to. Select Replace to replace the text, or Escape or Exit to cancel.

The Show command locates and displays all the carriage return characters in the file.

Once you have made the necessary changes, you should save the file to the disk with the Save command. Save renames the old version of your file with .BAK as the extension. This enables you to recover the original file if you ever need to.

To leave Edit File, press Escape, click on the close box using the mouse, or choose the Exit command.

USING PC SHELL TO PARK YOUR HARD-DISK HEADS

If you are going to move your computer, it is a good idea to park your hard disk read/write heads first. Parking the heads positions the read/write heads over an unused part of the hard disk, usually over the highest numbered cylinder on the drive. On a hard disk with more than one partition, the heads are placed at the end of the last partition. This prevents any data loss from the heads accidentally contacting the disk surface.

In PC Shell, choose the Park Disk option from the Disk pull-down menu. PC Shell opens a dialog box to confirm that the heads are parked, and reminds you to turn your computer off immediately to transport it. Do not use your computer for anything else after parking the heads because the heads will move to access disk information and will once again be positioned over the data area of the disk.

With PC Tools 6.0 you can also run the Park program directly from the DOS command line. Just type

PARK

and you will see the confirmation message

The hard drive heads are now parked.
You may now turn off your computer
and transport it. If you continue,
the heads will no longer be parked.

SUMMARY

In the first part of this chapter, I concentrated on the details of disk organization that provide the basis for subsequent chapters' discussions of hard-disk management and data recovery.

You are now familiar with the following PC Shell selections: Hex Edit and Edit File in the File menu; Disk Info, View/Edit, and Park Heads in the Disk menu; and Disk Map and File Map in the Special menu.

In the next chapter, you will learn how to back up your hard disk. In Chapter 4, you will learn how to unerase files that have been erased and how to recover from an accidental format of your hard disk.

3

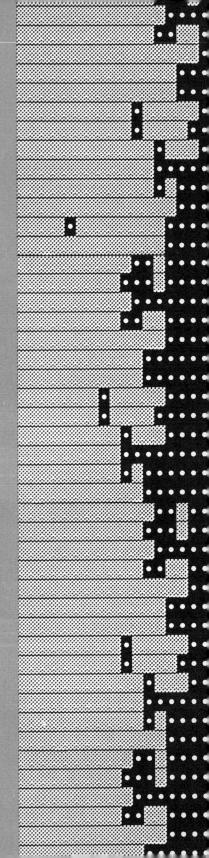

Backing Up
Your Hard Disk

3

Throughout this book, I remind you to back up your entire system before performing certain operations. For example, before running the file unfragmentation program for the first time, I suggest that you back up your system. A *backup* is an up-to-date copy of all your files that you can use to reload your system in case of an accident. Backups are insurance against anything happening to the hundreds or possibly thousands of files you might have on your hard disk. If the unthinkable did occur—you lost all of your system's data and didn't have backup copies—it could take you weeks or even months to recreate all that data, if indeed it could be recreated.

WHEN SHOULD I MAKE A BACKUP?

You should get into the habit of backing up your system regularly so that you never have to do any extra work as a result of damaged or missing files. How often you should make a backup depends on how much work you do on your computer. For example, computer programmers will do a lot of new work during a week, and because they stand to lose a lot of work in the event of an accident, they should back up their files on a daily basis, or even sometimes twice a day. A person running what-if financial analyses might back up his or her work every two or three days because that is as much as he or she can afford to lose. If you write only an occasional memo, however, you can probably get away with backing up your system once a week.

As a rule, most people make a full backup at the end of the work week, and smaller daily backups of the files that have changed during the day. This ensures that you have all your files on a backup disk somewhere. For example, if your hard disk crashes during the day on Thursday, you can restore last Friday's full backup, as well as the partial backups for Monday, Tuesday, and Wednesday. All you have lost is Thursday's work.

There are several other occasions when you should back up your entire system. If you are going to move your computer, you should make a complete backup of the hard disk. Even if you are only moving next door, your hard disk may not survive the trip. Similarly, if you are sending your computer in for any kind of service work, including work on the disk drives, you should have a complete system backup first.

Whenever you need to remove directories and files because you are running out of space on your hard disk, you should back up your hard disk completely (dating the backup) before making the deletions. You may need these files again sometime. Similarly, if someone leaves your company, a complete backup is a good way to preserve his or her work, allowing the replacement person to start work without any anxieties about the files on his or her disk.

Finally, if you are going to run a program such as a file unfragmenting program, which optimizes your hard disk file layout by rewriting all your files, be sure to have a new complete backup of your hard disk before you start running the program. Your hard disk and the optimizing program may be incompatible. Also, power outages and brownouts can occur at any time, even during the optimization itself.

BACKING UP YOUR FLOPPY DISKS USING DOS COMMANDS

If you have only a small number of files on your system, you can use the DOS commands DISKCOPY, COPY, or XCOPY to back up your files.

USING DISKCOPY TO BACK UP FLOPPY DISKS

The DOS DISKCOPY command makes an exact duplicate copy of your original floppy disk's contents. DISKCOPY copies the low-level raw data of your disk sector by sector, rather than file by file. For example, if your original disk was a system disk, your copy will also be a system disk. You don't even have to format the destination disk; DISKCOPY formats it during the copy process. In fact, you should use unformatted disks to save time. This way you will avoid copying a nonsystem disk to a system disk, and having to format another system disk as you are now short one copy.

Suppose drive A is the current drive and you type

```
DISKCOPY
```

without specifying the drive letter. DISKCOPY prompts you to change source and target disks during the copy process, and then asks if you want to copy another disk, as shown in Figure 3.1.

```
A:\>DISKCOPY

Insert SOURCE diskette in drive A:

Press any key when ready . . .

Copying 80 tracks
9 Sectors/Track, 2 Side(s)

Insert TARGET diskette in drive A:

Press any key when ready . . .

Insert SOURCE diskette in drive A:

Press any key when ready . . .

Insert TARGET diskette in drive A:

Press any key when ready . . .


Copy another diskette (Y/N)?
```

Figure 3.1: Copy process with DISKCOPY

 You cannot use DISKCOPY to copy a hard disk.

You can use individual drive letters to exert more control over the copy process. If you type

DISKCOPY A: B:

you can copy the contents of the disk in drive A onto the disk in drive B without changing any disks.

Although DISKCOPY is faster than COPY, it has several drawbacks. For one, it can copy data onto bad areas of the destination disk. Also, you cannot use DISKCOPY with

- Hard disks

- Network drives

- Different sizes of source and destination disks

To copy files from one disk type to another, you should use the COPY command.

USING COPY TO MAKE BACKUPS

If you want to back up files selectively, choosing a few files from a disk or directory on your hard disk, you can use the COPY command. COPY copies files by name rather than making a duplicate of the original disk. As always, you need to verify that the destination disk has sufficient space for the files you want to copy. When copying files to disks that contain files, be careful not to overwrite existing files. That is, if you are backing up a directory to a disk that holds the directory's previous backup, all files with matching file names will be overwritten by the new copies. When you want to keep your backup versions separate, it's easiest to use different disks.

Once you have chosen the correct destination disk, you can run the COPY command and name the files individually.

You can also specify the DOS wildcard characters instead of complete file names. For example, to copy all the files in the \BATCH directory on drive C to the disk in drive A, make \BATCH the current directory and type

COPY *.* A:

During the copy process, your files are read file by file and then rewritten to the disk in drive A. COPY writes the name of each file copied onto the screen, as shown in Figure 3.2. This means that the COPY command eliminates file fragmentation—the backup files' clusters are written consecutively for each file.

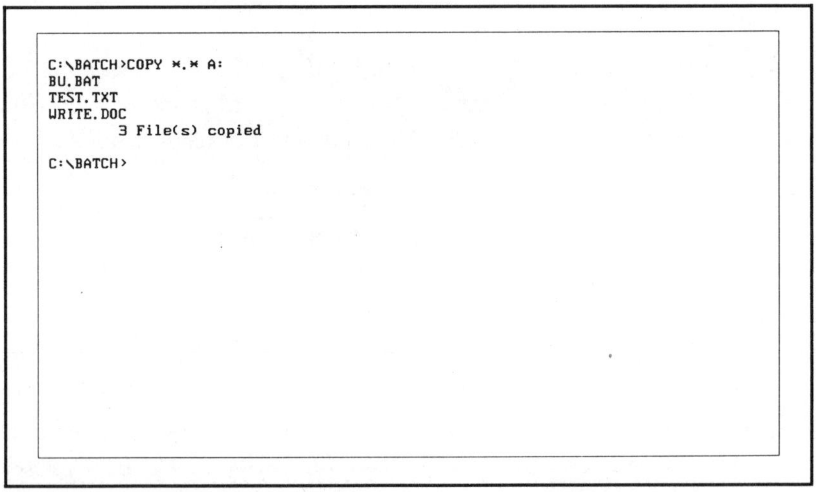

```
C:\BATCH>COPY *.* A:
BU.BAT
TEST.TXT
WRITE.DOC
        3 File(s) copied

C:\BATCH>
```

Figure 3.2: Copy process with COPY

USING XCOPY TO BACK UP FILES

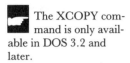 The XCOPY command is only available in DOS 3.2 and later.

The XCOPY command is even more powerful than the COPY command. XCOPY uses as much free memory in the computer as possible during the copy process. Instead of reading a file, writing it to disk, and then reading the next file (like COPY), XCOPY reads as many files as it can into memory and then writes them to disk. As with the COPY command, you must first ensure that there is enough space on the destination disk for all your files.

XCOPY also has several switches that make it more flexible. These switches are shown in Table 3.1.

Table 3.1: XCOPY Command Switches

SWITCH	OPERATION
/A	Copies those files whose archive bit is set
/D	Copies only those files whose date is the same or later than the date specified
/E	Creates subdirectories on the target when used with the /S switch
/M	Copies files whose archive bit is set and clears the bit
/P	Prompts before copying each file
/S	Copies files in subdirectories
/V	Forces DOS to check that all files have been written correctly
/W	Prompts for a keystroke before copying, allowing you to insert a new disk

BACKING UP YOUR HARD DISK USING DOS COMMANDS

As you have seen, DISKCOPY and COPY have limited usefulness when it comes to backing up your files. XCOPY, on the other hand, can duplicate your hard disk quite easily. XCOPY's only drawback is that it can easily require an enormous number of floppy disks. One alternative is to use the DOS BACKUP command for backing up hard disks, which condenses the files. The files now require less disk space for storage; you just use the RESTORE command to make them usable again.

USING THE BACKUP COMMAND

BACKUP allows you to copy a file or a group of files onto a set of floppy disks (or onto another hard disk) for archival purposes. The BACKUP command keeps track of which file is where on the backup floppy disks.

The general syntax of the BACKUP command is

BACKUP *source destination switches*

If you do not use any of the optional switches, BACKUP will back up all the files in the current directory. (You must always specify the destination directory.)

To back up all files in your word processing directory, specify the directory, including its path, as the first parameter. If you do not specify any files, DOS copies all the files in the directory to the backup disk.

BACKUP C:\WS4 A:

The exact wording of the BACKUP prompts depends on your version of DOS.

DOS responds with the message:

> Insert Archive Diskette 01 in Drive A:
> WARNING! All Files Will Be Deleted!
> Press Any Key to Continue, Control-C To Abort

This warning lets you confirm that you have inserted the right disk in drive A before DOS overwrites everything on the disk. Pressing Enter starts the backup process. DOS lists on the screen the complete path name of each file as it is written to the backup disk. If you have more files to back up than will fit onto a single disk, DOS prompts you to load another disk with the message:

> Insert Archive Diskette 02 in Drive A:

These steps are shown in Figure 3.3. As before, DOS warns you that the contents of the disk BACKUP is writing to will be overwritten.

During the backup process, DOS continues to ask for more disks until the entire directory has been backed up. You should carefully label each disk with its disk number, the date of the backup, any special switches you used, and the total number of disks in the backup. When you restore the backup onto your hard disk, the disks must be restored in the exact order in which you made them.

The files made by BACKUP are not standard DOS files. In the preceding example, in DOS 3.3 or later, all your word processing files are combined into one single file called BACKUP.*NNN*. A second file, CONTROL.*NNN*, contains the actual file names and file length data, as well as a description of the directory that contained them. These two .*NNN* files include a complete description of all the files you have backed up. The .*NNN* extensions are sequencing numbers so that you can distinguish the different disks made during a single BACKUP operation. Different disks in the same backup set have different sequence numbers: The first disk files have the extension .001, the next have the extension of .002, and so on.

You cannot use the DOS DEL or ERASE commands to delete files made by BACKUP, as these files are created with the read-only bit in the attribute byte set. See Chapter 5 for a complete discussion of file attributes.

⊙ Do not have the DOS commands SUBST, JOIN, APPEND, or ASSIGN active when you use BACKUP, as you may not be able to restore the files properly.

```
\WS4\INSTALL.CHL
\WS4\INSTALL.LFT
\WS4\INSTALLF.BAT
\WS4\INSTALLH.BAT
\WS4\INTERNAL.DCT
\WS4\ISOKIN.FRD
\WS4\JANET.SPR
\WS4\JAPAN
\WS4\JIM
\WS4\LASER1.DOC
\WS4\LASER2.DOC
\WS4\LEGAL
\WS4\LIDOKAS.REL
\WS4\LIFT.INS
\WS4\LIFT.PAT
\WS4\LIFTZ31.INS
\WS4\LINEA2.FRD
\WS4\MAIN.DCT

Insert backup diskette 02 in drive A:

Warning! Files in the target drive
A:\ root directory will be erased
Strike any key when ready
```

Figure 3.3: BACKUP prompting for another disk when the first is full

There are several useful switches you can use with the BACKUP command, as shown in Table 3.2.

Table 3.2: BACKUP Command Switches

SWITCH	OPERATION
/A	Adds files to a backup disk
/D	Backs up files by date
/F	Formats the destination disk if required
/L	Creates a log file
/M	Backs up modified files
/S	Backs up subdirectories
/T	Backs up files by time on date specified by /D. Specify *a* for A.M. or *p* for P.M.

RESTORING FILES FROM A DOS BACKUP DISK

You can use the RESTORE command to restore onto your hard disk files made by the BACKUP command. You can restore single files, complete directories and their subdirectories, or the entire disk. The RESTORE command has the general syntax:

RESTORE *source destination switches*

Because the files made by BACKUP have a special format, you cannot use COPY or XCOPY to load them onto your hard disk.

Remember, because these backup files are special files, you cannot use COPY or XCOPY to restore them.

When you use RESTORE, you must specify a complete path if the current directory is not the directory into which you want to restore files. If you do not specify a complete path and the files you have specified for restoration were not backed up from the current directory, you may receive the misleading error message

Warning! No files were found to restore

The RESTORE command has several optional switches, which are summarized in Table 3.3.

Table 3.3: RESTORE Command Switches

SWITCH	OPERATION
/A:*mm-dd-yy*	Restores files that were modified on or after *mm-dd-yy*
/B:*mm-dd-yy*	Restores files that were modified on or before *mm-dd-yy*
/E:*hh-mm-ss*	Restores files modified earlier than *hh-mm-ss*
/L:*hh-mm-ss*	Restores files modified later than *hh-mm-ss*
/M	Restores files that have changed or have been erased since the last backup
/N	Restores files that no longer exist on the destination disk
/P	Prompts you before restoring each file, if the file was modified since it was backed up
/S	Restores files in subdirectories

Backing up your hard disk is an important operation that you should not neglect. However, using the DOS commands to make or restore a backup is difficult and can be confusing. Fortunately, PC Tools offers an alternative.

BACKING UP YOUR HARD DISK WITH PCBACKUP

If you are using PC Tools 6.0, turn off your fax card before starting a backup. If a fax arrives in the middle of a backup, you will get unpredictable results.

PC Tools offers a fast and easy-to-use alternative to the DOS commands for disk backup. The PCBACKUP program can back up your disk, in whole or in part, either as a DOS-compatible backup or by using high-speed DMA.

PCBACKUP 6.0 is not compatible with backups made by PCBACKUP 5.5 or earlier.

DOS-COMPATIBLE BACKUPS

You can use the DOS-compatible selection to make a backup to any DOS-supported device, including floppy disks, another hard disk, or a tape drive. In fact, if you want to use anything other than floppy disks, you *must* use this method to make your backup.

The files in the backup are stored in a special way to reduce the amount of space they occupy, so you must restore the files before you can use them.

HIGH-SPEED DMA BACKUPS

Some PC-compatibles may not support DMA due to hardware limitations. If you are unsure of your system, run a test backup and try restoring the files to ensure that you can restore them properly. If not, use the DOS-compatible method.

To lighten the load on your computer's microprocessor, some parts of your system can transfer data to and from memory without going through the CPU. This operation is known as *direct memory access,* or *DMA,* and is handled by the DMA controller. One of the purposes of DMA is to allow the disk drives to read or write data directly without involving the CPU. DMA can speed performance considerably, because transfers can take place at the full speed of the bus and of memory.

DMA backups are much faster than DOS-compatible backups. However, you can only make them to floppy disks; you cannot use a tape or another hard disk. The backup files are recorded in a special format that DOS cannot read. PC Tools provides a program called PCBDIR that enables you to read disks made by DMA backup.

If you have a Copy PC II Deluxe Option Board installed in your system, PCBACKUP will use it to increase the speed with which it formats new disks during a DMA backup. The degree of improvement depends on your CPU, disk speed, and other factors, but can be as much as 20 to 30 percent.

MAKING A COMPLETE BACKUP

To start PCBACKUP from the DOS prompt, type

```
PCBACKUP
```

Notice that there are no spaces in the program name. DOS does not allow them.

The first time you run PCBACKUP, you can configure the program to your requirements and save the details of the configuration in a file that PCBACKUP calls PCBACKUP.CFG. The next time you run PCBACKUP, this file will automatically load your default settings.

CHANGING YOUR USER LEVEL (VERSION 6.0)

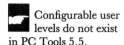
Configurable user levels do not exist in PC Tools 5.5.

In PCBACKUP Version 6.0 you can choose from three different user levels to customize your work environment to your own requirements. Select the User Level option from the Configure pull-down menu, and you will see the screen shown in Figure 3.4.

The three user levels are:

- Beginner
- Intermediate
- Advanced

Make your selection from this list, and select the OK button. The Advanced level is active by default. Use the Cancel button if you don't want to change your user level.

The user level determines the entries shown in the PCBACKUP Options menu. To keep the selections under Options to a minimum, choose the Beginner level. For a larger selection, choose the Intermediate level, and for maximum control, choose the Advanced level for the complete set of menu items. The Options pull-down menu selections by user level are shown in Table 3.4.

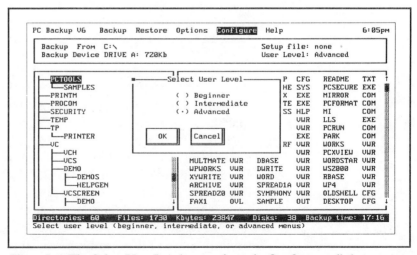

Figure 3.4: The Select User Level screen from the Configure pull-down menu

Table 3.4: The Options Pull-Down Menu Selections by User Level

BEGINNER	INTERMEDIATE	ADVANCED
Load setup	Load setup	Load setup
	Save setup	Save setup
	Backup Method	Backup method
	Reporting	Reporting
	Subdirectory inclusion	Compress
	Include/exclude files	Verify
	Attribute exclusions	Format Always
	Date range selection	Error Correction
	Overwrite warning	Standard Format
		Subdirectory inclusion
		Include/Exclude Files
		Attribute exclusions
		Date range selection
		Save History
		Time display
		Overwrite warning

As you become more familiar with the selections available in this menu, you will want to increase your user level.

PCBACKUP tries to determine the type of drives installed in your machine. On some systems, this information is not available and PCBACKUP defaults to 360K floppy disks. The first dialog box presents you with the options for your drive and for the backup type, DOS Compatible or High Speed DMA. Be careful to enter information only about the actual drive type and not about the type of disk you want to use for the backup. For example, enter a 1.2MB drive here, even though you want to make your backups to 360K disks using this drive. The target media type information is requested by the next dialog box. Enter your choice of disk type by clicking with the mouse, or using the arrow keys and pressing Enter.

If you have two floppy-disk drives of the same type, an additional dialog box will ask if you want to make a one-drive or a two-drive backup. If you can, choose the two-drive backup to save time when changing disks.

You can also choose to back up your system to another hard disk or to a removable device such as a Bernoulli box. To back up to another hard disk, you must choose the drive number and enter the complete path for the backup. If you are using a tape drive, select the removable drive option.

As mentioned, PCBACKUP saves this configuration in a file called PCBACKUP.CFG, which is kept in the same directory as PCBACKUP.

If you want to back up your whole disk, you are now ready to start the backup. The default configuration of drive C starts with the root directory and includes all subdirectories.

Select Start Backup (F5) from the Backup pull-down menu or click on the Start Backup command on the message line at the bottom of the screen. PCBACKUP prompts you to insert each disk in turn. The directory and file being backed up both appear highlighted on the main display, so you can watch the progress of the backup. The status line at the bottom of the screen also indicates the progress of the backup by showing the disk number, the track number of the disk, the percentage complete, and the time elapsed since you started the backup.

When the backup is complete, a directory for the entire backup set is written to the last disk. You should carefully number each of the disks in your backup, since the Restore selection will want you to load the backup disks in the same order.

At the end of the backup, you'll see a dialog box that contains statistics for the backup. This dialog box includes the total number of directories, files, and kilobytes backed up, the total number of disks used, the time the backup took to complete, and the average transfer rate in kilobytes per minute, as shown in Figure 3.5.

MAKING A PARTIAL BACKUP

You may not always want to back up your whole disk. Often you will want to back up only files that have changed, or files that changed after a certain date, or even a certain type of file. The

PCBACKUP Options pull-down menu, shown in Figure 3.6, makes this kind of selection easy.

The current settings of several of these choices are shown (in parentheses) to the right of the menu items.

LOAD SETUP   Once you have saved a configuration in a file, you can reload it into PCBACKUP with the Load Setup selection. This

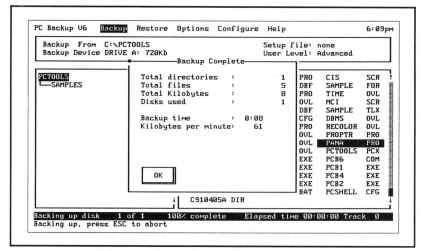

Figure 3.5: PCBACKUP screen of statistics for a partial backup

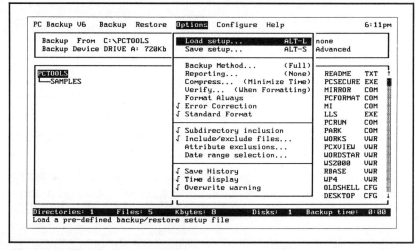

Figure 3.6: The Options menu

means that you can make several different types of backups without having to reconfigure the program. You just load the file and make the backup.

SAVE SETUP   After selecting from the many available options, save them in a file and load them with Load Setup rather than reconfiguring the program manually. When choosing a file name for the configuration file, choose one that you can remember easily. For example, you might save the configuration for backing up your word processing files in a file called WORDBACK.

The following list shows all the PCBACKUP options saved in the configuration file:

- Attribute exclusions
- Backup method (DOS-compatible or high-speed DMA)
- Backup type (Full, Full Continual, Archive, or Continual)
- Color selections
- Compression type (Minimize Disks or Minimize Time)
- Date range selections
- Disk media
- Disk type(s)
- Formatting type (Always or When Needed)
- Include/exclude files
- Overwrite warning
- Subdirectory inclusion
- Time display
- User level
- Verification type

BACKUP METHOD   You can select one of four backup methods: Full, Full Continual, Archive, or Continual. The default setting is for a Full backup.

- Full backs up all the files in all the directories you selected, regardless of the status of the archive bit in the file's attribute byte. When the backup is complete, the archive bit is reset.

- Full Continual is like a Full backup, but the archive bit in the attribute byte is left unchanged.

- Archive backs up files that have been created or modified since the last backup. The archive bit is reset at the end of the backup.

- Continual is the same as Archive, but the archive bit is not reset at the end of the backup.

REPORTING You can have PCBACKUP print a report when the backup is complete, and you can choose whether the report is sent to a disk file or to the printer. The default is off.

- None generates no report.

- Printer sends the report to the printer.

- Disk sends the report to a disk file called PCBACKUP.RPT in the directory from which PCBACKUP runs.

A sample report is shown in Figure 3.7.

COMPRESS You can set Compress to minimize the time the backup takes or to minimize the number of disks used for the backup. The default setting is Minimize Time.

- None gives you no compression.

- Minimize Spaces minimizes the number of disks made during a backup. Files are compressed as they are backed up to reduce the number of disks needed for the backup. Compression results depend on the type of files being compressed. Program files will not change very much. Data files, word processing files, and spreadsheet files will compress much more. This option works for both DOS-compatible and high-speed DMA backups.

- Minimize Time does as much compression as it can in the time allowed without slowing down the operation. The faster

```
PC Backup V 6  Directory Report
(c) Copyright 1989, 1990 Central Point Software, Inc. All Rights Reserved
Backup Performed on 04/05/1991  06:48p

Backup Method: High-Speed DMA
Media Type: 720 Kb
Verify When Formatting was ON.
Save Time Compression was ON.
Standard Backup Format, Error correction was ON.

Include/Exclude Selections:
    *.PRO
    *.COM
    *.CFG

Total Directories:    1
Total Files:         18
Number of Disks:      1

      Name              Size        Date        Time    Atrib Vol


Directory: C:\PCTOOLS\
PCSETUP.CFG            5,610   03/24/1990     06:00p   ----   1
PC-CACHE.COM         27,984   03/29/1990     06:00p   ----   1
MIRROR.COM           15,897   03/24/1990     06:00p   ----   1
REBUILD.COM          17,504   03/24/1990     06:00p   ----   1
PCFORMAT.COM         16,960   03/24/1990     06:00p   ----   1
MI.COM                4,256   03/24/1990     06:00p   ----   1
PCRUN.COM             3,020   03/27/1990     06:00p   ----   1
PARK.COM                649   03/27/1990     06:00p   ----   1
OLDSHELL.CFG            267   04/04/1991     11:07a   ----   1
DESKTOP.CFG           3,283   04/04/1991     11:07a   ----   1
SAMPLE.PRO            3,134   03/24/1990     06:00p   ----   1
HPLJF.PRO             1,290   03/24/1990     06:00p   ----   1
FAX.CFG              33,410   04/04/1991     11:07a   ----   1
EPSON.PRO             1,546   03/24/1990     06:00p   ----   1
PROPTR.PRO            1,398   03/24/1990     06:00p   ----   1
PANA.PRO              1,627   03/24/1990     06:00p   ----   1
PCB6.COM              6,480   03/28/1990     06:00p   ----   1
PCSHELL.CFG           2,606   04/04/1991     11:09a   ----   1
Total Bytes:   146,921

Total Compression:       38
```

Figure 3.7: A sample PCBACKUP report

your disk and CPU speed, the more compression will be accomplished. This option works only with high-speed DMA backups.

VERIFY   PCBACKUP will verify the data on your backup disks. The default setting is Verify When Formatting.

- None gives you no verification.

- When Formatting causes PCBACKUP to verify a disk as it is formatted. This is the most likely time to find a disk error.

- Always verifies the disk every time something is written to it. This selection will slow down the backup process, but you should choose it to be absolutely certain of a good quality backup.

FORMAT ALWAYS Formats the backup disk every time it is used. This is not usually necessary. The default for this command is off.

ERROR CORRECTION (VERSION 6.0)

The Error Correction and Standard Format selections are not available in PC Tools 5.5.

If you turn on Error Correction, a check mark appears to the left of the menu entry. With Error Correction turned on, PCBACKUP can recover from a multitude of errors on a damaged disk. To be able to do this, PCBACKUP stores additional information along with the backed-up files on each backup disk. This process takes slightly longer than a standard backup.

STANDARD FORMAT (VERSION 6.0)

PCBACKUP has two methods available for formatting the backup disks:

All disks formatted by PC Tools 5 and later were formatted using this nonstandard method. To use these disks be sure to select nonstandard—otherwise they will have to be reformatted.

- Standard uses the usual DOS method of formatting the backup disk.

- Nonstandard uses a formatting method that writes an additional sector of data per track on the disk. DOS cannot read disks formatted by this method.

A check mark to the left of the menu item indicates that Standard Format is turned on.

SUBDIRECTORY INCLUSION The Subdirectory inclusion selection includes all of a selected directory's subdirectories in the backup if it is on, or excludes them if it is off. The default is on. A check mark appears to the left of its name in the menu to indicate that Subdirectory inclusion is on. Selecting it again turns it off. Make this selection before using Include/exclude files.

INCLUDE/EXCLUDE FILES   Include/exclude files allows you to choose individual files for backup. The default is Include All Files. This is shown in the Include/Exclude editor by the DOS wildcard designation *.*.

The screen allows up to 16 lines of files to include or exclude, and the list is always processed from top to bottom. To exclude a file or a group of files, place a minus sign in the left-hand column of the screen. Table 3.5 shows examples of Include/Exclude options.

Table 3.5: Example Include/Exclude Options Using DOS Wildcard Characters

OPTION	RESULT
.	Includes everything on the disk, all files and subdirectories (setting Subdirectory Inclusion has no effect on this selection).
− *.*	Unselects everything on the disk.
.	Selects all files in the root directory.
\WORDPROC*.*	Selects all files in the \WORDPROC directory. If Subdirectory Inclusion is on, also selects all files in all subdirectories below \WORDPROC.
\LOTUS*.WK1	Selects all files in the \LOTUS directory with the extension .WK1, all Lotus worksheets, and if Subdirectory Inclusion is on, all files in all subdirectories below \LOTUS that also match.
−\WORDPROC*.BAK	Excludes all files with the extension .BAK in the \WORDPROC directory, and if Subdirectory Inclusion is on, excludes all files in all directories below \WORDPROC with the .BAK extension.

If you change the Subdirectory inclusion setting after making Include/Exclude choices, you must reenter the Include/Exclude screen and choose OK again to make this change affect the previously chosen files.

ATTRIBUTE EXCLUSIONS Attribute exclusions modifies any of the file-selection techniques in use in PCBACKUP. You can exclude hidden files, read-only files, or system files.

- Hidden Files excludes all hidden files from the backup. Hidden files are sometimes used on copy-protection schemes where they are usually location-specific. They do not like to be moved and will often refuse to work if you change their position. The Hidden Files setting default is on.

- System Files excludes all system files from the backup. The DOS files are system files, as well as being location-specific, and you should exclude them from the backup. The System Files setting default is on.

- Read Only files excludes all read-only files from the backup.

DATE RANGE SELECTION Date range selection allows you to back up files before, after, or between certain dates. Date range selection works with Include/exclude files. If Include/exclude files is off, Date range selection does nothing. If Include/exclude files is on and you make a Date range selection, only those files meeting both criteria are backed up. Specify the date as *MM/DD/YY,* entering both digits for each number.

SAVE HISTORY (VERSION 6.0)

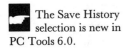
The Save History selection is new in PC Tools 6.0.

A file containing information on the files backed up, the time of the backup, and the type of backup performed is added to the last disk of each backup you make. If Save History is turned on, this file is also written to your hard disk. When you restore or compare files from your backup, the process goes much quicker if PCBACKUP can read the file from your hard disk, rather than asking you to insert the last floppy disk so that it can search for the history file.

TIME DISPLAY   You can choose whether or not to display the elapsed backup time. This may be a problem on some PC-compatibles, or if you are working on a network. The default is on.

- Setting Time display to On turns the time display on.
- Setting Time display to Off turns the time display off.

Choose Time display from the Options menu once to turn it on. Select it again to turn it off. A check mark to the left of the menu entry indicates that it is on.

OVERWRITE WARNING   The Overwrite warning warns you that the disk in use has already been used in a backup, and that existing files will be overwritten. The default is on.

- If you set Overwrite warning to On, as PCBACKUP attempts to write on a disk that contains backup files, the backup stops and you are asked to confirm whether you wish to overwrite the existing files.
- If you set Overwrite warning to Off, files are overwritten with no warning.

In the Backup pull-down menu there are two other ways of selecting files and directories for backup: backup From entry and cHoose Directories.

BACKUP FROM ENTRY   You can specify a particular path for backup with the backup From entry selection. The default setting is C:\, which means back up every file and directory. You can change the default by entering a new path. To back up all your PC Tools files, enter

    C:\PCTOOLS

To back up all your Lotus files, type

    C:\LOTUS

The display of files in the files list window changes to reflect your choices.

Once you have made all your choices from these selections, you can proceed with the backup. Choose Start Backup from the Backup pull-down menu (F5), or click on the Backup command on the message line at the bottom of the screen.

The status bar at the bottom of the screen also changes to reflect the number of files for backup and the number of disks needed.

CHOOSE DIRECTORIES   Select cHoose directories (F4) from the Backup pull-down menu, or click the mouse in the tree list window.

To choose all the files in your word processing directory, move the highlight to the \WS4 directory and press Enter or click the mouse. All files are now selected. You can use the Tab key or click in the file list window to select that window, and then start to select individual files.

CHANGING AND SAVING PCBACKUP CONFIGURATIONS

The commands in the Configure pull-down menu shown in Figure 3.8 are for changing the default settings in PCBACKUP.

The selection Choose Drive and Media lets you change the disk media designation, while Define Equipment lets you change the

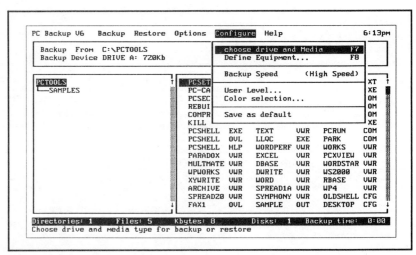

Figure 3.8: Configure pull-down menu

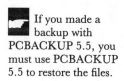

Selecting the high-intensity option can cause some monochrome monitors to start flashing in reverse video. This is unpleasant, so be careful.

drive specification and whether you want high-speed DMA or DOS-compatible backups.

If you are using a color monitor, or a monochrome monitor that can support shades of gray, the Color Selection choice helps you to change the default colors. The left-hand side of the screen lists the names of the windows, and the color choices are shown on the right.

Save as Default saves these changed items into the default PCBACKUP configuration file.

USING PCBACKUP IN A BATCH FILE

You can also load the configuration file into PCBACKUP if you are using a batch file or running PCBACKUP from the DOS command prompt. To make a backup that saves all your Lotus worksheet files, use the Options selection to select the method of archive, and use the Save option to keep this configuration information in a file called LOTUSBCK. Include the line

    PCBACKUP LOTUSBCK

in your batch file and PCBACKUP will prompt you to insert the backup disks in sequence. When the backup is complete, control is passed back to the batch file and execution continues at the next line.

USING PCBACKUP TO RESTORE FILES FROM YOUR BACKUP DISKS

If you made a backup with PCBACKUP 5.5, you must use PCBACKUP 5.5 to restore the files.

You use the commands in the Restore pull-down menu either to reload files onto a hard disk after a hardware problem or to move files from one machine to another. Figure 3.9 shows the Restore pull-down menu.

Restore assumes that you have already formatted the hard disk and loaded all the DOS files and the PC Tools files into their respective directories.

MAKING A COMPLETE RESTORE

Select Start Restore (F6) from the Restore pull-down menu, and you are prompted for disk 1 of your backup. You may be asked to

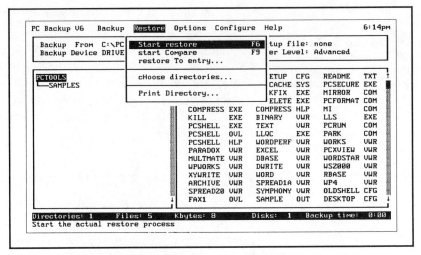

Figure 3.9: Restore pull-down menu

insert the last disk of the backup set so that the directory information can be read from this disk before the backup proceeds. You are prompted for each disk in turn as the restore process continues. Insert the disks in the sequence in which you made the backup.

If Restore detects that a file already exists on the hard disk, you have the following choices: Overwrite, Overwrite with Newer File Only, Skip this File, and Repeat for all Later Files.

- Overwrite overwrites the existing file on the disk with the file being restored.

- Overwrite with Newer File Only overwrites the file on the hard disk only if the backup file has a later date—that is, if the file on the backup disk is a more recent file.

- Skip this File prevents Restore from overwriting the file.

- Repeat for all Later Files adds capability to one of the first three commands, and keeps you from having to make the same choice repeatedly.

MAKING A PARTIAL RESTORE

Often a partial restore may be all you need. You might want to recover just one file or just one directory from your backup.

Select the Restore pull-down menu, and choose restore To entry. It is important to restore files and directories into the same directory from which they were backed up. restore To entry works just like the backup From entry selection just described. To restore the PC Tools files into their directory, type

C:\PCTOOLS

in the restore To entry dialog box. To restore your Lotus worksheet files, type

C:\LOTUS

into the restore To entry dialog box.

You can also use cHoose directories in the same menu to restore files and directories. You are prompted to insert the last backup disk so that the directory information can be read, and the tree and file list windows can be updated. In PC Tools 6.0, PCBACKUP lists the history files found on the hard disk. The list shows the drive letter the backup was made from, the name, date, time, and size of the backup, and the backup media type. If the list does not include the backup you want, select the Insert button, and you will be prompted to insert the last backup disk so that the directory information can be read, and the tree and file list windows can be updated. You can also choose to print a history report from a history file on the hard disk or from the inserted floppy disk or tape. PCBACKUP usually assumes that you want to restore everything in the backup, so all files and directories are highlighted. If you only want to restore a part of the backup, move the highlight onto the root directory and press Enter or click the left mouse button. This deselects all files and directories. Now you can choose which files to restore using the same mechanisms you used to make the backup. You can use the following options from the Options pull-down menu:

- Subdirectory inclusion
- Include/exclude files
- Attribute exclusions
- Date range exclusion

CH. 3

These commands work with Restore just as they did with Backup, but the conditions apply to the files you are restoring rather than to the files you are backing up.

Start the restore by selecting Start Restore (F6) or clicking on the Start Restore command. You are prompted to insert the appropriate disks, and when the restore is complete, the message

Restore Completed!

appears in a dialog box on the screen.

The tree and file list windows are updated to show the information from your backup disks.

If you lose a backup disk, continue with the restore operation anyhow. Restore will tell you that the disk is out of sequence, and will then continue to restore all the complete files. If a file crosses a disk boundary—with one part of the file on one disk and another part on another disk—and the disk is lost, the file cannot be restored.

Also, if you lose the last disk in the backup, Restore can rebuild the directory information it contained from the other disks in the set, so you can still make the restore.

Restore senses that the directory information for the backup set is missing and asks if you want to rebuild it. Rebuild reads all the disks in the set and makes a new directory. Rebuild then opens a dialog box and asks if you want to continue with the restore operation or write out the directory information to floppy disk. Save the directory information to a new disk so that you don't overwrite any of your backup files.

START COMPARE (VERSION 6.0)

 Start Compare is new in PC Tools 6.0.

After you have made a backup, or before you start to restore files, you can compare the files in the backup with the files on your disk. This is available as an extra security measure. PCBACKUP uses the history file for the comparison, and displays information in the Tree List window when you compare files.

First you must select Choose Directories from the Restore pull-down menu, and decide which backup set you are going to work with. When you first choose the backup, all files and directories are selected; use the mouse or the keyboard to unselect any files you want to exclude from the comparison. Next select Start Compare, and you are prompted to insert the appropriate backup disk that contains the files for the comparison. A special symbol appears next to each file. These symbols are shown in Table 3.6.

If the x symbol, indicating a problem exists with the backup, appears next to any of your files, check that there are no TSR programs running that might change a file during a backup. You can also try making the backup at a different speed, but be sure to do another compare afterwards to ensure that the backup is good.

Table 3.6: Start Compare Symbols Describing the Comparison

SYMBOL	MEANING
=	The backup file and the hard disk file are identical.
<	The backup file is older than the hard disk file, but the files are identical.
<<	The backup file is older than the hard disk file, and the files are not identical.
>	The backup file is newer than the hard disk file, but the files are identical.
>>	The backup file is newer than the hard disk file, and the files are not identical.
s	The size of the backup file is different from the hard disk file, but the date and time are the same.
-	The backup file is not present on the hard disk.
x	The backup file is different from the hard disk file, even though the dates and times are identical.

USING PCBDIR TO LOOK AT DMA BACKUP FILES

PCBDIR, provided with Version 5.5 and 6.0 of PC Tools, can read DMA backup disks from PC Tools Versions 5.0 through 5.1. However, it cannot generate a report from these disks.

When PCBACKUP makes a high-speed DMA backup, it does so in a form that DOS cannot read. For this reason, PC Tools includes a program called PCBDIR that lets you look at these backup disks. PCBDIR does more than just list the disks, however. If you forgot to label your backup disks, it can help you put them in the right sequence.

To run PCBDIR on a high-speed DMA backup disk in drive A, type

PCBDIR A:

You will see the information shown in Figure 3.10.

PCBDIR shows the date and time the backup was made, the number of the disk, and the number of files and directories in the backup.

```
C:\PCTOOLS>PCBDIR
PCBackup Directory Report V6
Copyright (c) 1990 by Central Point Software. All Rights Reserved.

What floppy drive contains the backup disk (default A:), Q to quit?A:

Disk is number 1 of a PC Backup set, backed up at 06:18p on 04/05/1991.
Disk was created with release 6.0 of PC Backup
The directory starts on track 3 (3h) of this disk.
This disk is recorded in DOS standard format.
Advanced Error Correction was ON for this backup.


What floppy drive contains the backup disk (default A:), Q to quit?Q


C:\PCTOOLS>
```

Figure 3.10: PCBDIR information on a high-speed DMA backup disk in drive A

BACKING UP WITH TAPE DRIVES

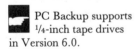 PC Backup supports ¼-inch tape drives in Version 6.0.

Although floppy disks are by far the most commonly used media for storing small numbers of backup files, other types of media are available.

Magnetic tape cartridges are used when a large amount of data has to be backed up, particularly in a business or scientific environment. These tape drives are fast and can store a large amount of data in a short time, often more than a megabyte a minute. They can be added to most computer systems easily as an internal or external drive by the addition of a single circuit board and some connecting cables. These drives often cost less than $1000, and the tapes themselves are inexpensive and easy to store.

In Version 6.0, PCBACKUP supports tape drives that use $1/4$-inch DC 2000 tape cartridges, including the IBM PS/2 Internal Tape Backup, the Compaq Internal Tape Backup, and the Irwin Model 2040 and 2080. PCBACKUP also supports QIC (Quarter-Inch Compatibility) 40 and QIC 80 tape drives from Mountain File-safe and ArchiveXL. These tape drives can only be used with computers using 80286 or later processors, and must be connected to the primary high-speed floppy-disk controller card inside the computer.

PCBACKUP will format a tape during a backup if necessary, but you can avoid this process and save a lot of time if you buy preformatted and certified tapes. It can take up to 90 minutes to format and certify a blank tape. If you do insert a blank tape, PCBACKUP rewinds the tape and tries to read the tape header. If this fails, the tape is retensioned, and PCBACKUP tries to read the header again. Finally, a dialog box appears displaying the message

Tape needs formatting and certification.

and you have the choice of formatting the tape, selecting a new tape, or cancelling the operation.

Making a backup with a tape is very similar to making a backup with floppy disks, the steps are essentially the same. Do not try to remove the tape from the drive when the tape is moving, as you might damage the tape. Leave the Verify When Formatting selection and the Error Correction selection in the Options menu set to their default On positions when using tapes to ensure the highest degree of data integrity.

You should use the Start Compare command after you have made your first tape backup to compare the files on the tape against the files on your hard disk. This comparison will alert you to any possible problems with the backup. Now is the time to discover any problems, not when you are battling to restore files after an accident with your hard disk. You can also set the Advanced user level Verify command to Verify Always. This makes an automatic comparison of the files on your hard disk against the files on your backup tape after the backup is complete, giving you an extra degree of certainty that your backup is good.

PCBACKUP creates tapes written in a proprietary format to enhance speed, file compression, and error recovery. You cannot use PCBACKUP to read tapes created by other backup programs; neither will they be able to read PCBACKUP tapes.

SUMMARY

In this chapter, I discussed why you should make a habit of backing up your hard disk on a regular basis. I explained the DOS commands for copying files, and the ways to use BACKUP and RESTORE. I described PC Backup's flexibility in making backups: from backups of a small number of files to backups of an entire disk. Finally, I covered the equally flexible Restore operations.

4

Unerasing
Files and
Data Recovery

4

In this chapter, I discuss some of the mishaps that can befall your data and how you can recover from them. Both floppy and hard disks can be mechanically damaged by careless handling, files can be deleted accidentally, and disks can be reformatted inadvertently. The PC Tools programs provide several elegant solutions to these problems. First, however, I'll give you some tips on how to prevent such problems from occurring.

TAKING CARE OF YOUR DISKS

Disks, both hard and floppy, can deteriorate through extended use. Floppy disks in particular can be easily damaged by careless handling.

SAFEGUARDING FLOPPY DISKS

Here are some suggestions for handling floppy disks:

- When you are not using a floppy disk, keep it in its jacket in a disk storage tray or in its box.

- Do not leave floppy disks where they will get hot, such as on a window sill, on top of your monitor, or in a car parked in the sun. The disks may warp and become unusable.

- Keep disks away from devices that emit magnetic fields, such as motors, paper clip holders, and magnetic keys.

- Do not touch the recording surface of the disk.

- Write on disk labels before attaching them to the disks. If you do write on a label that is on a disk, use a soft felt-tip pen, not a pencil.

- Keep backup copies of all distribution disks, and do not keep them with the original disks. You can often find a local company that specializes in archiving data in a secure storage area. Such companies use precisely controlled temperature and humidity to preserve the media in storage. They also usually have excellent security and fire protection.

HANDLING HARD DISKS

Your hard disk is not immune from problems either. Here are some suggestions for hard-disk care:

- Do not move a hard disk while you are using it.
- Use the Park Disk head-parking program in PC Shell before turning the computer off. This is especially important if you are going to move the computer.

RECOVERING FROM HARD-DISK FORMATTING PROBLEMS

If you accidentally reformat your hard disk, all your programs and data will be lost. With the PC Tools programs Mirror and Rebuild, however, you can recover data from a reformatted hard disk.

USING MIRROR TO SAVE A COPY OF THE SYSTEM AREA

The FORMAT commands supplied with Compaq DOS up through Version 3.2, and AT&T's MS-DOS up through Version 3.1 actually erase all the data on the hard disk.

When you run the DOS FORMAT command on a hard disk, it clears the root directory and the file allocation table (FAT) of all entries but does not overwrite the data area on the disk. However, even though the data is still there, you normally have no way of accessing it.

Note that you cannot use Mirror and Recover to recover data from floppy disks formatted with the DOS FORMAT command because this command overwrites all the data on the floppy.

If you have reformatted the disk and started to load programs onto it from your floppy-disk masters, you may have overwritten the MIRROR.FIL file, in which case complete recovery might be impossible.

MIRROR makes copies of the FAT and the root directory of your hard disk and puts the copies into a file called MIRROR.FIL in the root directory. The size of this file is proportional to the number of files on your disk; for 10 megabytes of files, this file is approximately 40K.

You can only achieve complete recovery if the MIRROR.FIL file is absolutely accurate and up to date. You can run Mirror from the DOS command prompt, or install it into your AUTOEXEC.BAT file so that it runs every time you start your computer. Alternatively, you can run Mirror at the end of every session to keep MIRROR-.FIL up to date. To run Mirror from the DOS prompt, enter

MIRROR *drive parameter*

where *drive* is the letter of the drive you want Mirror to work on and *parameter* is one or more of the optional parameters you can use with Mirror. These optional parameters are

- /1 specifies that Mirror should save only the latest FAT and root directory information in the MIRROR.FIL file.

- /PARTN makes a floppy-disk copy of your partition table information.

- /T*drive* enables delete tracking. *Drive* is the drive letter to track. Delete tracking is discussed in full later in this chapter.

To have Mirror copy the system area of drive C, enter

MIRROR C:

Mirror normally keeps two copies of your FAT and root directory. Each time Mirror runs, it renames the old file as MIRROR.BAK and creates a new one called MIRROR.FIL that contains the latest information. This provides extra protection. If you want Mirror to keep only the latest information in a single file, enter

MIRROR C: /1

However, you should only do this when space on your hard disk is at a premium.

USING REBUILD TO RECOVER FILES AFTER AN ACCIDENTAL FORMAT

If you have deleted only a few files by accident, run the Undelete Files selection from the Special menu in PC Shell.

Suppose you run Mirror regularly to save information on your FAT and root directory into the MIRROR.FIL file. If you accidentally reformat your hard disk, it is relatively easy to recover your files and directories with Rebuild.

The only time you should ever run Rebuild is to recover your system after an accidental format. Rebuild displays a screen warning of the hazards of running it at any other time.

If you are unsure of when your MIRROR.FIL and MIRROR-.BAK files were made, you can use Rebuild with the special /J parameter to check the files before recovering your system. When you use the /J parameter, Rebuild merely looks at the dates of the two Mirror files and reports this information to you. You can then choose which of the two files to rebuild your system with. To look at the two Mirror files on drive C, enter

REBUILD C: /J

The opening Rebuild dialog is shown in Figure 4.1.

If you do not wish to proceed with the recovery, you can press the Escape key to leave Rebuild and return to the DOS prompt. If you want to reconstruct your hard disk, choose one of the files for Rebuild to use. Press L to use the last (or later) Mirror file or press P to use the prior (or previous) Mirror file, and the recovery process begins. Since Rebuild searches your disk directly for the Mirror files, the disk does not need to be readable by DOS for Rebuild to work properly.

When Rebuild completes the reconstruction of your system, you should run the DOS CHKDSK command as a final precaution.

Your disk does not have to be readable by DOS for Rebuild to work properly.

```
PC Tools Deluxe - REBUILD  V6
(C) Copyright 1987-1990  Central Point Software, Inc.
Unauthorized duplication prohibited.

Restore the SYSTEM area of your hard drive with
the image file created by MIRROR.

    WARNING !!        WARNING !!

This should be used ONLY to recover from the inadvertent use
of the DOS 'Format' command or the DOS 'Recover' command.
Any other use of REBUILD may cause you to lose data!  Files modified
since the last use of MIRROR may be lost.  To recover lost or
corrupted files, directories, etc., use PC Tools DISKFIX instead.

Just checking this time.

The LAST time MIRROR was used was at 17:46 on 04-05-91.
The PRIOR time MIRROR was used was at 08:11 on 04-05-91.

If you wish to use the LAST file as indicated
above, press 'L'. If you wish to use the PRIOR
file as indicated above, press 'P'. Press ESCAPE
to terminate REBUILD.
```

Figure 4.1: The opening Rebuild dialog

Rebuild recovers your FAT and root directory information. It does not recover files in subdirectories below the root. You should use Undelete Files for this task.

CHKDSK looks at the internal organization of your disk and reports any remaining file fragments that it finds as unallocated clusters. If CHKDSK finds any errors, the Mirror files were probably not absolutely up to date. In other words, there were files on your disk that were not detailed in the Mirror files. To look for these errors with CHKDSK, enter

CHKDSK

If CHKDSK finds any errors, run it again using the /F parameter as follows:

CHKDSK /F

This will fix the errors.

RUNNING REBUILD WITHOUT A MIRROR FILE

If you don't have a Mirror file on your hard disk, Rebuild tries to recover your FAT and root directory using the information that it finds on the disk. This will be much slower and rather less reliable than recovery using a Mirror file. To run Rebuild, enter

REBUILD *drive parameters*

where *drive* is the letter of the drive you are trying to recover and *parameter* is either /P, /L, /?, or /TEST.

- Use the /P option to direct all Rebuild output to your printer.

- Use the /L parameter to list every file and subdirectory REBUILD finds during the process. You can also use the /P parameter to direct all lists to the printer.

- The /? parameter displays a short Rebuild help screen.

- The /TEST parameter allows you to simulate the Rebuild without actually doing anything. This option can be very useful if you are unsure of the state of your Mirror files. You can run a test Rebuild, running it again in real mode if you like the results.

Rebuild needs your input whenever it cannot find all the pieces of a fragmented file. Rebuild asks if it should truncate the file or delete it altogether. If you truncate the file, you can usually save at least a part of it. On the other hand, if you delete the file you can always try the Undelete Files option in the PC Shell Special menu to work on the file individually. The choice you make depends on how much you know about the contents of the file. Truncating a program file is downright dangerous and can have unpredictable results. Truncating a text file, in contrast, is much less hazardous and you do recover a portion of your file.

If Rebuild does not ask any questions about a file, the file is probably intact and recovered.

Finally, run CHKDSK to check for any remaining errors.

PC FORMAT—A SAFE FORMAT PROGRAM

PC Format provides a faster, easier to use alternative to the DOS FORMAT command. It adds many useful safety features, including the ability to preserve the original contents of the disk you are formatting so that you can recover the original data on the disk.

You already learned what happens when you run the DOS FORMAT command on a hard disk. The FAT and root directory entries are destroyed. On a floppy disk, FORMAT writes a character into every location on the disk, completely destroying the disk's original data.

Using PC Format with a floppy disk allows Rebuild to recover the original contents of the disk, including the first letter of all the file names.

If you use PC Format on a floppy disk, the program first tries to read the disk. If it cannot find any data or if tracks 0 and 1 are empty, PC Format overwrites every track on the disk. If PC Format finds any data on the disk, it leaves the data intact but clears the FAT and the first character of all the file names in the root directory. It stores the first character of the file names in a special area in the root directory.

You cannot use PC Format to perform low-level formatting of your hard disk.

Similarly, if you use PC Format on your hard disk, the program does not destroy the original data on the disk. It clears the FAT and the first character of the file names in the root directory, and saves this information in a special place in the directory.

If you used the PC Setup install program to load PC Tools onto your hard disk, the installation program renames the DOS FORMAT command to FORMAT!, and makes a small batch file called

FORMAT that loads PC Format. Now when you type

FORMAT

the batch file loads PC Format rather than running the DOS FOR-MAT command.

To format the floppy disk in drive B, enter

FORMAT B:

PC Format always lets you change your mind before it starts the formatting process.

Figure 4.2 shows the resulting screen.

PC Format identifies the type of drive—in this case a 5¼″ 360K floppy—and selects the correct format mode of 9 sectors in each of the 40 tracks. PC Format checks the disk for existing data by reading tracks 0 and 1 before writing anything onto the disk. If they are empty, PC Format overwrites every track. In this case, since the disk already contained data, PC Format asks

Are you SURE you want to do this?

If you answer yes, the formatting starts. A small display of disk head number, cylinder number, and percentage complete shows the progress of the format.

```
C:\>FORMAT B:

C:\>PCFORMAT B:
PC Tools Disk Formatter v6
Copyright 1987-90 by Central Point Software, Inc.  All rights reserved.

Will format drive B:  (physical # 01h, type= 360k 5.25-inch)

Formatting 9 sectors, 40 cylinders, 2 sides.
Press Enter when ready...

Diskette may already contain data.

Are you SURE you want to do this?
If so, type in YES; anything else cancels.
? YES
Format completed.

    362496 bytes total disk space.
    362496 bytes available on disk.

Format another diskette (Y/N)? No
```

Figure 4.2: PC Format formatting a floppy disk in drive B

You can use PC Format with several optional parameters directly from the DOS command prompt to perform specific functions. Table 4.1 lists the optional PC Format parameters for floppy disks, and Table 4.2 lists those for hard disks.

Table 4.1: PC Format Parameters for Use with Floppy Disks

PARAMETER	USE
drive	Specifies the drive for formatting.
/1	Selects single-sided format.
/4	Formats a 360K floppy disk in a 1.2MB drive.
/8	Formats the disk with 8 sectors per track.
/DESTROY	Formats the disk and erases all data.
/F	Specifies a full format. PC Format reads the data on each track, formats the track, and rewrites the data. This may be slower than the other modes, but it can clean up poor disks. The FAT is cleared, but Rebuild can still recover the original data on the disk.
/F:*nnn*	Formats the disk to the specified size: 160, 180, 320, 360, 720, 1200, or 1400K.
/N:*xx*	Specifies the number of sectors to format. Must be used with the /T parameter.
/P	Prints the information on the screen to LPT1.
/Q	Quickly reformats an already formatted disk, erases the FAT and root directory.
/R	Reformats and rewrites each track.
/S	Copies the DOS system files after formatting to make the disk bootable.
/TEST	Simulates a format without writing to the disk.
/T:*xx*	Specifies the number of tracks to format. Must be used with the /N parameter.
/V	Adds a volume label. PC Format asks for the label when the format is complete.

Table 4.2: PC Format Parameters for Use with Hard Disks

PARAMETER	USE
drive	Specifies the drive for formatting.
/P	Prints the information on the screen to LPT1.
/Q	Quickly reformats an already formatted disk.
/S	Copies the DOS system files to the disk after formatting to make the disk bootable. Before using /S, boot the computer with a floppy disk containing the version of DOS you want transferred to the hard disk.
/TEST	Simulates a format without writing to the disk.
/V	Adds a volume label. PC Format prompts you for the label when the format is complete.

If you use PC Format to format a floppy disk, you can probably use Rebuild to recover the original data. The only data lost is the FAT, which Rebuild can reconstruct as long as the disk did not contain any fragmented files.

PC Format is a considerable advance over the DOS FORMAT command, and adds many useful safety features, including the ability to recover the original data on the disk if necessary.

USING PC SHELL TO FORMAT FLOPPY DISKS

As an alternative to PC Format, you can use one of the selections available in PC Shell to format your floppy disks. Suppose you run PC Shell memory-resident and are in the middle of an application program when you realize that you have to format a floppy disk before you can continue with your main application. You can hotkey into PC Shell, format the floppy disk, and return to your foreground application.

Insert a new floppy disk into your floppy-disk drive, and choose Format Data Disk from the Disk pull-down menu. Confirm which drive you are using, and PC Shell presents all the possible options available with your drive hardware, as shown in Table 4.3.

Table 4.3: Formatting Options Available Under PC Shell's Format Data Disk Option

160K	single-sided	8 sectors per track	40 tracks
180K	single-sided	9 sectors per track	40 tracks
320K	double-sided	8 sectors per track	40 tracks
360K	double-sided	9 sectors per track	·40 tracks
720K	double-sided	9 sectors per track	80 tracks
1.2MB	double-sided	15 sectors per track	80 tracks
1.44MB	double-sided	18 sectors per track	80 tracks

The 1.2MB and 1.44MB options are usually only available on computers that use the 80286 or a later microprocessor.

Choose the desired format option and select Continue. The progress of the format is shown on the screen in the Disk Initialization box. You can see exactly which track on which side of the disk is being formatted. When formatting is complete, you can enter an 11-character volume label to identify the disk. Then you are offered the choice of making a bootable system disk or not. Finally, PC Shell lists the number of bytes of disk space available and the number of bad sectors on the disk. Choose the Next box to format another floppy disk or the Exit box to return to PC Shell.

You can use Make System Disk in the same menu to make bootable system floppy disks, if your disks are already formatted.

Make System Disk transfers onto the floppy disk the DOS system files that are needed to make the disk bootable. Insert the floppy disk into drive A and choose Make System Disk from the Disk menu. Confirm your choice of disk, and PC Shell will complete the transfer of files. These files must be in a very specific location on the disk. If this location is already in use, the file transfer will fail and you will have to reformat the disk and retry Make System Disk.

RECOVERING FROM PARTITION TABLE PROBLEMS

Every formatted hard disk contains at least one partition. Some people divide large disks into smaller partitions and may install different operating systems in the separate partitions. The information on how your disk is partitioned is saved in a table on the hard disk. If this table is ever damaged or lost, DOS will not recognize the drive and you will see the terrifying error message

Invalid drive specification

when you try to access the drive.

SAVING PARTITION TABLE INFORMATION

MIRROR/PARTN only saves information for standard DOS partitions; it cannot recognize or save non-standard third-party partitioning schemes.

You cannot prevent accidents from damaging your partition table. However, you can use Mirror with a special parameter to save a copy of your disk's partition table to a floppy disk as insurance. To back up your partition table, insert a floppy disk into drive A and enter

MIRROR /PARTN

When you use Mirror with /PARTN, the partition table information is written to the floppy disk in a file called PARTNSAV.FIL. To save FAT and root directory entries, you must run Mirror again, this time including the drive letter of the drive for which you want Mirror to save the information. Figure 4.3 shows the dialog involved in making a copy of your partition table.

Once Mirror has copied your partition table on the floppy disk, you should carefully label the disk and put it in a safe place.

```
C:\>MIRROR /PARTN

PC Tools Deluxe - MIRROR  V6
(C) Copyright 1987-1990  Central Point Software, Inc.
Unauthorized duplication prohibited.

Disk Partition Table saver.

The partition information from your hard drive(s) has been read.

Next, the file PARTNSAV.FIL will be written to a floppy disk.  Please
insert a formatted diskette and enter the name of the diskette drive.
What drive? A

Successful.

C:\>
```

Figure 4.3: Mirror backing up your partition table

If you change any of the formatting information on your hard disk, or change the details of your partitions, you must execute

MIRROR /PARTN

again to record the changes.

Now if you see the DOS error message

Invalid drive specification

you can use Rebuild to reload the backup copy of your partition table onto your hard disk by entering

REBUILD /PARTN

Rebuild first checks whether the drive parameters on the hard disk match those on the floppy disk. If the parameters don't match, Rebuild will not restore the partition table information. If the parameters match, Rebuild continues with the restoration.

When Rebuild is finished, it prompts you to load a DOS disk in drive A and reboot the computer so that DOS can load the valid partition table. You can now run Rebuild again, this time to recover your FAT and root directory information.

RECOVERING ERASED FILES

Especially if you use wildcards in file names, it is easy to delete more files than you intended. You may even delete the entire contents of the directory. For example, both EDLIN and WordStar create .BAK files when files are modified or saved. Most people delete these files to save space, relying on their backup disks for copies of the original files. Suppose in this case you mistype

DEL *.BAK

as

DEL *.BAT

Instead of deleting your .BAK files, you have just deleted all your batch files.

Careful disk organization can help prevent some of these accidental erasures. To protect your batch files, for example, you should keep them in a directory separate from your EDLIN or WordStar files. No matter how good your organization is, however, sooner or later you will erase a file by accident or want to recover a file that you erased intentionally. This is where PC Tools comes into its own.

WHAT REALLY HAPPENS WHEN YOU DELETE A FILE?

Before describing how the PC Tools programs do their job, I'll explain precisely what happens when you delete a file. When you use DEL or ERASE on a file, the file's entries are cleared from the FAT. DOS also changes the first character of the file name in its directory to a Greek sigma character (ASCII E5 hex or 229 decimal) to indicate to the rest of the DOS system that the file has been erased. The file's entry, including its starting cluster number and its length, remains in the directory, hidden from your view because of the sigma character. The data itself is still in its original place on the disk. DOS does not do anything to the data until it is instructed to write another file over the same clusters. Thus, the first cluster of a file can be found and recovered quite easily as long as it has not been overwritten.

To illustrate this, make a very small text file on a blank formatted floppy disk in drive A. Open PC Shell, select drive A as the current drive, and choose Edit File from the File pull-down menu. Enter the following short piece of text:

This is a short piece of text.

Save the file as TESTFILE.TXT, and exit from the Edit File. In the main PC Shell display, you can see that the disk in drive A contains one short file. Use the More File Info selection from the File pull-down menu to look at the details of the file. Figure 4.4 shows the More File Information display for this file.

Figure 4.4: More File Information display for a small text file

Next, delete the file by selecting it in the main PC Shell display, and then using Delete File from the File pull-down menu or returning to DOS and entering

DEL TESTFILE.TXT

Now reopen PC Shell and look at the root directory of the disk in drive A. Notice that the message

no entries found

is shown where the file was, and that the file list is empty. Select View/ Edit Disk from the Disk pull-down menu, and look at sector 5, the original starting sector of the root directory. Note that the file name's first character has been changed to a sigma character, and that the rest of the file name entry is still intact, as shown in Figure 4.5.

Next, look at sector 12. The original text,

This is a short piece of text.

is still on the disk even though the file has been erased, as shown in Figure 4.6.

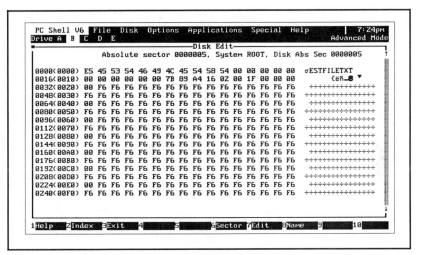

Figure 4.5: Looking at an erased file in the root directory

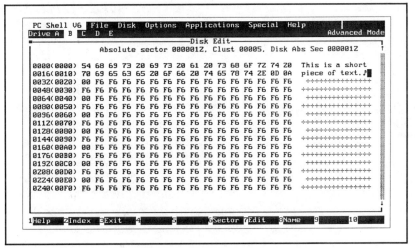

Figure 4.6: Original text of erased file is still on the disk

WHAT HAPPENS WHEN YOU ADD A NEW FILE?

See Chapter 6 to learn how to reduce file fragmentation with Compress.

When you add a new file to your disk, DOS looks for the next available piece (cluster) of free disk space. If the file is small enough to fit into this space, DOS slots it in. If the file is larger, DOS splits it into several pieces, placing it in clusters that are not numbered consecutively. In other words, the file becomes fragmented.

Thus, saving a new file onto the disk destroys the deleted file's data. If the new file is larger than the old one, the old file is completely obliterated. If the new file is smaller than the old one, some unknown amount of the old file will remain on the disk until it is finally overwritten during another write-to-disk operation.

The most important point to remember about file recovery is that you must not save anything on the disk until you have completed the recovery operation. Do not even copy PC Tools onto the hard disk; instead, run it from a floppy disk, installing it on your hard disk only when the recovery is completely finished. By following this rule, you will not overwrite the erased file's data, and will increase the chances of a complete recovery.

> Do not save anything after you delete a file inadvertently, or you may be unable to recover the file.

USING PC SHELL UNDELETE FILES TO RECOVER A FILE

> In PC Shell 6.0 the File menu has a selection called Undelete File. It works the same as Undelete Files from the Special menu.

I'll demonstrate how to restore erased files by using a text file rather than a program or binary file. You can examine a text file by several different methods in DOS or in PC Tools, and most people can immediately see when the contents of a text file (unlike a program file) begin to make sense.

To demonstrate how to use Undelete Files in PC Shell's Special pull-down menu, continue with TESTFILE.TXT, the small text file that you created and deleted on drive A.

Select Undelete Files from the Special pull-down menu, and confirm that you are in the correct directory by selecting Continue. You are presented with four choices: FILE, SUB-DIR, CREATE, and CANCEL, as shown in Figure 4.7.

Choose the FILE option. Select the file and then press Go. The next screen, shown in Figure 4.8, gives details of all the deleted files contained on the current drive.

This example contains only one file. The first letter of the file name has been replaced by a ? character, as it is unknown. Undelete asks you to provide a suitable beginning letter for the file, so enter T and then choose UNDELETE. Next you must choose between AUTO-MATIC or MANUAL recovery. Choose AUTOMATIC, and

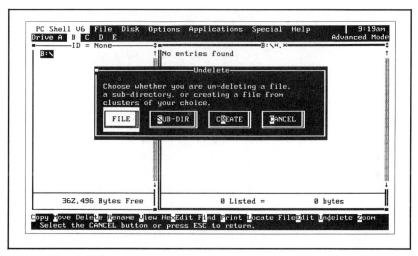

Figure 4.7: The Undelete menu choices

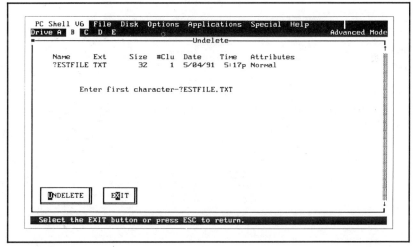

Figure 4.8: The Undelete screen

Undelete will recover the file if it can be recovered automatically. If the file cannot be recovered automatically, you will be prompted to use manual recovery methods, which are covered shortly. Choose Continue to return to the main PC Shell screen. You will see that the file TESTFILE.TXT has been completely restored.

This method of file recovery is known in PC Tools as the standard DOS method. A much more certain way of recovering erased files is to use the information collected by the delete tracking program.

HOW TO INSTALL DELETE TRACKING

You can use Mirror to install a small memory-resident delete tracking program that intercepts all DOS DEL and ERASE commands. The program saves several pieces of information about the file before it is actually deleted, including the file's name, size, and date, and a list of the file's cluster numbers. Once this information is stored in the delete tracking file, PCTRACKR.DEL, the DOS DEL or ERASE operation continues and the file is erased.

If you are using the DOS commands SUBST or JOIN, do not use delete tracking. If you are using ASSIGN, make sure that you install ASSIGN before you start delete tracking.

To install the delete tracking program for drive C, enter

> The Undelete Files option in PC Shell also uses information from the PCTRACKR.DEL file to supply the missing first letter of a deleted file and to help recover badly fragmented files.

```
MIRROR /TC
```

You can use delete tracking to protect more than one drive at a time. To install delete tracking on drives A and C, enter

```
MIRROR /TA /TC
```

The delete tracking file PCTRACKR.DEL is always created in the root directory of your disk. If the disk has more than one partition, PCTRACKR.DEL is kept in the root directory of the first partition. The delete tracking file is proportional to the size of the disk media you are using. See Table 4.4 for a list of disk types, delete tracking file sizes, and the number of file entries the delete tracking file can hold.

If you need to keep information on a different number of entries in the delete tracking file, you can specify the number of entries the file can hold (up to 999) by adding another optional item to the DOS command line.

To create a delete tracking file that can hold information on up to 999 entries for drive C, enter

```
MIRROR /TC-999
```

Table 4.4: Disk Drive Type, Delete Tracking File Size, and Number of Entries in Each File

DELETE TRACKING		
DISK TYPE	**FILE SIZE**	**NUMBER OF ENTRIES**
360K floppy	5K	25
720K floppy	9K	50
1.2MB floppy	14K	75
1.44MB floppy	14K	75
20MB hard disk	18K	101
32MB hard disk	36K	202
Over 32 MB hard disk	55K	303

If delete tracking cannot save the deleted file directory information into the PCTRACKR.DEL file, it beeps twice. If the PCTRACKR-.DEL file fills up completely, entries are overwritten, starting with the oldest entries.

RECOVERING ERASED FILES WITH DELETE TRACKING INSTALLED

After you install delete tracking, Undelete Files works in a much more powerful way. As an example, you will erase and then recover a file with delete tracking installed.

Place a freshly formatted floppy disk in drive A. Use Copy File in the File pull-down menu to copy the README.TXT file distributed with PC Tools from the \PCTOOLS directory to drive A. Then exit PC Shell back to DOS. Install delete tracking for drives C and A by entering

MIRROR /TC /TA

as shown in Figure 4.9.

Now return to PC Shell, select drive A, and delete the READ-ME.TXT file. Run Undelete Files, choose the File option, and

note that the next screen is different from the one described in
the standard DOS method of file undeletion. A dialog box, shown
in Figure 4.10, tells you that a delete tracking record exists (the
PCTRACKR.DEL file) and that you may undelete files using the
delete tracking method. Choose DEL TRACK to use information
from the PCTRACKR.DEL file in recovering README.TXT.

```
C:\>MIRROR /TC /TA

PC Tools Deluxe - MIRROR  V6
(C) Copyright 1987-1990  Central Point Software, Inc.
Unauthorized duplication prohibited.

Creates an image of the SYSTEM area.

Drive C being processed.

MIRROR successful.

PC Tools Deluxe - Delete Tracker V6
(C) Copyright 1987-1990  Central Point Software, Inc.
Unauthorized duplication prohibited.

The following drives are supported:
Drive A - Default
Drive C - Default

Installation complete.

C:\>
```

Figure 4.9: Using Mirror to install delete tracking on drives A and C

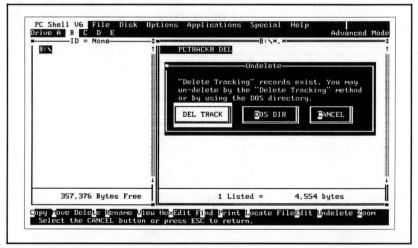

Figure 4.10: Selecting the delete tracking method for file recovery

Erased files ready for recovery are listed on the screen this time with their names shown in full, as in Figure 4.11. Notice that the first letter of the file name has been provided from the delete tracking file. In the example, only one file is shown on the screen, so go ahead and press G to undelete it.

The @ character at the end of the file name in Figure 4.11 indicates that the file can be recovered automatically. If you are using the delete tracking method, this symbol also means that none of the file's clusters are in use by another file, and the file will be recovered in its entirety. A * character would indicate that some of the file's clusters are available and others are in use by a file. If neither character is present, file recovery may be impossible.

If Undelete Files cannot recover the file automatically, you can try the manual method. Undelete Files collects the clusters it considers most likely to belong to your file, and you decide whether or not to add them to the file. In this mode, you can add the current cluster to the file, skip the current cluster without adding it to the file, save the clusters, search for particular characters, select a new cluster, or edit the cluster sequence by moving or removing a cluster from the file. If your file was fragmented, you may not want to add all the clusters into your file. With Edit, you can reorder the sequence of the clusters, or even remove one or more clusters.

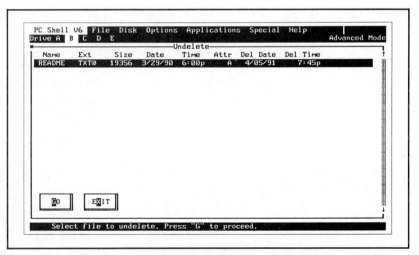

Figure 4.11: Using delete tracking to recover an erased file

PC Tools 6.0 includes a DOS command line version of Undelete Files simply called Undelete. You can use it if you want to undelete a file quickly without loading PC Shell. The general form of the command is

UNDELETE *drive parameters*

where *drive* is the drive you want to undelete files from, and *parameters* are chosen from the list shown in Table 4.5.

Before using the file recovery parameters of Undelete, you should use the /LIST option to review all the files that Undelete might attempt to recover. You might have deleted some of the files a long time ago, and you may not want to see them ever again. Others,

Table 4.5: Parameters for the DOS Command Line Version of Undelete (Version 6.0)

PARAMETER	USE
drive	The drive you are undeleting files from; defaults to the current drive.
file name	DOS file name to undelete. You can use DOS wildcard characters.
path	The path defining the directory where you want to undelete files.
/ALL	Undeletes all the deleted files it can find in the current directory without any prompting.
/DOS	Undeletes the files without using delete tracking, prompting you for your approval for each file.
/DT	Undeletes the files tracked by delete tracking, prompting for your approval for each file.
/LIST	Lists all the deleted files available for undeletion.
/? or /HELP	Displays a Help screen.

however, you will want to recover. Choose the files you want to undelete from the list and then use the /DT or /DOS parameters to do the undeleting. You must use either /DT or /DOS; you cannot use them together as they are mutually exclusive.

If the file you are trying to recover is fragmented into several pieces, then the recovery process will be much more complex. The manual method of file recovery is explained in detail in the next section.

RECOVERING PARTIAL FILES

Recovering files is not always as straightforward as was recovering TESTFILE.TXT. DOS may overwrite all or part of the erased file with another file before you realize that you want to recover the erased file. Whether recovery is possible depends on many factors, including the length of the new and erased files, and the existence or nonexistence of the erased file's directory entry.

However, the most critical aspect of this kind of file recovery is how much you know about the contents of the erased file. If you know nothing about the file, it may be impossible to determine whether you have recovered it completely. If you are familiar with the file's original contents, there is a good chance that you will be able to identify the parts of the file.

As an example of a partial file-recovery operation, we need to write a file, delete it, overwrite it with another file, and then try to recover the original file. By assuming that delete tracking is not installed, we make this recovery process as difficult as possible, and you will see in a moment that you cannot use the standard DOS recovery method either—you must use manual recovery techniques to recover what you can of the original file. This is a complex procedure and I'll describe it in detail.

Start by formatting a floppy disk with the DOS FORMAT command or by using PC Format with the /DESTROY option. (Do this to make sure that no data remains on the disk.) Then load PC Shell, select the \PCTOOLS directory and the README.TXT file. Choose the Copy File option from the File pull-down menu, select drive B as the destination drive, and copy the file over. Change to drive B and use the More File Info option in the File menu to look at the file, as shown in Figure 4.12.

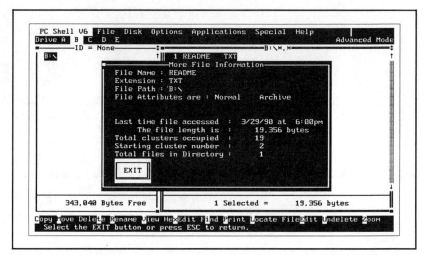

Figure 4.12: The More File Information display for the README.TXT file on drive B

The README.TXT file is a normal text file, 19,356 bytes long. It is the only file on the disk, so it starts at cluster number 2 and is 19 clusters long. Remember this information, since you will need some of it when you try to recover the file.

So that you are familiar with the contents of this file, load Edit File from the File pull-down menu and display the contents of READ-ME.TXT. Press PgDn three times until the description of PC-Cache is in the display. Try to remember some of the text in this general area. This screenful of text is shown in Figure 4.13.

Now delete README.TXT with the Delete option from the File pull-down menu or with the DOS DEL command. To use the DOS command, enter

DEL B: README.TXT

Next, create a small text file on the floppy disk. To do this, open PC Shell, reload Edit File, and enter

This is more text.

into a new file called TEXT.TXT, as shown in Figure 4.14.

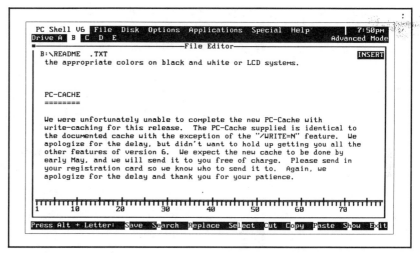

Figure 4.13: First part of the README.TXT file

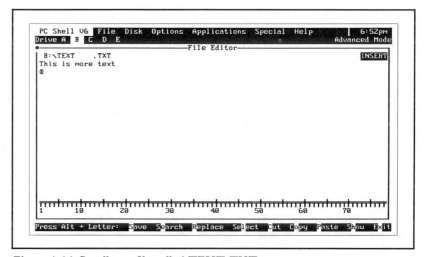

Figure 4.14: Small text file called TEXT.TXT

This new file will overwrite some of the space previously occupied by the README.TXT file.

Now try to recover the original README.TXT file. First see if anything can be recovered quickly. Select Undelete Files, select File, and note the dialog box containing the message

No File to Process

Different versions of DOS may produce different results here.

Undelete Files cannot find any information on README.TXT because the directory entries of file name, file size, and starting cluster number for the README.TXT file were overwritten when you created the TEXT.TXT file. You need to use more complex methods of file recovery.

Since TEXT.TXT is the first file on the disk and is only a short file, there is a good chance that it only occupies the first available cluster on the disk, which is cluster 2. Select More File Info from the File pull-down menu to confirm this. As you can see from Figure 4.15, the TEXT.TXT file is only 20 bytes long, occupying 1 cluster, cluster number 2.

The directory entries for the original file were overwritten when you created the TEXT.TXT file, but some of the original data must still be on the disk if the TEXT.TXT file only occupies the first cluster.

Next you use the Create option in Undelete to make a new set of directory entries with which to rebuild the file. Create a new file called MYFILE.TXT.

The recovery process now becomes completely manual. Undelete Files loads the next available cluster on the disk, displaying its contents on the screen. You must choose whether to add the cluster to the file or reject it and look at the next one. At this point, knowing the contents of the file is very important to the recovery process. If you're not familiar with the file, you won't recognize this text as part of the README.TXT file.

The contents of the first cluster are shown in Figure 4.16. Notice the text

WRITE = N

on the right side in the ASCII area of the display, and compare this with Figure 4.13, which shows the original contents of README.TXT. The same text occurs about halfway down the first page of README.TXT, indicating that the recovery process is on target so far.

Add this first cluster to the file, and continue to add clusters until the display contains F6 characters rather than text. This means that Undelete has run off the end of the file into the newly formatted area of the disk. Back up one cluster and save the file. You have now recovered as much as possible of the original README.TXT file.

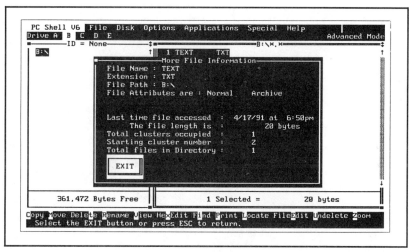

Figure 4.15: More File Information display for TEXT.TXT

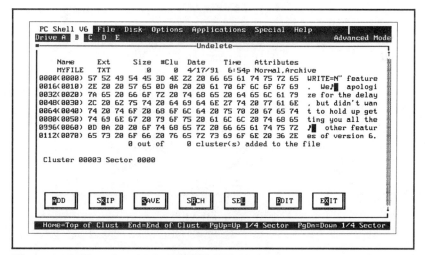

Figure 4.16: First cluster of MYFILE.TXT being recovered manually

Return to the PC Shell main screen and note that there are now two files in the display for drive B: the short file TEXT.TXT and the file you created, MYFILE.TXT.

Select MYFILE.TXT and then select More File Info from the File pull-down menu to look at this file. The resulting display is shown in Figure 4.17.

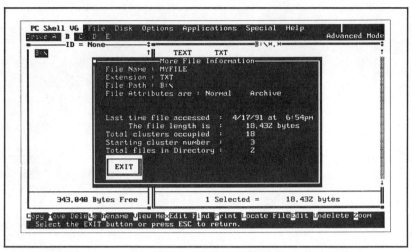

Figure 4.17: More File Information display for MYFILE.TXT

MYFILE.TXT starts in cluster number 3, is 18 clusters long, and occupies 18,432 bytes. In other words, the original README.TXT file lost its first cluster when the file was overwritten by the TEXT-.TXT file.

It is impossible to recover the whole README.TXT file because the first part of the file has been completely overwritten by MYFILE.TXT. You will have to recreate that part of the file. This has also been a simple recovery example because the README.TXT file was not fragmented. A fragmented file is less likely to be successfully recovered after it is erased, since it is harder to find and identify the pieces of the file. If the file has some characteristic text, you can try searching for the string with the Search (Srch) selection in Undelete. Again, this will only be fruitful if the file contains very specific text strings that you can remember even after you have erased the file.

RECOVERING AN ERASED DIRECTORY

If a directory contains any files, you cannot delete it.

To recover files, you must sometimes first recover a directory. Undelete can recover subdirectories as well as files. Indeed, the process is exactly the same as recovering files. Once you have recovered the directory, all its files can be restored as long as they have not been overwritten.

DOS treats the removal of a directory as it treats the removal of a file. The first character is set to the same special character, and the removed directory's entry remains in its parent directory (unseen, of course), just like a removed file's entry.

As an example, suppose you erased all of your Lotus 1-2-3 spreadsheets that were in the C drive's \123 directory, removed the directory, and then discovered that you hadn't intended to delete this directory. Undelete will not be able to find the spreadsheet files to restore them, since their names, starting cluster numbers, and file lengths are all stored in the \123 directory. You must recover the directory before you can recover the files. Select the parent directory that contained the \123 directory (the root directory in this example) and run Undelete. After confirming that you are in the right place on the right disk, choose the SUB-DIR selection.

If delete tracking was on when the files and directory were deleted, it will be easy to recover the directory. Just select the DEL TRACK option; the rest of the operation is automatic. Figure 4.18 shows the Undelete screen used to recover the \123 directory.

Run Undelete again to recover the Lotus files in the \123 directory. Figure 4.19 shows this file-recovery operation.

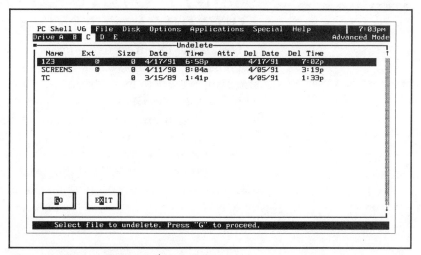

Figure 4.18: Undeleting the \123 directory

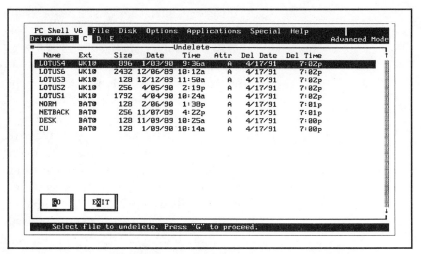

Figure 4.19: Recovering Lotus files after recovering the \123 directory

If delete tracking was not in use, recovery is a little slower and requires more input from you. You must supply the starting letter for the directory name and also for each of the file names before recovery is complete.

USING DISKFIX TO REPAIR YOUR DISKS (VERSION 6.0)

The DISKFIX program is a major new program, released for the first time with PC Tools 6.0. It is a disk maintenance and repair program you can use to fix problems with your floppy or hard disks. As with the other programs in the PC Tools package, DISKFIX is easy to use, with pop-up windows and full keyboard and mouse support. You don't have to have extensive knowledge of complex disk hardware to be able to take advantage of DISKFIX; just follow the instructions on the screen and the program will guide you through the most complex recovery operations. It is a very powerful program, but it is very easy to use. Start the program from the DOS command line by typing

DISKFIX

As the program starts it tests your computer hardware in a variety of ways to ensure that the disk drives are installed and configured correctly. If DISKFIX finds any problems with the information from your partition table, CMOS memory, or the boot sectors for any of the defined disks, you will see an error message displayed in a dialog box on the screen. Next DISKFIX gives you the opportunity to fix the problem now or come back and fix it later. The choice is yours. If you choose to repair the problem now, you are asked to choose the disk you want to analyze from a list on the screen. Select the disk with the arrow keys or click on the disk with the mouse. As DISKFIX examines the drive, it displays a status box on the screen as shown in Figure 4.20.

See Chapter 2 for a complete description of how disks work.

DISKFIX analyzes the following areas of your disk:

- DOS Boot Sector. DISKFIX looks at the boot sector to make sure it is not damaged in any way.

- Media Descriptors. DOS reserves a byte in the BIOS Parameter Block for the media descriptor, a number that indicates the type of disk. DISKFIX checks that the media descriptor is appropriate for the disk being checked.

- File Allocation Tables. The File Allocation Table (FAT) is a list of the addresses of all directories and files on your disk.

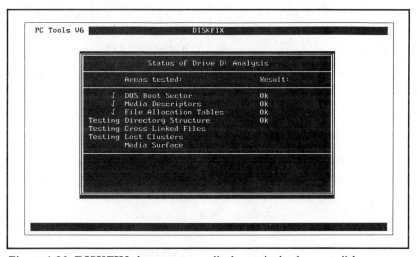

Figure 4.20: DISKFIX shows a status display as it checks your disk

Because it is the index to all your program and data files, DOS keeps two copies of the FAT on each disk. DISKFIX tests that there are no read errors in either of the copies of the FAT. If it finds a read error, DISKFIX copies the good FAT over the FAT containing the read error. Next, DISKCOPY verifies that the two copies of the FAT are identical, and that they only contain legal DOS entries. If the FATs are not identical, DISKFIX identifies the one with the fewest errors. At the end of the FAT checking, both copies of the FAT will be identical and will contain only legal entries.

- Directory Structure. DISKFIX reads all the directories on your disk and looks for illegal file names, file size, FAT errors, and cross-linked files.

- Cross-Linked Files. DISKFIX tests for cross-linked files, where two files are using the same entries in the FAT. If there are a large number of cross-linked files, fixing them might take a few minutes.

- Lost Subdirectories. If the FAT was damaged, or if there were errors in the root directory, you might have lost some subdirectories. The search for lost subdirectories can take several minutes, so be prepared for a short wait. DISKFIX puts any lost directories it finds into the root directory and names them LOST0000, LOST0001, LOST0002, and so on.

- Lost Clusters. These are clusters on the disk marked as in use in the FAT, but they are not actually allocated to a file anywhere. You can ask DISKFIX to convert these lost clusters into files. These files will be called PCT00000.FIX, PCT-00001.FIX, PCT00002.FIX, and so on, and they will be written into the root directory.

Next, DISKFIX asks if you want to test the disk media surface itself. If you select yes, DISKFIX tries to read every sector on the disk, and with large disks this process can take some time to complete. If it finds a read error, DISKFIX marks the cluster as bad in the FAT so that the bad area on the disk will not be used by DOS in the future. If the bad part of the disk is already in use by a file, DISKFIX copies as much as it can to a safe area of the disk, and replaces any information it could not read with dash characters (-) to help identify the damaged piece of the file. As this media surface scan is taking place, you can watch its progress on your computer screen with the display shown in Figure 4.21.

When DISKFIX completes the analysis, you can print a report of the scan either to your printer, or to a file if you want to look at it later. This file is called DISKFIX.RPT. The report details problems found with your disk, and any corrective action taken to fix the problem.

At this point, the main DISKFIX menu appears as shown in Figure 4.22. If no problems were encountered with your disk when you started the program, you will go to the main menu almost immediately.

I have already described the first two entries in the DISKFIX main menu, Fix a Disk and Surface Scan. They are available from this menu so that you can run them on disks other than the one you loaded the program from.

The next selection in the menu, Revitalize a Floppy, can often recover data that DOS cannot read. Sometimes the address marks on a disk can be faint and difficult to read, and as a result DOS reports read errors whenever it tries to read that area of the disk. DISKFIX can read the disk in a different way, and so it often can read data that DOS could not. In fact DISKFIX reads the data from the floppy disk, then reformats the disk and rewrites the original data back onto

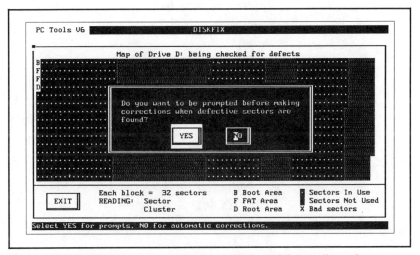

Figure 4.21: DISKFIX shows a graphical display of the media surface scan

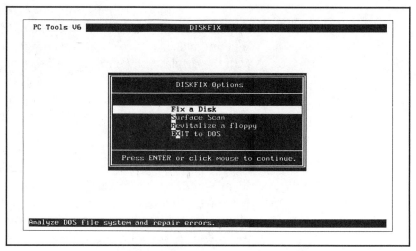

Figure 4.22: DISKFIX main menu

the disk again. A graphical screen shows the progress of this revital-
ization process.

With the combined power of Undelete Files and DISKFIX, you
should be able to fix almost any file- or disk-related problem you are
likely to encounter.

SUMMARY

In this chapter, I discussed the importance of taking care of
floppy and hard disks. You also learned how to use several PC Shell
commands, including Undelete Files; PC Format, the safe format
alternative to the DOS FORMAT command; Mirror and Rebuild,
which provide protection against file loss due to accidental hard-
disk erasure; and DISKFIX, a powerful disk maintenance and
repair utility program.

As you now know, file recovery is by no means certain. Many
aspects of the process influence the success of any recovery attempt.
Although the file-recovery process can be more difficult than the
examples in this chapter (recovering deleted program files that have
been partially overwritten may prove to be impossible), you should
have enough knowledge of the PC Tools recovery programs to
attempt most recoveries on your own. If you can't rescue it with PC
Tools, chances are that the file can't be recovered.

5

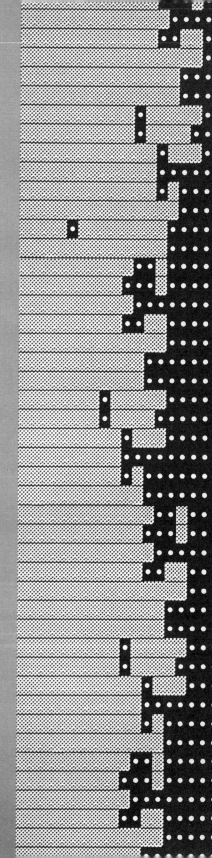

Organizing
Your Hard
Disk with
PC Shell

One of the toughest problems in managing your hard disk is deciding how to organize your files into directories. You want to implement a system that allows you and others to find files easily. PC Shell contains several selections to help you to organize and work with files. First, however, you should know how the file system in DOS works.

THE DOS DIRECTORY STRUCTURE

The most useful feature of DOS's file system is its ability to organize directories hierarchically. What this means is that directories can contain subdirectories as well as files; in fact, you can consider a subdirectory to be another type of file.

All disks start with the root directory, which is like the main root of a tree, with all the other directories branching out beneath it.

THE ROOT DIRECTORY

You should be careful to install as few files as possible in the root directory—AUTOEXEC.BAT, CONFIG.SYS, and COMMAND-.COM being the three main exceptions to this rule. In this way, you will be able to find your way around the disk easily and quickly, and DOS will run more efficiently.

ORGANIZING YOUR HARD DISK

Don't clutter up your root directory with files; place them in subdirectories, reserving the root for other directories. Subdirectories of the root directory are commonly referred to as directories.

The key to successful hard-disk management is organization. You should group similar files in their own directories rather than putting all your files in the root directory. Placing all your files in the same directory defeats the purpose of DOS's hierarchical file system, which is to enable you to find the file you want rapidly.

Keep the files of each software package you install on your system (the program files, device drivers, help files, and so on) all in the same directory. For example, if you are a Lotus 1-2-3 user, create a directory called \123 in the root directory and install Lotus 1-2-3 into it. If necessary, you can create additional subdirectories below the \123 directory. Suppose you want to separate your quarterly budget files from all your other Lotus files. You could place them in a subdirectory of \123 called \BUDGETS. Note, however, that you would only want to separate an easily identifiable group of files and that this group should contain more than just a few files. Otherwise, you will quickly forget where your files are. By the same token, you don't want to create too many directories or levels of subdirectories.

I recommend that you limit yourself to three levels: root, subdirectories, and subdirectories of those subdirectories. With any more, it will be time-consuming to move through your directory structure.

When you want to use a file or directory, you tell DOS where it is in the hierarchy. In other words, you give DOS the file or directory's *path*. For example, to move from the root to your newly created \BUDGETS directory, you would type

```
CD\123\BUDGETS
```

at the DOS prompt.

For more information about the PATH command, see Chapter 1.

When you organize your directory structure, make sure you install all the DOS files except for COMMAND.COM, CONFIG.SYS, and AUTOEXEC.BAT in a directory under the root directory. You should not install them in the root itself. Use the PATH command in your AUTOEXEC.BAT file to tell DOS where to look for certain files such as device drivers.

LISTING FILES AND DIRECTORIES

Perhaps the first step in organizing your hard disk is to take a look at the directory structure that already exists. I'll briefly discuss the DOS commands that allow you to do this, and then explain how to do the same thing—plus some things that you can't do with DOS—with much less effort by using PC Tools.

USING THE DOS DIR COMMAND

The DOS DIR command lists the names of all the files and subdirectories in a directory. DIR also lists the file size in bytes, the date and time of the file's creation or last modification, and the number of bytes remaining on the disk. DIR does not list hidden files. If the disk has a volume label, DIR shows the label text in the first line of the listing; otherwise, DIR reports

Volume in drive *n:* has no label

To make a DIR listing of the root directory on drive C, type

DIR

from the root directory. Figure 5.1 shows a typical listing from DIR.

If the listing flashes by so you can read only the last part, you can press Ctrl-S to stop and then restart the listing. You can also make DOS present only one screenful at a time. For example, list the files in the \DOS directory by entering

DIR \DOS/P

Each screenful will then be displayed until you press any key, and then the next screenful will be displayed.

To make a wide listing that gives only file and directory names, use the /W switch as shown in Figure 5.2. Directories in this display do

If you want to print the DIR listing rather than display it on the screen, use the re-direction facilities in DOS and type

DIR > PRN

```
C:\UC>DIR

 Volume in drive C is DYSON
 Directory of  C:\UC

 .            <DIR>      12-27-89   4:10p
 ..           <DIR>      12-27-89   4:10p
 UCH          <DIR>      12-28-89   2:35p
 UCS          <DIR>      12-28-89   2:35p
 DEMO         <DIR>      12-28-89   2:39p
 UCSCREEN     <DIR>       1-15-90   1:18p
 UCTCZS   LIB  145920     7-01-89  12:00p
 UCTCZL   LIB  167936     7-01-89  12:00p
 UCTCZC   LIB  163840     7-01-89  12:00p
 UCTCZM   LIB  150016     7-01-89  12:00p
        10 File(s)    6813696 bytes free

C:\UC>
```

Figure 5.1: A typical DIR listing

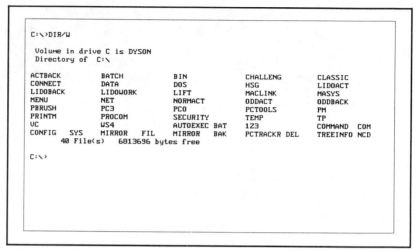

```
C:\>DIR/W

 Volume in drive C is DYSON
 Directory of  C:\

ACTBACK      BATCH       BIN          CHALLENG      CLASSIC
CONNECT      DATA        DOS          HSG           LIDOACT
LIDOBACK     LIDOWORK    LIFT         MACLINK       MASYS
MENU         NET         NORMACT      ODDACT        ODDBACK
PBRUSH       PC3         PCO          PCTOOLS       PM
PRINTM       PROCOM      SECURITY     TEMP          TP
VC           WS4         AUTOEXEC BAT 123           COMMAND  COM
CONFIG   SYS   MIRROR   FIL    MIRROR   BAK   PCTRACKR DEL   TREEINFO NCD
       40 File(s)    6813696 bytes free

C:\>
```

Figure 5.2: A wide listing made with DIR/W

not have the usual <DIR> notation and may be easily confused with files.

USING THE DOS TREE COMMAND

The DOS TREE command summarizes the directory information for all the directories on a disk, and presents this data in an outline form. To make a TREE listing of your disk, type

TREE

Using the /F switch will make TREE list all the files in each directory or subdirectory. This listing will be too long to fit on the screen. You can send the listing to your printer instead of displaying it on the screen by typing

TREE/F > PRN

The output produced by this command will not be broken into neat pages; it will be an exact copy of what would have appeared on the screen.

USING PC SHELL TO LIST
FILES AND DIRECTORIES

PC Shell greatly expands on the DOS DIR and TREE commands. The PC Shell startup screen, which shows the tree and file lists, is shown in Figure 5.3.

The left side of the screen, marked with the disk volume label, shows a graphic representation of the directory structure on your disk, highlighting the currently selected directory. The right side of the screen shows the full path name of the current directory and lists the names of all files in the directory. As you select different directories in the tree list on the left side of the display, the files list on the right is automatically updated to show the files contained in the new directory. Use the Tab key to move between the two windows or click with the mouse on the screen you want to move to.

Sometimes these directory or file lists are too long to fit in the window, so you have to scroll the display to see everything. You can scroll either side of the display independently. You can use ↑ and ↓ to move one line in the window at a time, use PgUp or PgDn to move a complete window at a time, or use Home to go to the top of the list and End to go to the end of the list.

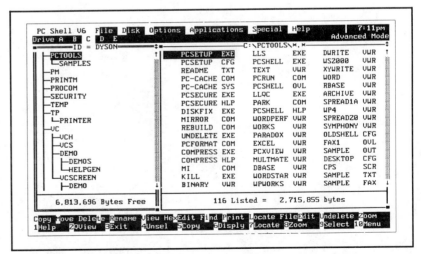

Figure 5.3: PC Shell opening screen

With the mouse, scrolling is even easier. Press the right mouse button and drag the mouse up to move up the screen or move it down to move down the screen. Alternatively, you can move by clicking on the scroll bars. You will become familiar with these two windows very quickly, because this is where you choose the files, disks, or directories that you will work on.

Most of the PC Shell commands that deal with files require that you select the file or files you want to work with before you choose the command. Before you can work on any files with the other commands in PC Shell, you must know how to select and unselect files.

To select a file using the keyboard

- Use the arrow keys to highlight the file you want, and press Enter to confirm your choice. The files you select are numbered in sequence.

- Alternatively, you may number or renumber your own selections. Move the cursor to the file name, type the number of your selection, and press Enter. PC Shell adjusts the numbering accordingly.

To select a file using the mouse

- Position the highlight bar on a file and click the left mouse button.

- Press the right mouse button, position over the first file to select, and then press and hold down the left mouse button. Now drag the highlight over the additional files you want to select. As you include files, they are numbered in sequence. When you have selected all the files, release both mouse buttons.

To unselect all previously selected files with a single keystroke, press F4. To unselect files individually using the keyboard

- Use the arrow keys to highlight the file or files you want to unselect, and press Enter to confirm your choice. The files you leave selected are renumbered in sequence.

To unselect a file or files using the mouse

- Click on the file you want to unselect.

- Press the right mouse button, position over the first file to unselect, and then press and hold down the left mouse button. Now drag the highlight over the additional files you want to unselect. As you unselect files, any remaining files are renumbered in sequence. When you have unselected all the files, release both mouse buttons.

USING MORE FILE INFO   The file list shows you the file name and its position in the directory, but doesn't tell you very much about the file itself. To find out more about the file, use More File Info from the File pull-down menu. I'll use the README file as an example.

Use the mouse or the cursor keys to make \PCTOOLS the current directory, and then select README.TXT. To choose More File Info, type F followed by I, or click on each of the two menu entries.

Figure 5.4 shows the More File Information dialog box for the README.TXT file.

The display contains the following information:

- File name

- Extension

- Full path name

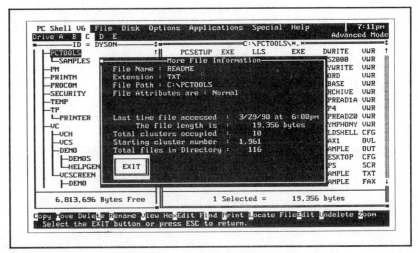

Figure 5.4: More File Information for README.TXT

- File attributes
- Time the file was last accessed
- File length in bytes
- Total clusters
- Starting cluster number
- Total number of files in the directory

The status line at the bottom of the screen lists summary information, including the number of files in the current directory, the total number of bytes they occupy, and the amount of free space left on the disk in bytes. If you select a file or files and then run More File Info, the right side of the status line lists the number of files selected and the total amount of disk space they occupy in bytes.

You can find out much more useful information by using More File Info than you can by using just the DOS DIR command. But what if you want to display and print this information for all the files in the directory? Use Print File List from the File pull-down menu. Select the directory you want to print and choose Print File List. I chose the \DOS directory, and Figure 5.5 shows the result.

The disk's volume label is printed in the upper-right corner of the printout, followed by the full path name of the directory. The files are arranged in columns, with file name and extension, size in bytes and clusters, last access date and time, and file attributes. (Note that the starting cluster is not listed in this display.)

The summary information given at the end of the printout includes number of files listed, number of files selected, total number of files in the subdirectory, their total size in bytes, and remaining free space on the disk.

MAKING, CHANGING, AND REMOVING DIRECTORIES

Creating and deleting directories and moving between directories are essential tasks for hard-disk users. You can accomplish these

```
PC Shell Version 6                  Directory Print        ID = DYSON
-------------------------------------------------------------------------
Path=C:\DOS
   Name      Ext    Size #Clu   Date      Time  Attributes
   ASSIGN    COM    1561    1  3-17-87  12:00p     A
   BACKUP    COM   31913    2  3-18-87  12:00p
   BASIC     COM    1063    1  3-17-87  12:00p
   BASICA    COM   36403    1  3-17-87  12:00p
   CHKDSK    COM    9850    2  3-18-87  12:00p
   COMMAND   COM   25307    3  3-17-87  12:00p
   COMP      COM    4214    1  3-17-87  12:00p
   DEBUG     COM   15897    2  3-17-87  12:00p
   DISKCOMP  COM    5879    1  3-17-87  12:00p
   DISKCOPY  COM    6295    1  3-17-87  12:00p
   EDLIN     COM    7526    1  3-17-87  12:00p
   FDISK     COM   48216    1  3-18-87  12:00p
   FORMAT    COM   11616    2  3-18-87  12:00p
   GRAPHICS  COM    3300    1  3-17-87  12:00p
   LABEL     COM    2377    1  3-17-87  12:00p
   MODE      COM   15487    1  3-17-87  12:00p
   MORE      COM     313    1  3-17-87  12:00p
   PRINT     COM    9026    1  3-17-87  12:00p
   RECOVER   COM    4299    1  3-18-87  12:00p
   RESTORE   COM   34643    2  3-17-87  12:00p
   TREE      COM    3571    1  3-17-87  12:00p
   AUTOEXEC  BAT     256    1  4-05-90   2:19p     A
   CONFIG    SYS     256    1  4-05-90   2:14p     A

   23 files LISTed   =  198478 bytes    23 files in sub-dir =   198478
    0 files SELECTed =       0 bytes    Available on volume =
```

Figure 5.5: Print Directory for the \DOS directory

common operations faster with PC Shell than you can with DOS, and you can see the results of your changes instantly. I'll quickly cover the DOS commands for these operations and then illustrate the more powerful PC Shell alternatives.

USING THE DOS COMMANDS

To make a new directory called \123 from the root for your Lotus files, type

    MKDIR 123

You can also abbreviate this command to

MD 123

DOS makes the new \123 directory, assigning its creation time and date. If you make a DIR listing now, you will see an entry whose format differs slightly from that of the file entries. The \123 directory had a creation time and date, but no file size. Instead, the designation <DIR> appears in the listing. This confirms that \123 is not a file but a directory. To make this new directory the default directory, type

CHDIR 123

for change directory. You can also abbreviate this command to

CD 123

The \123 directory is now the current, or default, directory. To make the root directory the default directory once more, type

**CD **

When you create a directory, DOS automatically places into it two special entries. These entries (known as . and ..) are shorthand for the full path name of the new directory (.) and the parent directory (..). Thus, for your new \123 directory, . is equivalent to \123, and .. is equivalent to the root directory (\). Although you can change to the root by typing

**CD **

you can also change to the root from the \123 directory by typing

CD ..

since the root is its parent directory.

As long as the directory contains only the . and .. entries, DOS considers it empty and you can delete it. If the directory is not empty when you try to remove it, DOS responds with the message:

Invalid path, not directory,
or directory not empty.

Use DOS's DEL or ERASE command to delete the files from the directory. For example, to remove all the files from a directory, type

DEL *.*

Because this is a potentially dangerous command, DOS has a built-in safety net, and prompts you with

Are you sure? (Y or N)

You have to confirm that you want to erase all the files or abort the DEL command.

If the directory also contains subdirectories, you will need to delete all their files and then remove each subdirectory individually before you can delete the parent directory. For instance, to remove \123's \BUDGETS directory, once it is empty, type

RMDIR BUDGETS

from the \123 directory. You can also remove it by changing to the root and typing

RD 123\BUDGETS

(RD is short for RMDIR.)

If you no longer use a directory, you should remove it. Your hierarchical structure will be easier to work with if it is not cluttered up with old, unused entries. Removing unused directories will also conserve some disk space.

USING PC SHELL TO
MANIPULATE DIRECTORIES

PC Shell includes all the functions of DOS's MD, CD, and RD commands, but is more flexibile and easier to use.

Choose Directory Maintenance from the Disk pull-down menu and notice the small arrow pointing to the right, indicating that the item has a submenu. Figure 5.6 shows this display.

Using this submenu, you can

- Add a subdirectory
- Rename a subdirectory
- Delete a subdirectory
- Change the current directory (not in Version 6.0)
- Prune and graft
- Modify attributes of a directory

For more information on file attributes, see the section "Looking at File Attributes" later in this chapter.

To add a new directory, choose Add a Sub Directory from the Directory Maintenance submenu. Use the arrow keys or a mouse to select the parent directory below which you want to make this new directory. Choose from the directories listed in the tree list display, or select the Continue button if you want to use the current directory. Type in the name (and the optional extension) of your new directory, and press Enter or click on Continue. Your new directory takes its place in the tree list shown on the left of the PC Shell screen.

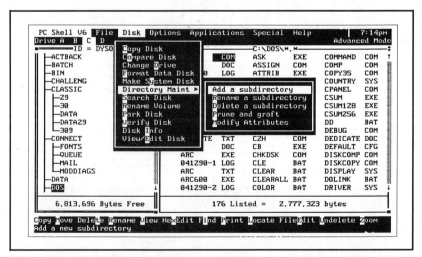

Figure 5.6: The Directory Maintenance submenu

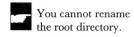 You cannot rename the root directory.

Similarly, if you want to rename an existing directory, select Rename a Sub Directory from the Directory Maintenance submenu and make your choice from the directories shown in the tree list. Type in the new name for this directory (and the optional extension), and press Enter or click on the Continue box. If the name you choose already exists, go back to the Subdirectory Rename box to enter another name.

If you want to delete a directory, choose Delete a Sub Directory from the Directory Maintenance submenu, and choose from the directories shown in the tree list. PC Shell prompts you to confirm your choice and then deletes the directory if it is empty. Remember that you cannot delete the root directory.

You cannot delete a directory that still contains files. Use Delete File in the File pull-down menu to empty the directory, and then try again.

The Prune and Graft option includes an operation that amounts to moving a directory and its files and subdirectories to a new location on your directory structure.

First, choose the directory to be pruned from the directories in the tree list, or select Continue if the current directory is the one to prune. The directory for pruning is marked with a > character. A Sub Directory Prune and Graft dialog box appears. From the tree list choose the directory to graft the moved directory onto, or select Continue to use the current directory. Confirm your choice and return to the Directory Maintenance submenu.

SORTING FILES WITHIN DIRECTORIES

Even on a well-organized disk, the accumulation of directories and files often forces you to look through long directory listings to find the desired directory or file. You can improve this situation by sorting directory listings. Sorting directory entries into groups based on criteria that you choose may speed your work. You can sort the information listed in a directory by adding switches to the DOS DIR command. In PC Shell, however, you can manipulate the contents of any directory more easily and in more ways.

USING DIRECTORY SORT

By using Directory Sort from the Special pull-down menu, you can sort the files in a directory by name, extension, date, time, or number in ascending or descending order. The Sort options are shown in Figure 5.7.

If you select files in the file list display before using Directory Sort, the files are each assigned a sequence number. You can sort the directory using this sequence number as the sort method to arrange the files in the exact order you require. This is completely independent of their file name or extension. To use this option

1. Select the files you want to sort in the file list display in the correct sequence. PC Shell assigns a number to each file.

2. Choose Directory Sort from the Special pull-down menu.

3. Select By Select Number in the list of sort fields. This is always an ascending sort.

To sort by one of the other criteria, choose the sort field first from By Name, By Extension, or By Date/Time, then choose the direction of the sort, either Ascending or Descending. PC Shell performs the

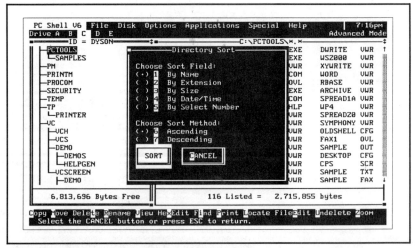

Figure 5.7: Sort options in Directory Sort

sort and then asks you to choose from the following:

- View allows you to look at the results of the sort before they are written to your disk. Use this option to ensure that the sort performed as expected.

- Cancel allows you to change your mind and unsort the files.

- Update allows you to write the sorted directory to your disk.

- Resort allows you to specify new sort options and re-sort the directory using these criteria.

WORKING WITH FILES AND DISKS

In PC Tools 6.0, many commands in the File pull-down menu have had the word "File" added to them. Copy becomes Copy File, Compare becomes Compare File, and so on.

So far, we have looked at PC Shell commands that operate on complete directories. Now we'll review the commands that work with files and disks—such as Copy File, Move File, Delete File, and Compare File. You need to be familiar with these operations to manage your hard disk effectively.

COPYING AND COMPARING FILES

You use the Copy File command to make additional copies of a file or a group of files. You can copy files to a different directory, to a different disk, or to the same disk with a different name. Copy File will also format the destination disk if it is unformatted.

First, select the directory you want to copy files from in the tree list, highlight the files you want to copy in the file list display, and then choose Copy File from the File pull-down menu. Select the drive and, from the tree list, select the directory to which to copy the files.

If there are files with identical names in the group you want to copy and in the destination directory, you have five options:

- REPLACE ALL replaces all the files in the destination directory that have the same names as files in the selected group, without asking for confirmation each time.

- REPLACE FILE replaces each file with the same name, but asks for confirmation on each file replacement.

- NEXT FILE moves to the next file. The current file is not copied.
- SKIP ALL aborts the copy process and returns you to the main PC Shell screen.
- EXIT returns you to the main PC Shell screen.

The Compare File command compares the contents of two or more files, usually to see whether two files located in different directories are identical. You can also use Compare File to verify whether two programs on two different disks with different dates are just replicas of one another created at different times.

Suppose you want to see if the copy of AUTOEXEC.BAT in your root directory is identical to the file in your word processing directory. First, select the root directory in the tree list and then select the AUTOEXEC.BAT file in the file list. Choose the File pull-down menu and the Compare File command. From the File Compare dialog box, select drive C as the second drive, since all the files for comparison in this example are on drive C. Next, PC Shell asks if you want to compare files with Matching Names or Different Names. In this example, choose the Matching Names option. Select the directory that contains the second copy of AUTOEXEC.BAT. If you chose Matching Names, the files are compared. If you chose Different Names, PC Shell asks you for the name of the file to compare to. Type the name and extension and select Continue to proceed. If you selected more than one file, the files are processed in turn.

If Compare File finds a difference between the two files that are identical in size, it displays the sector number and a byte offset of the position of the difference, as well as the ASCII value of each difference. If the files are different in size, it shows the original file name and the path to the comparison file. Then Compare File states that the comparison was unsuccessful because the files were of different sizes.

MOVING AND RENAMING FILES

When you copy a file, an exact replica of the file is made in the destination directory, and the original is preserved intact. That is, after the copy operation, there are two copies of the file in different places. Sometimes you may want to move rather than copy a file. The Move File command is designed for exactly this purpose. At other times, you may want to change the name of the copy by renaming the file with the Rename File command.

Moving a file is like copying a file, but the original file is deleted when the Move File operation is complete. First, select the files you want to move from the tree list and the file list, and then select Move File from the File pull-down menu. Choose the destination drive and directory. PC Shell moves the files to the destination directory and deletes the original source files. If you try to move files to the same directory that the originals occupy, PC Shell responds with a dialog box containing the message

File already exists.

You may then choose to Replace All, Replace File, Next File, Skip All, or Exit.

Renaming a file is even easier than moving it. Select the file or files you want to work with from the file list and select Rename File from the File pull-down menu.

If you selected one file, its current name is shown in the File Rename window and you are asked to enter the new name and extension. If you selected several files, you can change their names or extensions globally, or one at a time.

- Global: Enter the new file name or extension. For example, to change all your file extensions from .DOC to .TXT, put the DOS wildcard character * in the name box, TXT in the extension box, and select RENAME.

- Single: Enter the file name and extension to use and select RENAME. Choosing NEXT FILE displays the next file from the list of selected files.

VERIFYING FILES

You can Verify a file to ensure that it is readable after a copy or move operation. Select the files for verification from the file list, and choose Verify File from the File pull-down menu. Verify File reads each sector in the file to ensure that the whole file can be read without errors. If you specified a group of files, each file is checked in turn for errors. If Verify File finds an error, the sector number containing the error is displayed.

DELETING FILES

There is a complete discussion of file attributes later in this chapter.

At some point, you will want to throw away a file or group of files. Use the Delete File command for this. Delete File can erase files that have the hidden, system, or read-only bits set in their attribute byte. If you want to delete more than one file, first choose your "victims" in the file list, and then select Delete File from the File pull-down menu. The File Delete dialog box is displayed for the first file in the list, and if you chose one file, two options are offered: DELETE and CANCEL. If you select more than one file, you have four options:

- DELETE erases the file.
- NEXT FILE skips over this file and displays the next file.
- DELETE ALL erases all the files you selected without any further dialog.
- CANCEL ends the deletion and returns you to the main PC Shell display.

When all the files have been deleted, you return to the main PC Shell screen.

COPYING AND COMPARING DISKS

Both source and target drives must be of the same drive and media type when you are copying an entire disk.

Often it is easier to copy a whole disk in one operation than to copy all the files individually. The Copy Disk option in the Disk menu is designed for this. First, select the source drive and the target drive. PC Shell prompts you to change disks if you are making a copy using a single drive. As the Copy proceeds, the display shown in Figure 5.8 indicates progress.

As the copy is made, a character is displayed opposite each track; F shows that the disk is being formatted, R indicates that the disk is being read, and W shows that the data is being written to the disk. When the copy is complete, you return to the PC Shell main screen.

Figure 5.8: The Copy Disk display shows progress

To confirm that the disk is an exact copy, you can use Compare Disk to check the copy against the original. This works much like Copy Disk. The main difference is that R indicates that the disk is being read, and C indicates that the comparison is taking place. If a dot appears in the track window, that track has been compared successfully.

PRINTING FILES

Often you will want to print a file without using a word processor, or, with a binary file, you might want to dump it to the printer in ASCII and hex. Print File can handle both of these tasks. Choose the file or files you want to print in the file list and then choose Print File from the File pull-down menu.

You can then use one of these three options to print the file:

- Print as a Standard Text File prints a simple ASCII text file.

- Print File Using PC Shell Print Options formats the output according to the settings shown in Table 5.1.

- Dump each sector in ASCII and HEX displays the decimal and hex equivalents.

Try running README.TXT through Print File, selecting a different option each time to see how the output varies.

Table 5.1: Settings for Text Formatting in Print File

SETTING	FUNCTION
Lines per Page	Specifies the number of lines per page. Default is 66.
Margin Lines Top and Bottom	Specifies the number of lines for the top and bottom margins. Default is 4.
Extra Spaces Between Lines	Specifies the number of blank lines to leave between each printed line. Default is none.
Left Margin	Specifies number of spaces in from left margin where printing starts. Default is 1.
Right Margin	Specifies number of spaces in from left margin where printing stops. Default is 80.
Page Headings	Choose Yes for page headings. You are prompted to enter the heading text. Default is Off.
Page Footings	Choose Yes for page footings. You are prompted to enter the footer text. Default is Off.
Page Numbers	Choose Yes for page numbering, No for unnumbered pages. Default is Off.
Stop Between Pages	Select Yes if you are using single sheets of paper rather than continuous paper. Default is Off.
Eject Last Page	Select Yes if you want to eject the last printed page automatically. Default is On.

If you select the first option, the file is printed as a long piece of text without any page breaks or any other formatting.

When you use the second setting, the file is divided into numbered pages and is much nicer to look at.

If you select the third option, each sector is numbered sequentially with the count starting at sector zero at the beginning of the file. On the left side of the printout, the decimal byte offset count is shown next to the hex byte offset count. This is the byte number starting with zero at the beginning of the file. In the center of the printout, the file's data are listed in two columns of 8 bytes each separated by a hyphen for easier reading. On the right, the data are shown again, this time in ASCII.

LOCATING FILES

Sometimes you know the name of a file but can't remember where it is. Sometimes you can't even remember the whole name. The DOS DIR command is of little use here; however, you can use PC Shell to locate lost files.

Locate File in the File pull-down menu can find files anywhere on your disk, and it can even find files belonging to common applications programs such as word processors or spreadsheets. You can use it to locate all the .EXE files in a directory, or to group all your Word-Perfect files together. Locate File recognizes files made with the following applications programs:

Locate File in PC Tools 5.5 is much less capable; it finds files in any directory by searching for specific names and extensions only.

dBASE

Desktop Notepad

DisplayWrite

Excel

Lotus 1-2-3

Paradox

R:BASE

Symphony

Microsoft Word

WordPerfect

Microsoft Works

XyWrite III Plus

Select Locate File from the File pull-down menu and choose Specify File Name(s) at the top of the list. You can use the DOS wildcard characters (? or *) in place of one or several characters in the file name if you can't remember the full name, or if you want to list all the files with a particular extension.

Type the file name AUTOEXEC with the extension .BAT into the Filespecs box for this example. Another window with the prompt

Search For:

opens after you enter the file name; ignore this window for the moment and just press the Enter key. Figure 5.9 shows the files found by Locate File.

Locate File found three files with the file name AUTOEXEC-.BAT: one in the root directory used when you boot the computer, the original file supplied with DOS located in the \DOS directory, and a working version in the word processing directory.

To find the files made by a particular applications program, choose the program name from the list of names in the File Locate window. Files are found on the basis of characteristic file-name extensions. For example, Microsoft Word adds the extension .DOC to all its files, dBASE uses .DBF, Lotus 1-2-3 uses .WK1, and so on. So when you ask Locate File to find all your Word files, it finds all the files ending in the extension .DOC.

But Locate File is even more powerful than a simple file finder; it can also find specific text inside a file. You can ask it to find which of your Lotus spreadsheet files contains the phrase ''Advertising Budget,'' or which Word file is addressed to ''Dear Mr President.''

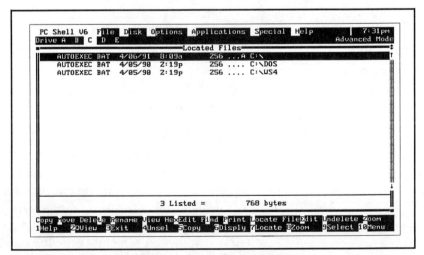

Figure 5.9: Locate File finds three AUTOEXEC.BAT files

Choose an application program from the list in the File Locate window, type the text you want to search for into the Search For window, and press Enter. Locate File finds all the files that contain your search string and lists them on the screen along with their file size, create time and date, and full path name.

You can use any of the commands available from the message bar or from pull-down menus in the Located Files window; you can select files and then compare, delete, copy, or move them.

You can also launch an applications program from the Located Files window just as you can from the File List window. If you have Lotus 1-2-3 on the PC Shell Applications menu associated with files with the extension .WK1, and you have a group of Lotus files in the Located Files window, you can press Ctrl-Enter to launch Lotus 1-2-3 on your selected or highlighted file. This loads Lotus 1-2-3, starts the program running, and opens the file you had selected as the current spreadsheet.

You can also view the contents of a file in the Locate File window. Use the arrow keys or the mouse to select one of the files, and press F2 for Quick View to see the file displayed in the correct file viewer format. PC Shell has several different viewers for different database, spreadsheet, and word processing formats, as well as a viewer for .PCX graphics files made by programs like PC Paintbrush. I will go into more detail on viewing files in the next section.

If you want to add your own choice of applications programs to the list used by Locate File, or change some of the search criteria used, use the function keys associated with the File Locate window. Four function keys are shown on the message line: Add, Edit, Delete, and Move.

- Add. Choose this function key if you want to add an entry to the list. A window opens so you can enter the Group Name as you want it to appear in the File Locate list. Type a ^ character before the letter you want to use as the selector letter. The character after the ^ is shown in bold or in a different color when it is displayed in the File Locate list.

  Enter the Filespecs you want to use for the search into the next window. If you are a programmer and you want to find all your C language source code you might enter *.C or *.ASM into this window.

- Edit. Choose Edit if you want to change the file search criteria already in use in one of the existing groups. You can change the Group Name or the Filespecs with Edit.

- Delete. If you want to delete an entry from the File Locate list, use Delete.

- Move. Use Move if you want to move one of the entries to a new place in the list. For example, if you want to put the Group Name you use most commonly at the top of the list for easy access, use Move.

If you want to save any of the changes you made to the File Locate list, remember to use Save Configuration in the Options pull-down menu before you exit PC Shell.

VIEWING FILES

If you select one or more files from the main PC Shell display, and then choose Quick File View from the File pull-down menu, you will see the file displayed on the screen in its native format. PC Shell can display files in many different forms, depending on whether they are database, spreadsheet, or word processor files. Table 5.2 lists all the file types that PC Shell can display.

If the file is a Lotus worksheet file, Quick File View loads the 123 Viewer and displays the file in spreadsheet format. Figure 5.10 shows a Lotus worksheet file displayed by the 123 Viewer. The name of the file you are viewing is shown in the top left corner of the screen.

You can select the commands on the message line by clicking on them with the mouse.

- Launch starts the appropriate application program running and loads the chosen file as the data file.

- Search allows you to enter a search string.

- Zoom/Unzoom changes the width of the display. When the display is unzoomed you can see the list of selected files as

Table 5.2: Quick File View Displays These Program Files in Their Native Formats

DATABASE VIEWERS	WORD PROCESSOR VIEWERS
Clipper	Desktop Notepad
dBASE	DisplayWrite
dBLX	Microsoft Word
FoxBASE	MultiMate
Paradox	WordStar
R:BASE	WordStar 2000
	WordPerfect
	XyWrite
SPREADSHEET VIEWERS	**MISCELLANEOUS VIEWERS**
Borland Quattro	ARC files
Lotus 1-2-3	Binary Files
Lotus Symphony	LHARC files
Microsoft Excel	.PAK files
Microsoft Works	.PCX files
Mosaic Twin	PKZIP files
	Text files

well as the contents of the current file. If you zoom, the file viewer takes the whole screen.

- NextF loads and displays the next file from the list of selected files.

You can also use the keys shown in Table 5.3 to navigate through the spreadsheet. Use the Home, End, PgUp, and PgDn keys to move vertically through the worksheet. Use Ctrl-← and Ctrl-→ to scroll left or right one window at a time horizontally.

You can use the mouse to move through the worksheet. To move horizontally along the rows, press the right mouse button and drag the mouse to the right or to the left. To move vertically along the

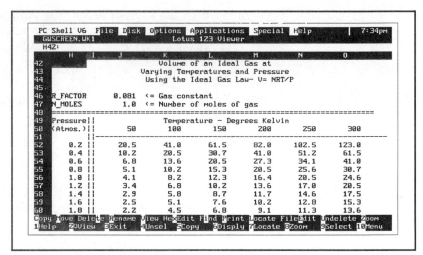

Figure 5.10: A Lotus spreadsheet file displayed by the 123 Viewer

Table 5.3: Keys for Moving Through Your Spreadsheet

KEY	FUNCTION
Right Arrow (→)	Move right one cell
Left Arrow (←)	Move left one cell
Up Arrow (↑)	Move up one row
Down Arrow (↓)	Move down one row
Home	Move to the first cell in the spreadsheet
End	Move to the last cell in the spreadsheet
PgUp	Move up one window
PgDn	Move down one window
Ctrl-→	Move right one window
Ctrl-←	Move left one window

columns, press the right mouse button and move it up or down. You can also move through the worksheet using the horizontal or vertical scroll bars.

If the file is a dBASE (or dBASE-compatible) file, Quick File View loads the dBASE Viewer, as shown in Figure 5.11.

The file name is shown in the upper-left corner of the screen, with its full path name. The number of the displayed record and the total number of records in the database are shown in the upper-right corner of the screen.

In addition to the commands you saw with the 123 Viewer, there are several database-specific commands now available on the message bar. Choose them by clicking on them with the mouse.

- Info displays a dialog box containing statistics about the database file you are viewing: the name of the file, the date of the last update, the size of the header record, the size of the data record, the number of fields and records, and the names, types, and sizes of all the fields. You can use the Home, End, PgUp, and PgDn keys to move through the field names. You can also scroll through the field names with the mouse using the scroll bar. Press Escape or click on the close box to leave the Data Base Statistics box.

- Goto allows you to go straight to the record you specify by record number.

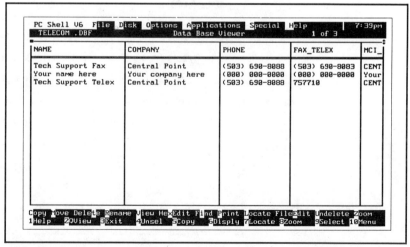

Figure 5.11: A dBASE file displayed by the Data Base Viewer

- Edit/Browse alternates between Browse mode where all the records in the database are displayed horizontally, field by field, and Edit mode where all the fields for one record are shown vertically on the screen.

If you are viewing an R:BASE file, some of these commands are slightly different.

- Tables displays a dialog box containing information on the tables in the R:BASE file and the number of rows and columns in each table.
- Goto allows you to go straight to the record you specify by row number.

You can also use the keystrokes shown in Table 5.4 to move through the records in the file.

Table 5.4: Keys for Moving Through Your Database

KEY	FUNCTION
EDIT MODE	
Right Arrow (→)	Display the next record
Left Arrow (←)	Display the previous record
Up Arrow (↑)	Move up one field
Down Arrow (↓)	Move down one field
PgUp	Move up one window
PgDn	Move down one window
Home	Go to the beginning of the record
End	Go to the end of the record
/	Toggle between the first and last record

If the file you want to view is a text file or a word processor file, Quick File View loads the Text Viewer, as shown in Figure 5.12. If

Table 5.4: Keys for Moving Through Your Database (Continued)

KEY	FUNCTION
BROWSE MODE	
Right Arrow (→)	Move right one field
Left Arrow (←)	Move left one field
Up Arrow (↑)	Move up one record
Down Arrow (↓)	Move down one record
PgUp	Move up one window
PgDn	Move down one window
Home	Go to the beginning of the database
End	Go to the end of the database
/	Toggle between the first and the last record

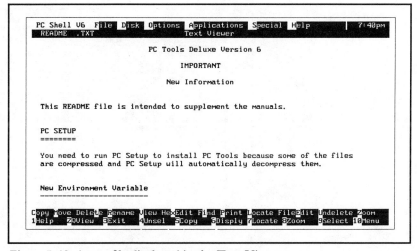

Figure 5.12: A text file displayed in the Text Viewer

your word processor is in the list shown in Table 5.2, Quick File View loads a special file viewer for that word processor file type. These special viewers are very similar to the Text Viewer.

There are no special function keys associated with the Text Viewer, or with the specific word processor viewers. You can use the keystrokes shown in Table 5.5 to move through a text file.

If you select a binary file, Quick File View loads the Binary File Viewer, as shown in Figure 5.13.

You can use these same commands to move through a binary file displayed in the Binary File Viewer.

Table 5.5: Keys for Moving Through Your Text or Binary Files

KEY	FUNCTION
Up Arrow (↑)	Move up one line
Down Arrow (↓)	Move down one line
PgUp	Move up one window
PgDn	Move down one window
Home	Go to the beginning of the file
End	Go to the end of the file

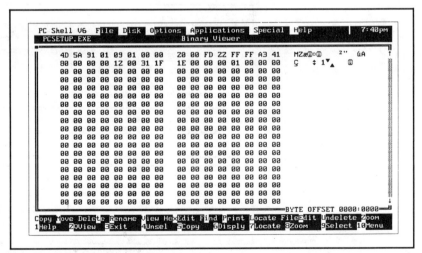

Figure 5.13: A binary file displayed in the Binary File Viewer

The Binary File Viewer looks a little different from the other viewers, and the data on the screen is divided into three columns. The two columns on the left show the hex data in the file, and the column on the right contains the ASCII characters equivalent to this hex data. There are no new function keys on the message line in the Binary File Viewer. The file name, size in bytes, create date and time, and attributes are all shown on the screen just above this Viewer.

If the file you want to view is made by one of the popular file-compressing utility programs like ARC or PKZIP, you will see another file viewer, as shown in Figure 5.14.

The ARC File Viewer lists data for each of the original files inside the ARC file, including the file name, size in bytes, the compression method, the percent reduction in size, current size in bytes, the file date and time, and the CRC (Cyclical Redundancy Check)—a kind of checksum. The ZIP File Viewer shows very similar information for files made by PKZIP.

This time the Info selection from the message line displays a dialog box containing information on the file, including the name and date, the number of original files, the original size of all the files, their current size, and the ratio between the two sizes to indicate the amount of space saved.

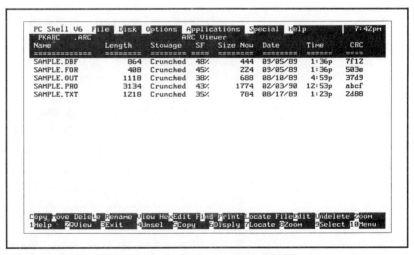

Figure 5.14: An ARC file displayed in the ARC File Viewer

FINDING TEXT WITHIN FILES

You may remember a particular piece of text in a text file, but not remember the name of the file that contained the text. You can use the Text Search command in the File pull-down menu to search selected files. You can also use the Search Disk command from the Disk menu to extend the search across an entire disk.

USING TEXT SEARCH   Text Search allows you to search through one or more of your files for text known as a *search string*. This search string can consist of any words or letters up to a maximum of 32 characters, and you can use F9 to toggle between entering the search string in ASCII or in hex.

Select the file or files you want to search before you start Text Search. Remember that the ASCII search is not case sensitive, so upper- or lowercase letters are treated the same. The hex search, on the other hand, matches the characters you enter exactly. So that you can check your hex entry, the corresponding ASCII characters are displayed on the line below as you enter the hex text for the search.

There are three search options:

- All Files extends the search to include all the files in the current directory.

- Selected Files searches only the files you selected before starting Text Search.

- Unselected Files searches all the files you didn't select before starting Text Search.

Select one of the options. Once the text is found there are two options:

- Select File and Continue marks the file containing the match for the search string as a selected file. When you return to the file list window, the file will be selected. This option allows you to collect all the files containing the search string together at the same time.

- Pause Search suspends the search when a match for the search string is found.

Now press Enter to start the search. When a match for the search string is found, the file is added to the list of selected files if you chose Select File and Continue. If you chose the Pause Search option, the bottom line of the screen shows the following selections:

- Search (F7) continues the search in the same file.

- Edit (F8) loads the Hex Editor and displays the file in sector format. The cursor indicates the position of the first byte of the search string.

- Next (F9) continues the search with the next file.

See Chapter 2 for more information on viewing and editing files.

USING SEARCH DISK   If you know the text is on the disk somewhere but you don't remember the file name, you can use Search Disk from the Disk pull-down menu.

Choose Search Disk from the Disk menu, and enter up to 32 characters to search for. Again, the text is not case sensitive. If you want to enter the search string in hex, press F9 and enter the string in hex. An exact match is made if you enter your search string in hex. As the search proceeds, a small horizontal display indicates progress.

When Search Disk finds a match, it displays the following options on the bottom line of the screen:

- Search (F7) continues to search for more matches.

- Name (F8) displays a small dialog box containing the name of the file. This allows you to go back and look at the file in detail when the search is complete.

- Edit (F9) loads the Hex Editor in sector mode, with the cursor indicating the starting character of the search string. You can view or edit the contents of the sector, and save your work when you have finished.

LOOKING AT FILE ATTRIBUTES

You can use a file's attributes to prevent it from being changed, deleted, or even seen. There are many reasons you might want to do this. You might want to hide a file so others don't know that it exists. If you are not the only person working on your computer or you are working on a local area network, you may want to restrict access to files containing sensitive data, such as payroll information or personnel records. You may want to make important files read-only so that you cannot erase then accidentally.

You can use the DOS ATTRIB command to provide some measure of protection. However, PC Shell has a much more complete and powerful set of capabilities.

WHAT ARE FILE ATTRIBUTES?

File *attributes* are characteristics that you can establish for your files, as follows:

- A read-only file cannot be written to or erased by the normal DOS commands. However, you can use read-only files with other DOS commands. For example, you can print them if they are text files. They also appear in the listings made by DIR. Very few commercial software packages use the read-only bit.

- Hidden files do not appear in listings made by DIR and can't be used with most DOS commands. Nonetheless, you can copy hidden files by using the DISKCOPY command, which makes a sector-by-sector duplicate of the original disk. To erase hidden files from a floppy disk, you must invoke the DOS FORMAT command, which is not always desirable since it destroys all the files on the disk.

- A system file is a hidden, read-only file that DOS uses and that cannot be written to or erased.

- The volume label identifies the disk and is an entry in the root directory.

- A subdirectory entry has an attribute that differentiates it from files.

- The archive bit indicates whether a file has been changed since it was last backed up. If it has been changed or has just been created, the archive bit is set. After a file has been copied by the BACKUP command, its archive bit is turned off. This is how BACKUP distinguishes the files that it has and hasn't backed up.

THE ATTRIBUTE BYTE

A file's attributes are recorded in its attribute byte. The attribute byte is part of a file's entry in a directory. Unlike the other entries, however, the attribute byte settings are not displayed in the usual DIR listing. Each different attribute has an associated bit. An attribute is turned on, or set, if the value of the bit equals 1. Each bit in the byte may be set or reset individually without affecting the other bits.

Table 5.6 shows the meaning of each bit in the attribute byte.

Table 5.6: The Attribute Bits

ATTRIBUTE	BIT NUMBER
Read-only file	0
Hidden file	1
System file	2
Volume label	3
Subdirectory	4
Archive bit	5
Unused	6
Unused	7

USING THE DOS ATTRIB COMMAND

The ATTRIB command is only available in DOS 3 and later.

To look at the status of a file's read-only and archive attributes with the DOS ATTRIB command, type

ATTRIB *MYFILE.TXT*

Assuming that *MYFILE.TXT* is a newly created file, DOS will return the current setting

A C:*MYFILE.TXT*

The A shows that the archive bit is set to on, indicating that the file will be backed up the next time BACKUP runs. The read-only bit is not set, which means that the file can be read, updated, or deleted.

You can use the ATTRIB command to set or reset a file's read-only and archive bits. None of the other attributes are accessible from ATTRIB.

To manipulate the attribute bits with ATTRIB, you can specify the following parameters:

- + R makes the file read-only by setting the read-only bit on.

- – R enables you to read and write to the file by setting the read-only bit off.

- + A sets the archive bit on.

- – A sets the archive bit off.

For example, typing

ATTRIB + R – A MYFILE.TXT

will set the read/write attribute bit on and set the archive bit off. Suppose you now use ATTRIB to look at the settings of the bits, by typing

ATTRIB MYFILE.TXT

The command will return:

R   C:\MYFILE.TXT

USING PC SHELL TO CHANGE FILE ATTRIBUTES

In PC Shell, you can use Attribute Change from the File pull-down menu to view and change a file's attributes as well as the last write date and time.

Select the files you want to work with in the files list in PC Shell, choose the File pull-down menu, and start Attribute Change by typing A, or by clicking on the menu item with the mouse.

A File Attribute window opens and lists the names of the files you chose, along with their attributes and creation date and time. A letter appears in the HSRA (hidden, system, read-only, archive) column if that particular bit is set. Eight files from the root directory of my hard disk are shown in Figure 5.15.

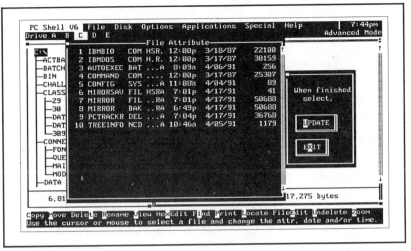

Figure 5.15: Attribute Change lists files and displays attribute settings

The DOS system files IBMBIO.COM and IBMDOS.COM have three attribute bits set, representing the hidden, system, and read-only bits. You should not change these bits on these particular files.

To change an attribute using the mouse, just click on the attribute letter to toggle its setting on or off. To change the date or time, move to the entry and type in the new date or time. Dates are entered as two digits, so May is 05, and October is 10. (The leading zero does not show on the screen, but you must type it in.)

To change an attribute using the keyboard, use the arrow keys to select the attribute you want to change and then press H, S, R, or A to toggle the appropriate attribute on or off. Move to the date or time entries with the arrow keys and enter the new values.

Finally, select Update to write your changes to your disk, or choose Exit to abandon your changes and return to the main PC Shell screen.

SPECIAL CONCERNS WITH READ-ONLY FILES   Beware of
making too many files read-only, as many commercial software packages have an installation program that configures parts of the software to your system's hardware. These programs write the details of your hardware system back into their own files. If you alter these files to read-only and then reconfigure the program in some way, the program will attempt to update its files with the new information, find that they are now read-only, and an error will occur. Some programs are smart

enough to produce a meaningful error message. If you try to use EDLIN on a read-only file, you will be told

File is READ-ONLY

dBASE III PLUS, on the other hand, may issue the more obscure message

File cannot be accessed.

SPECIAL CONCERNS WITH HIDDEN FILES Applications programs differ in their response to hidden files. WordStar will load a hidden text file, but other word processors may not. To edit a hidden file you may first have to reset the hidden bit to make the file visible.

Some commercial software packages use the hidden-files attribute as a part of their copy-protection schemes. If you do not remove the software according to the directions in the manual, these hidden files may remain on your disk, occupying valuable space.

You should resist the temptation to make too many files into hidden files. If you do, the saying "out of sight out of mind" may become painfully evident. For example, there is no point in hiding batch files or program files; you will soon forget their names and will be unable to use them. If a directory is cluttered with files you do not often use, don't hide them by setting the hidden bit; instead, copy them into another directory. Then add that directory's name into your path statement so that the files will be available when you do want to use them.

IDENTIFYING YOUR DISKS WITH VOLUME LABELS

Each disk has an entry in the root directory called the volume label. It is most often used to add a global title that applies to the whole disk. For example, you might call a floppy disk that contains word processing work MEMOS, or a disk containing Lotus 1-2-3 spreadsheets BUDGETS.

CREATING AND
VIEWING VOLUME LABELS IN DOS

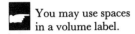
You may use spaces in a volume label.

The volume label can have up to 11 characters, which DOS displays in uppercase. To create a volume label, use the LABEL command. For example, enter

LABEL A:BUDGETS

to add the volume label BUDGETS to a floppy disk in drive A. You can also view a volume label by typing

LABEL A:

The exact wording of this message depends on the version of DOS you are using.

DOS will reply with the message

Volume in drive A is BUDGETS
Type a volume label of up to 11 characters or
Press Enter for no volume label update:

You can add a volume label to a floppy disk immediately after you finish formatting it if you specify the /V switch with the FORMAT command. For example, type

FORMAT A:/V

After the formatting process is complete, the following prompt appears:

Format complete
Volume label (11 characters, ENTER for none)?

You can now enter the volume label.

You can also use the VOL command in DOS to look at the contents of the volume label. Type

VOL A:

and DOS replies with

Volume in drive A has no label

if a volume label has not been specified for this disk. DOS will report

Volume in drive A is BUDGETS

if the disk contains the label BUDGETS.

USING PC SHELL TO CREATE AND VIEW VOLUME LABELS

You can use Rename Volume in PC Shell to review or change a disk's volume label. If you select Rename Volume from the Disk pull-down menu, a window opens showing the text of the current volume label. Figure 5.16 shows the Disk Rename window and the volume label of a hard disk.

Enter the new volume label and then select RENAME to write the new label to the disk, or CANCEL to ignore the new label.

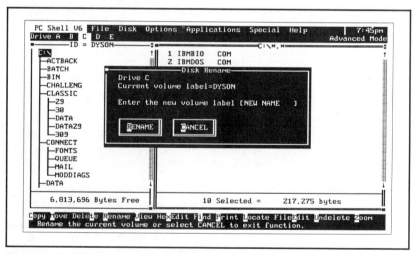

Figure 5.16: Disk Rename dialog window

SUMMARY

In this chapter, I described the hierarchical directory structure in DOS and the DOS commands used with files and directories.

You can use many of the PC Shell selections to help manage your hard disk. Some of the programs extend the capabilities of their DOS equivalents, but many of them are totally new capabilities that can greatly simplify your life.

6

Viewing
Your System
and Improving
Performance

There are several PC Tools programs that you can use to examine and quantify your computer system's performance. This chapter describes these programs and teaches you how to increase your computer's performance. It also discusses file fragmentation and a program for unfragmenting your files. It explains what to do when you encounter disk errors and other related hardware failures. Finally, the last section describes how you can speed up disk accesses with PC-Cache, and encrypt and compress your files with PC Secure.

INVESTIGATING YOUR HARDWARE AND EVALUATING PERFORMANCE

The System Info option from the Special pull-down menu in PC Shell reports on your PC's hardware configuration and calculates a performance index. If your job entails installing, demonstrating, or troubleshooting hardware or software products on unfamiliar PCs, this program is ideal. Running System Info is a quick and efficient way to learn about your hardware that will save time and prevent frustration.

To run System Info, choose the Special pull-down menu in PC Shell, and select or click on System Info. Figure 6.1 shows a report made by System Info for an AT-compatible computer.

Figure 6.1: System Info report on an AT-compatible computer

What follows is a line-by-line description of the System Info report:

- Computer: System Info gets the name of the computer from the ROM BIOS, and can recognize all of the IBM models and most of the compatibles.

- BIOS programs dated: The date that the ROM containing the BIOS (basic input/output system) was made or changed. The BIOS is a layer of software that loads from ROM and lies between the computer's hardware and DOS. The BIOS handles the basic input and output functions in the computer.

- Operating system: The version of DOS being run.

- Number of logical disk drives: The number of disk drives available on the system. May include a RAM disk in your computer's memory. This number is also controlled by the LASTDRIVE statement in your CONFIG.SYS file. If you do not have a LASTDRIVE specification, the number will often default to E or 5.

- Logical drive letter range: Displays the range of letters available for the drives you have connected.

- Serial Ports: Gives the number of installed serial interface ports. DOS used to support two serial ports, but beginning with DOS 3.3 the number increased to four. You can use the serial ports for different serial devices, including a modem, a mouse, a serial printer, or a digitizer. They handle data one bit after another in a serial form.

- Parallel Ports: Gives the number of installed parallel interface ports. The parallel port is normally used to connect the system printer and handles 8 data bits at once. The data transfer rate of a parallel port is generally higher than that of a serial port.

- CPU Type: The name of the microprocessor used in your PC. The microprocessor is the computer's engine. It turns information read from the files on the disk into instructions that it can execute, and it executes them very quickly. The IBM PC, IBM PC/XT, and their compatibles use the Intel 8086 or 8088 microprocessor. The PC/AT machine and its compatibles use the Intel 80286. More recent machines use the Intel 80386, or the 80486 chip.

- Relative speed (orig PC = 100%): The processing speed of the CPU in your computer compared with that of a standard IBM PC running at 4.77 MHz. To perform this test, System Info executes a set of instructions that might occur in a standard off-the-shelf application package. You can only use this figure to compare two systems in a general way, since System Info does not attempt to measure disk system performance.

In Figure 6.1, System Info was run on an AT-compatible computer. Note that this PC uses an Intel 80286 microprocessor, which gives a relative speed of 690 percent when compared to the IBM PC/XT.

The PCjr does not have a socket for a math coprocessor.

The 80486 has an on-chip floating-point unit as a part of its circuitry. Software written for the 80387 math coprocessor will run on the 80486 on-chip floating-point unit without any modifications.

- Math co-processor present: The Intel microprocessors used in PCs are designed so that other chips can be added to them, increasing their power. One such additional chip is a math, or floating-point, coprocessor. The PC has a socket on the main motherboard designed specifically for this coprocessor.

  Each Intel chip has a matched math coprocessor. The 8087 is used with the 8086, the 80287 is used with the 80286, and the 80387 is used with the 80386. These coprocessors take over some of the number crunching from the main microprocessor, increasing the speed and accuracy of the calculations. As well as simple add, subtract, multiply, and divide operations, math coprocessors can do trigonometric calculations such as sine, cosine, and tangent. Generally, a math coprocessor is 5 to 50 times faster than the regular processor. (These coprocessors are not the same as the third-party add-in accelerator boards that occupy a slot in the chassis and actually take over the original microprocessor's work by replacing it with a faster processor.)

- User programs are loaded at HEX paragraph: The point in the computer's memory where your applications programs are loaded. As this number increases, DOS and your memory-resident programs are taking up more room so the space available for your application programs decreases.

- Memory used by DOS and resident programs: The amount of memory occupied by both DOS and your memory-resident programs. As you use more memory for resident programs, the amount of space remaining for regular applications programs shrinks.

- Memory available for user programs: The amount of memory available for your regular applications programs.

- Total memory reported by DOS: The amount of memory DOS reports as available.

- PC Shell has found the total memory to be: PC Shell actually checks the amount of memory available. If you see a difference between this amount and the previous figure, you may have some hardware switches set to the wrong configuration. Alternately, a program like a RAM disk or print spooler may have taken memory for its own use.

- Video Display Adapter: The name of the video display adapter in use. There are five major types of video adapter boards:

    The monochrome display adapter (MDA)

    The color graphics adapter (CGA)

    The Hercules graphics adapter, also known as the monochrome graphics display adapter (MGDA)

    The enhanced graphics adapter (EGA)

    The video graphics array (VGA), which was introduced with the IBM PS/2 computer

- Extended memory installed: Details the amount of memory you have installed in your computer.

- Additional ROM BIOS found at HEX paragraph: Describes whether or not you have any expansion boards plugged into your computer that contain extensions to the BIOS. If none are found, this line is not displayed. In Figure 6.1, the additional ROM BIOS found at hex paragraph C000 is for a hard disk.

System Info alone justifies the purchase of PC Tools—it saves time and prevents frustration when you are working on an unfamiliar computer.

USING MEMORY MAP

Memory Map, another option in the Special pull-down menu, also shows details of how memory is used. You can use this information to work out how much memory each of your resident programs uses.

For more information on memory-resident programs, see Appendix D.

Memory Map lists the type, size, and location of memory blocks, as well as the names of the programs that own them. Memory Map gives you four different ways of looking at this data:

- The program memory blocks

- The program memory blocks with a list of interrupt vectors

- All of the memory blocks

- All of the memory blocks with a list of interrupt vectors

Figure 6.2 shows an example of the third type of display.

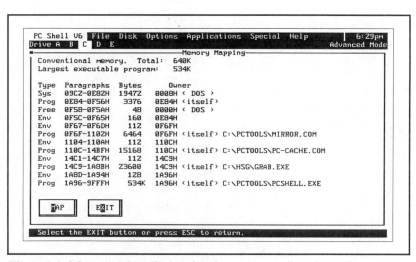

Figure 6.2: Memory Map display showing memory allocation

- At the top of the screen the amount of conventional memory is shown as 640K.

- 534K is the largest executable application program that will fit into that 640K after DOS and all the ancillary programs have been loaded.

- Type can be one of the following:

    Env: The DOS environment space, or a program's copy of the environment

    Free: Unallocated memory

    Prog: Applications program

    Sys: System program, a portion of DOS

    Env is short for environment. In DOS, the environment is a section of memory used primarily to keep the settings of the DOS PATH, SET, and PROMPT commands. When a program is loaded, it is given its own copy of the DOS environment. The program may modify its copy of the environment, but this will not affect the original copy of DOS maintained by the command processor. Any program that remains resident in memory retains its copy of the environment, which is not updated by any subsequent commands that alter DOS's copy of the environment.

- The hex starting and ending paragraph numbers represent the actual memory space occupied by the program. Paragraphs are 16-byte chunks of contiguous memory.

- Bytes shows the number of bytes (or kilobytes) in use by the program.

- The owner is the name of the program using this space. Note that the full path name is given in some cases.

Before describing the other display formats you can use to view memory apportionment in your computer, I need to make a short digression to describe interrupts—what they are for and how they work.

We want computers to work on the job we have sent them, but also to respond quickly to any request we make, such as pressing a key at the keyboard. The mechanism that accomplishes this task is known as an *interrupt*. An interrupt is an event that causes the processor to temporarily suspend its current activity and branch to a service routine somewhere in memory. After the service routine performs its task, control returns to the suspended process. Interrupts on DOS machines can be divided into two types, based on whether they are generated by hardware or by software. Interrupts are always channeled through a common internal vector table. By replacing interrupt routines, a memory-resident program can monitor hardware events and software service requests. For example, virtually all programs read the keyboard through interrupt 16H, which normally points to a service routine in the BIOS. It becomes a simple matter to change the response of the system to keyboard read requests by rerouting this vector through an alternative procedure. In PC Tools, these replaced vectors are called *hooked* vectors, and they are listed for each program if you choose the fourth display selection in Memory Map. Figure 6.3 shows such a display for the programs that were shown in Figure 6.2.

For example, in Figure 6.3, the Mirror program is using several software interrupts. Interrupt 25H is the DOS absolute disk read; it

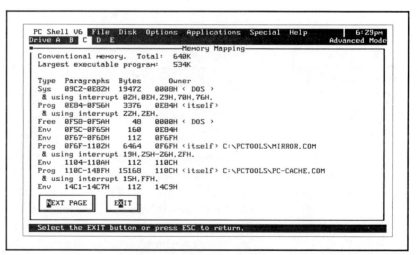

Figure 6.3: Memory Map display listing programs and DOS interrupt vectors

reads data from a logical disk sector into a specified memory location. Interrupt 26H is the DOS absolute disk write, which writes data from a specified memory buffer to a logical disk sector. With these services available, you can begin to see how powerful the memory-resident portion of Mirror can be, although it only occupies 6464 bytes in memory.

WHAT IS FILE FRAGMENTATION?

DOS manages the reading and writing of files on your disk. Files are written to the disk in groups of sectors called clusters. If you write a short file to disk, it occupies the first available cluster. When you write another short file to the same disk, this file occupies the next available cluster. If you now increase the first file's size above that of a cluster and save it with the same file name, DOS fragments this file by splitting it into two pieces, one occupying the first cluster and one occupying the third cluster.

However, the disk heads have to move to different locations on the disk to read or write a fragmented file. This takes more time than reading the same file from a series of contiguous clusters. By reducing or eliminating file fragmentation, you can increase the performance of your disk.

Another benefit of unfragmenting a disk is that DOS is less likely to fragment files that you subsequently add to your disk. Moreover, it is easier to undelete files that are in one piece. On the other hand, unfragmenting, or *optimizing,* your disk will probably make it impossible to recover any files that were deleted before the optimization.

To remove the effects of file fragmentation, all the files on the disk must be rearranged to consist of contiguous clusters. You can do this yourself by copying all the files and directories to backup disks, reformatting the hard disk, and reloading all the files onto the hard disk. This is a tremendous amount of tedious work, however. It is much easier to use the Compress program, which was designed for dealing with file fragmentation.

If there are erased files on the disk that you want to recover, do so before you unfragment the disk.

REPORTING FILE
FRAGMENTATION WITH COMPRESS

Have Compress prepare a report on the degree to which a file, directory, or disk is fragmented before you decide to reorganize your system. Daily and weekly fragmentation reports will indicate how fragmentation on your disk is changing over time and how often you should run Compress on your particular system. Compress can also change the order in which files or directories are recorded on the disk.

To activate Compress, type

COMPRESS

Compress will not run on a Novell Netware file server or on any networked drive.

at the DOS prompt or choose Compress Disk from the Applications pull-down menu in PC Shell. The main Compress screen is shown in Figure 6.4. Compress maps your disk in terms of allocated and unallocated clusters, and marks the boot record, FAT, and root directory as specific items. Several shortcut function keys are shown on the message bar at the bottom of the screen. The pull-down menus and function-key shortcuts work as they do in PC Shell, so once you can use PC Shell, you can use Compress.

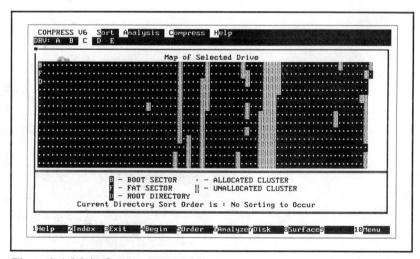

Figure 6.4: Main Compress screen

To make a report on the entire disk, select the Analysis menu and choose Disk Analysis or press (F7). The resulting display is shown in Figure 6.5.

Figure 6.5 indicates that 14026 clusters are in use by files, 2305 are available for use, and 2 clusters are marked as bad but fortunately are not being used. You can tell that this is the case by examining the last item in this list. The number of bad clusters within files is 0, therefore the 2 bad clusters have been marked as bad and are unavailable for use. There are 1835 files on the disk; 94 of them are fragmented, which gives a fragmentation factor of 1 percent. The number of non-contiguous free-space areas indicates how the unallocated free space on the disk is distributed. This number should be kept as small as possible so that the free space exists in a small number of large pieces, rather than a large number of small pieces.

To look at the individual files on your disk in detail, choose the File Analysis option from the Analysis pull-down menu. Figure 6.6 shows a display for the \PCTOOLS directory on a hard disk.

The full path name of the directory is shown in the upper-left corner of Figure 6.6, and the remaining area of the screen is occupied by the files in the directory. Files are listed in the order in which they occur in the directory, along with the number of clusters in the file,

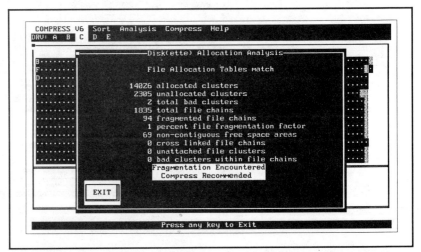

Figure 6.5: Compress Disk Allocation Analysis report for a hard disk

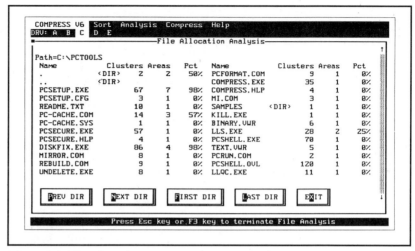

Figure 6.6: File Allocation Analysis display for the \PCTOOLS directory on a hard disk

and the number of areas the file is divided into. An unfragmented file shows a 1 in this column. A percentage fragmented figure is also given for each file in the directory.

Use ↑ and ↓ to move one line at a time through the display. PgUp and PgDn move up or down one window, and Home and End move to the ends of the listing. Alternatively, use the mouse and the scroll bars to move through the list of files.

You can also move through the whole disk one directory at a time by using the PREV DIR or NEXT DIR selections. You can go directly to the root directory with FIRST DIR, or to the end of the disk with LAST DIR. To leave the File Allocation Analysis screen, press Escape or EXIT (F3).

PRECAUTIONS TO TAKE BEFORE RUNNING COMPRESS ON YOUR HARD DISK

Be sure to make a complete hard-disk backup before you use Compress to reorganize your files.

Before you make Compress reorganize the files on your hard disk, you must take a few precautions:

- Make a complete backup of your hard disk in case there is an incompatibility between your system and Compress. Problems can occur because of the enormous number of potential combinations of hard disks and disk controllers.

- Run the DOS CHKDSK command and Surface Analysis (F8), described later in this chapter, to find and hopefully fix any hardware-related file or disk problems. This will give Compress a clean system to work with.

- Do not turn your computer off while Compress is running. You can only interrupt Compress by pressing Escape. Compress may continue running until it finds a safe and convenient place to stop.

- Make sure that you turn off and disable any memory-resident software that might access the disk while Compress is running. For example, some programs save your work to the hard disk automatically at set time intervals. You must turn off this type of software.

If you are using the DOS FASTOPEN utility, or any other disk buffering program, you will probably have to reboot your computer after running Compress. This is because Compress changes directory and file locations when it optimizes the disk, and FASTOPEN may not find the files where it expects to. If you see the message

File not found

after running Compress, reboot your PC and try again.

UNFRAGMENTING FILES ON YOUR HARD DISK WITH COMPRESS

Choose the Compress pull-down menu to display the options available during compressions. Figure 6.7 shows the Compression menu. First select a compress technique from the list of options:

- Unfragment only unfragments all your files but does not collect all the free space on your disk into one large segment.

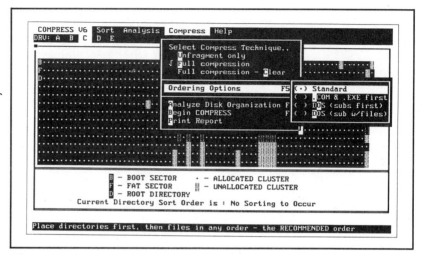

Figure 6.7: Compression pull-down menu

The next file you write on your disk may be badly fragmented as DOS tries to fill in many small areas of your disk. This selection runs quickly, but the benefits from it will not last long since any new files are likely to be fragmented.

- Full compression unfragments your files and collects all the free space in one place on your disk. This is generally more useful than the Unfragment Only selection.

- Full compression - clear does everything a Full Compression does, and also erases all data in the unused sectors. Recover any erased files before selecting this option since you will not be able to recover them afterwards.

Next choose the ordering sequence you want to use (F5) from the list of preset options:

Putting program files near the outer edge of the disk will help prevent future fragmentation.

- Standard puts your files into the most convenient order for Compress to use, making Compress run faster.

- .COM & .EXE First moves all your program files towards the front of the disk. Program files tend to stay the same size (unless you are doing software development, in which case they always grow bigger) and should not need to be rewritten.

- DOS (subs first) puts your files into what PC Tools calls DOS ordering. This means that all the files in any given subdirectory will be kept together. This is a good selection for optimizing hard-disk performance, as data and program overlay files are kept close together. This selection is only available in PC Tools 5.5.

- DOS (subs with files) positions each subdirectory just before its files. Use this method if you tend to add and delete entire directories rather than single files.

Now that you have chosen a compression technique and the ordering options for file arrangement, you can check to see if the compression is really needed with the Analyze Disk Organization (F6) selection of the Compress pull-down menu. This option looks at your compression choices and compares them with what it finds on the hard disk. If there is a difference, it recommends that you proceed with the compression. This also prevents a second disk optimization when nothing has changed.

Print Report makes a report to the printer or to a disk file COMPRESS.RPT. You must choose to make a report before starting the compression. The report details how long the optimization took, the options you selected, and the number of used, unused, and bad clusters on the disk. If you want to write the report to a file, you must send it to a disk other than the one you are compressing.

SORTING DIRECTORIES WITH COMPRESS

The PC Shell program contains an option for sorting directories, but this is a slow way of sorting all of the directories on your hard disk. Compress has a Sort menu that you can use so that the sorting is done with the optimization. Figure 6.8 shows this Sort pull-down menu.

You can sort directories by Date/Time, File Name, Extension, or Size, and you can select Ascending or Descending sorts. If you sort by extension, files are arranged in alphabetical order within extension type. This is often a convenient way of grouping your files since it keeps similar file types together. You can also select No Sorting.

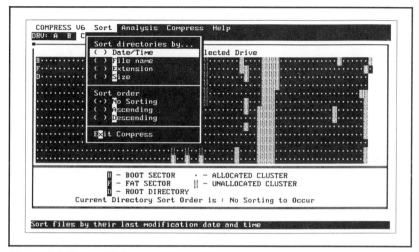

Figure 6.8: Sort pull-down menu

RUNNING COMPRESS

Select Begin COMPRESS (F4) from the Compress pull-down menu; a warning screen reminds you to disable all memory-resident programs and stop all disk activity. The warning screen also recommends that you make a complete backup before optimizing your disk.

Optimization can take a long time, especially if you are unfragmenting an entire hard disk. Monitor the Percentage Complete and Elapsed Time displays to get an idea of how long it will take to complete the job. Press Escape to stop the optimization.

As the compression proceeds, the Disk Map on the screen changes dynamically to reflect the new disk structure. At the end of the compression, the left side of the screen should be full of clusters-in-use characters and the right side should be full of free-space characters. If you selected the Unfragment Only option, there might be some areas of free space amongst your files.

A very small number of files may still be fragmented when the compression is finished because they extend across a hidden or system file. Compress will not move either the hidden file or the regular file that spans it so as not to interfere with any copy-protection schemes.

Finally, before leaving Compress you should make a new Mirror file to record the new file and directory arrangement on your hard disk. Your old Mirror file is now completely out of date, and the success of a future file or disk recovery depends on a current Mirror file. Compress reminds you that you need to make a new Mirror file, so do this now.

USING COMPRESS AUTOMATICALLY FROM A BATCH FILE

You can run Compress by including it in a batch file and using several optional parameters to automate the operation. Remember, however, that after accidental deletion unfragmented files are almost always easier to recover than fragmented files. If you have deleted files on the disk that you want to try to restore, you must rescue them before running Compress. Compress will almost always write over the deleted files at some point in its operation, practically eliminating the chances of a successful file recovery.

The general form for running Compress from the DOS prompt or in a batch file is

See Appendix A for a complete list of all optional parameters for all PC Tools programs.

Compress *drive parameters*

where *drive* is the letter of the drive you want to compress. If you don't enter a drive letter, Compress assumes that you want to use the current drive.

You can use the following optional parameters to aid in automatic operation.

You can specify your choice of compression selections with the following options:

/CC   Compress performs a full compression and clears all unused sectors.

/CF   Compress performs a full compression.

/CU   Compress unfragments your disk using the minimum compressions option.

You can specify the physical file ordering from the DOS prompt or from a batch file with the following options:

/OD   Compress performs standard DOS ordering—that is, files are kept close to their parent directory.

/OO   Compress places each subdirectory immediately before its own files.

/OP   Compress locates program files (*.EXE, and *.COM) at the front of the disk. Program files do not normally grow once you have installed them, so placing them at the front of the disk will prevent them from becoming fragmented again in the future.

/OS   Compress uses standard ordering; files are placed where it is most convenient for the program. This is the fastest ordering option, and is the one you will use most often.

You can select the type of sort from the DOS prompt or from a batch file with the following options:

/SE   Compress sorts by file extension.

/SF   Compress sorts by file name.

/SS   Compress sorts by file size.

/ST   Compress sorts by file time.

Finally, you can specify the sort order with one of the following parameters:

/SA   Compress performs an ascending sort.

/SD   Compress performs a descending sort.

COMPRESS AND COPY-PROTECTION SCHEMES

Some copy-protection methods that rely on hidden files insist that the hidden files stay in exactly the same place on the disk. If your copy-protection method uses hidden files and you move them to another location on the disk, your application program will often refuse to work—it thinks that you are using an illegal copy of the file.

with the system attribute bit set, so as not to interfere with the copy-protection systems. Also, Compress will not move the DOS hidden files (IBMBIO.COM and IBMDOS.COM) that DOS places at the beginning of all bootable disks. If an application uses some other location-specific copy-protection scheme, the only way to be absolutely sure that Compress will not interfere with it is to remove the software package completely before running Compress, and then reinstall it after Compress is done.

CHECKING YOUR DISKS WITH SURFACE ANALYSIS

Disk errors can appear in a variety of forms, and you can use the Surface Analysis program to help isolate—and in some cases solve—problems associated with read errors. Because Surface Analysis actually reads or attempts to read the data from each cluster on the disk, it differs from the DOS CHKDSK command, which only tests for logical errors in the data contained in the FAT and the directories.

When a disk-read error occurs, DOS can respond with a variety of messages. The typical DOS prompt following such a device error is

   Abort, Retry, Ignore, Fail?

although the actual selections in this sequence depend on which version of DOS you are using and the nature of the error. If you choose Abort, DOS terminates execution of the program that initially performed the read. Retry tells DOS to try the operation again. Choosing Ignore causes DOS to return to the application without an error code, giving the illusion that the operation has been performed. Choosing Fail causes DOS to return control to the original application with a code indicating failure. Sometimes Fail will be disallowed and promoted to Abort, and sometimes Ignore will be disallowed and promoted to Abort or Fail.

RUNNING SURFACE ANALYSIS

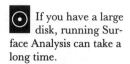 If you have a large disk, running Surface Analysis can take a long time.

Select Surface Analysis (F8) from the Analysis menu. This selects the disk-read test, which reads every part of the disk, including the

~~Compress recognizes and does not move these hidden files or files~~ system area of boot record, FAT, and the root directory, and the data area, which consists of the file space and the unused or erased file space. Because it checks the entire disk, this option can take a long time to run. You are asked if you want to make one or several passes across the disk. If your disk has hard errors (errors that occur every time an area of the disk is accessed), one pass should be sufficient to find them. If your disk has soft errors (which only occur occasionally), more passes will be needed. The number of the cluster and sector currently being tested is shown on the screen as the program runs, as are the elapsed time and the percent complete.

The completed Surface Analysis display is shown in Figure 6.9. When the program is running, press Escape to interrupt it at any time. In the figure, Surface Analysis found two bad clusters. If a cluster is already marked as bad, Surface Analysis continues the scan. Because the cluster is already marked as bad, there is no danger that it will be used by DOS in the future. This is not usually an indication of deteriorating disk conditions, since most hard disks have a few clusters marked as bad by the low-level formatting program.

> Certain bad-cluster errors can be corrected with programs like SpinRite from Gibson Research Corporation or Disk Technician from Prime Solutions, Inc.

If the number of errors that Surface Analysis uncovers increases, you should replace or repair the hard disk as soon as possible. If the problems are reported from a floppy disk, you should try cleaning

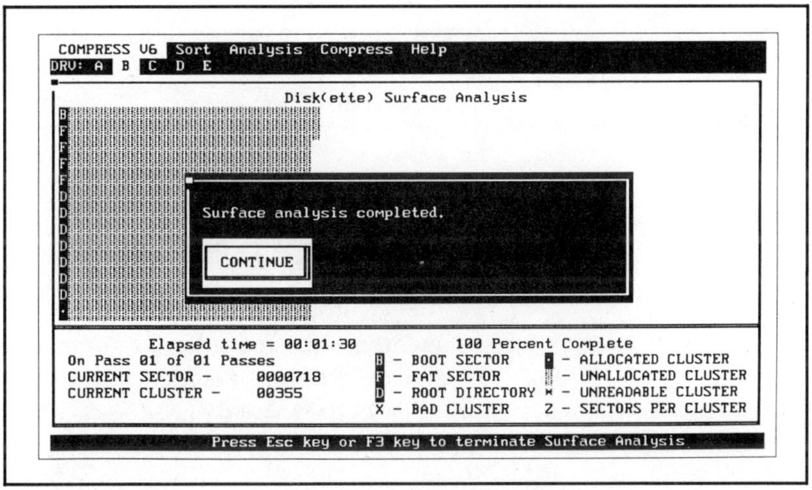

Figure 6.9: Surface Analysis display for the disk-read test

the disk heads. Then reformat the disk and run Surface Analysis on it again to see if the errors have been removed.

If Surface Analysis finds a cluster that it cannot read but that was not marked as bad by the low-level formatting program, it locks the cluster out of the list of available clusters in the FAT so it cannot be used in the future by DOS.

If Surface Analysis finds an error in a cluster in use by a file, it moves the file to a safe area of the disk and marks the original area as bad so that it cannot be used in the future.

The degree of danger any error represents really depends on where the bad cluster is on your disk. If the error is in the system area of the disk, in the boot record, in either of the FAT's, or in the root directory, you could potentially lose all the data on the disk. If it is a hard disk, this can be a great deal of data to lose (another reason you should always have up-to-date backups). If the bad cluster contains the boot record, the hard disk may refuse to boot. The system area on a disk cannot be copied to a safe area of the disk because the three components of the system area must be in a specific place on the disk. In this situation, make a complete hard-disk backup if you do not already have one, reformat the disk with the DOS FORMAT command or with PC Format, and reload the contents of the hard disk.

For a floppy disk, back it up and reformat it. If that doesn't work, throw the disk away. Never use a dubious disk as a backup disk. Make your backups onto error-free disks only. When you need to reload your system from your backup disks, you cannot tolerate any errors.

Now that you have optimized the organization of your files on your hard disk, you can use PC-Cache to speed up disk access times.

USING PC-CACHE TO INCREASE DISK PERFORMANCE

PC-Cache is designed to speed up your work by retaining the most frequently requested information in memory rather than reading it from disk each time it is requested. This cuts down on the number of times DOS has to read or access your disks. You use PC-Cache from the DOS prompt since it does not have a full-screen option.

You must install
PC-Cache after
Mirror but before any
other memory-resident
programs. See Appendix D for more details on
memory-resident programs and loading order.

See Appendix A for
a complete list of
PC-Cache optional
parameters.

If you used PC Setup to install PC Tools, PC-Cache will be installed in the correct sequence. If you do the installation yourself, make sure to place PC-Cache after the Mirror program and before any other memory-resident programs such as PC Shell, Desktop, and so on.

To see a list of the PC-Cache parameters, type

PC-Cache /?

Figure 6.10 shows the list of parameters.

To run PC-Cache from the DOS prompt, type

PC-CACHE *parameters*

where you choose parameters from the list in Table 6.1.

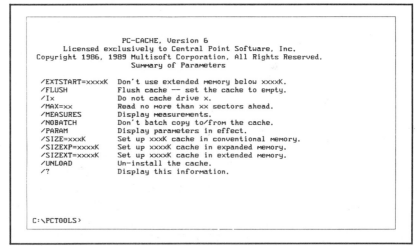

```
                    PC-CACHE, Version 6
        Licensed exclusively to Central Point Software, Inc.
    Copyright 1986, 1989 Multisoft Corporation, All Rights Reserved.
                    Summary of Parameters

    /EXTSTART=xxxxK  Don't use extended memory below xxxxK.
    /FLUSH          Flush cache -- set the cache to empty.
    /Ix             Do not cache drive x.
    /MAX=xx         Read no more than xx sectors ahead.
    /MEASURES       Display measurements.
    /NOBATCH        Don't batch copy to/from the cache.
    /PARAM          Display parameters in effect.
    /SIZE=xxxK      Set up xxxK cache in conventional memory.
    /SIZEXP=xxxxK   Set up xxxxK cache in expanded memory.
    /SIZEXT=xxxxK   Set up xxxxK cache in extended memory.
    /UNLOAD         Un-install the cache.
    /?              Display this information.



    C:\PCTOOLS>
```

Figure 6.10: List of optional PC-Cache command-line parameters

Table 6.1: PC-Cache Parameters

PARAMETER	MEANING
/EXTSTART = *nn*K	Specifies the start of the cache buffer in extended memory. EXTSTART must be larger than 1MB—that is, 1024K. PC-Cache is compatible with VDISK.SYS.

Table 6.1: PC-Cache Parameters (Continued)

PARAMETER	MEANING
/FLUSH	Empties the cache.
/I*drive*	Specifies the drive or drives that should not be cached.
/INFO (Version 6.0)	Displays a table showing the size of your hard drives, and the type and size of the cache. You cannot use this parameter if PC-Cache is already installed; remove it first with /UNLOAD and then run /INFO.
/MAX = *nnn*	Specifies the number of sectors that the cache can save in a single read operation. The default is 4, and selecting a number between 8 and 16 will optimize the cache for large applications.
/MEASURES	Displays cache performance information.
/PARAM	Displays the parameters used when the cache was installed.
/PARAM*	Displays PC-Cache setup information, including the number of sectors transferred at a time, and the type and size of the cache.
/PAUSE (Version 6.0)	Used under special circumstances if you are having problems with PC-Cache. Follow the directions on the screen.
/QUIET (Version 6.0)	Turns off the PC-Cache startup information, so that PC-Cache can be used in batch files.
/UNLOAD	Removes the cache as long as the cache was the last TSR loaded.

Table 6.1: PC-Cache Parameters (Continued)

PARAMETER	MEANING
/WRITE = *nn* (Version 6.0)	Specifies the delay, in seconds, before write operations are sent to the disk. Use this parameter carefully, because if you set the delay to be too long, you might loose data by turning your computer off before it has finished writing all your data.
/?	Displays a help screen showing all PC-Cache's parameters. Use this to confirm the version number of the PC-Cache you are using.

PC-Cache supports standard memory (up to 640K), expanded memory (memory that conforms to the Lotus/Intel/Microsoft expanded memory specification), or extended memory (AT-style memory above 640K). When a cache is created in expanded or extended memory, a small amount of standard memory is also used. You may use only one SIZE parameter; you cannot mix standard, expanded, and extended memory. You can specify the size of the cache with one of the parameters listed in Table 6.2.

Table 6.2: PC-Cache Size Parameters

PARAMETER	MEANING
/SIZE = *nnn*K	Specifies the amount of standard memory for the cache. If no size is given, the default is 64K.
/SIZEXP = *nnn*K	Specifies the amount of expanded memory for the cache. The smallest size is 10K and the default is 256K.

Table 6.2: PC-Cache Size Parameters (Continued)

PARAMETER	MEANING
/SIZEXT = *nnn*K	Specifies the amount of extended memory for the cache. This parameter can only be used on computers using Intel's 80286 and 80386 processors. The default is 256K.
/SIZEXT* = *nnn*K (Version 6.0)	Allows PC-Cache to decide the best method for accessing extended memory.

For example, to install a cache of 128K in standard memory and ignore floppy-disk drives A and B, add the following line to your AUTOEXEC.BAT file:

PC-CACHE /IA /IB/SIZE = 128K

To install a cache of 256K in expanded memory, include the line

PC-CACHE /SIZEXP = 256K

To make a cache of 256K in extended memory, use the line

PC-CACHE /SIZEXT = 256K

Reboot your computer after you have changed AUTOEXEC.BAT so that the new cache will be installed. Remember, you can only use one /SIZE statement in the cache specification.

To see how well your cache is performing after you have been using it for a while, use the /MEASURES parameter from the DOS prompt, as follows:

PC-CACHE /MEASURES

The results are shown in Figure 6.11.

```
C:\PCTOOLS>PC-CACHE /MEASURES

    PC-CACHE, Version 6
    Unauthorized duplication prohibited.
    The PC-CACHE program is already installed.
    Measurements are as follows:
            36   logical transfers.
            23   physical transfers.
            13   transfers saved.
            36   percent saved.


C:\PCTOOLS>
```

Figure 6.11: PC-Cache display using the /MEASURES parameter

PC-Cache lists the following performance indicators:

- Logical Transfers are the number of data transfers that have occurred between the cache and the current application.

- Physical Transfers are the number of data transfers that have occurred between the disk and the current application.

- Transfers Saved are the number of physical transfers saved by using PC-Cache. This is the difference between the logical and physical transfers.

- Percentage Saved is the number of saved transfers expressed as a percentage.

To see which parameters were used to install the cache, use the /PARAM option to display the parameters currently in effect, as shown in Figure 6.12.

You can use a similar option, /PARAM*, to display information about your drives, the sizes of your drives, and the status of extended memory. You must remember to include the * character, which is not a wildcard or a placeholder—it's just a character.

```
C:\PCTOOLS>PC-CACHE /PARAM

  PC-CACHE, Version 6
  Unauthorized duplication prohibited.
  The PC-CACHE program is already installed.
  PC-CACHE has been set up as follows:

        Perform batch copies to/from cache.
        Read a maximum of  4 sectors ahead.
        No caching of drive A.
        No caching of drive B.
        256K Extended memory cache at  2176K has been set up as follows:
                          Conventional        Extended
        DOS/Resident          62K                0K
        PC-CACHE              15K              256K
        Available            564K             1152K
        Total                640K             1408K


C:\PCTOOLS>
```

Figure 6.12: The /PARAM option displays the current PC-Cache parameters

PC-CACHE AND BERNOULLI BOXES

If you are using a Bernoulli box, you can install a cache for it by adding a special device driver specification to your CONFIG.SYS file. This device driver, called PC-CACHE.SYS, allows PC-Cache to watch transfers to and from your Bernoulli box. You should place the device specification immediately after the line that specifies the Bernoulli driver (IDRIVE.SYS or RDC.SYS or equivalent). Add the line

DEVICE = PC-CACHE.SYS

to your CONFIG.SYS file and reboot your computer. You will see a short message from PC-CACHE.SYS during the startup sequence if it is installed correctly. Load PC-Cache as you would normally.

USING PC SECURE

> PC Tools 5.5 cannot decrypt files made with 6.0. Version 6.0 can decrypt files made with 5.5.

As an operating system, DOS has virtually no built-in security features. If you keep confidential files such as payroll records or personnel files on your computer, you may want to encrypt them for increased security. Also, you can use one of the selections in PC

Secure to employ a data compression technique called block-adaptive Lempel-Ziv-Welch compression to shrink your files and use your disk space more effectively.

THE DATA ENCRYPTION STANDARD

If you want to know more about DES, see the U.S. Department of Commerce/National Bureau of Standards, Data Encryption Standard, Federal Information Processing Standard Publication 46, 1977, which contains full details of the algorithm.

PC Secure uses the DES (data encryption standard) to encrypt and decrypt files. The DES encryption scheme is a block cipher that works by a combination of transposition and substitution. It works on blocks of 8 bytes (64 bits), encrypting or decrypting them using a 56-bit user-supplied key. With a 54-bit key, there are about 7.2×10^{16} possible keys. Due to the algorithm's complexity and length, it is not reproduced here.

Since the DES algorithm cannot be shipped outside the USA, PC Secure is shipped overseas with the encrypt/decrypt option removed. File compression/expansion is still active and can give some security, although that is certainly not its prime purpose and the result is not as secure as a file encrypted with DES.

DES was developed after years of work at IBM, rigorously tested by the National Security Agency, and finally accepted as being free of any statistical or mathematical weaknesses. This suggests that it is impossible to break the system using statistical frequency tables or to work the algorithm backwards using mathematical methods. DES is used by federal departments and most banks and money-transfer systems to protect all sensitive computer data.

DES has the following features:

- It has remained unbroken despite years of use.

- It completely randomizes the data in the file.

- Even if you know some of the original text, you cannot use it to determine the encryption key.

- After DES encryption, it is virtually impossible to decrypt the file without the key.

COMPRESSING FILES

Do not confuse references in this section to file compression (which actually makes a file smaller) with the Compress program in PC Tools (which unfragments and rearranges files on your disks).

Using DES encryption increases security by scrambling the contents of a file. However, one of the other selections in PC Secure allows you to compress your files—that is, to actually make them smaller so that they occupy less space on your disk. You will see the biggest change in size with text files, and you will see little if any change with program or other binary files. PC Secure uses a block-adaptive Lempel-Ziv-Welch (LZW) compression method. This method can be done in one pass across the file, unlike Huffman coding (another common data compression technique often used by fax machines), and does not require that a translation table be stored or transmitted with the compressed file. You can transmit a compressed file by modem or back up a compressed file to a floppy disk much faster than you can process the larger original.

ENCRYPTING YOUR FILES

PC Secure is another member of the PC Tools family that uses full-screen data entry techniques with full mouse and keyboard support. You can load PC Secure through the Applications menu in PC Shell, or you can run it from the DOS prompt by typing

   PCSECURE

CREATING A KEY   The first time you run PC Secure, you are asked to create a master key. The key can be either a combination of alphanumeric characters or hex numbers. If you enter alphanumeric characters, the key must be from five to 32 alphabetic or numeric characters long. The key is case sensitive, so computer, Computer, and COMPUTER are three different keys. Keys must be longer than five characters, since it is too easy to guess keys of less than five characters.

As you type in your alphanumeric key, for security reasons PC Secure displays a * instead of the character you enter. You are asked to confirm your key by typing it a second time.

Press F9 if you would rather enter your key directly in hexadecimal. If you choose this option, the key must be exactly 16 characters long. In hexadecimal entry, you only type your key once; you are not asked to confirm it. Also, in this mode the characters are displayed as you enter them.

Consider the following when choosing your keys:

- Do not choose a key that others might easily guess.

- Don't lose your keys.

- Don't tell other people about your keys.

The worst keys are the obvious ones: initials, place names or people's names, phone numbers, birth dates, or complete English words

> If you lose the key or password used to encrypt a file, you will never be able to decrypt the file again, so be very careful.

(there are a limited number of words in the English language and a computer can try them all very quickly). The best keys are longer rather than shorter, and usually contain a combination of letters and numbers. Your key should be easy for you to remember but meaningless to anyone else.

The key is stored in the PCSECURE.EXE file for safekeeping, and it will be used to encrypt any file except those encrypted in expert mode.

You can use PC Secure to encrypt and compress all sorts of files. You cannot, however, use it on files that are already compressed by utilities like ARC or other encryption schemes (if you run PC Secure on these files, they will probably grow slightly larger). You can compress Lotus spreadsheet files by up to 60 or 70 percent, and word processing files by 50 to 60 percent. The kind of results you get will depend on the types of file you work with.

Do not encrypt or compress applications that use some sort of copy-protection scheme. PC Secure will compress and encrypt the file, but the application will not run if certain information is not accessible. You can use PC Shell File and Disk commands as well as the DOS equivalents to copy, delete, back up, and restore encrypted files. You can even run the hard-disk optimizing program Compress on PC Secure files. Remember that the compressed or encrypted files are binary files, so be careful to select the appropriate file-transfer method if you want to transfer the file to another computer over a modem. You cannot use ASCII transfer methods on a binary file; use XMODEM if it is available.

PC Secure is also compatible with standard DOS networks, but you should be careful not to place a decrypted file on the network server disk where others may find it. Copy the encrypted file to your local station and decrypt the file there to maintain security.

CHOOSING ENCRYPTION OPTIONS Before proceeding, you should choose the encryption selections you need from the Options pull-down menu shown in Figure 6.13.

Your selections are indicated by a check mark to the left of the item in the menu. If there is no mark, the option will not be used when you start file encryption.

- Full DES Encryption gives the file the full 16 encryption rounds as defined in the standard.

Since encrypted or compressed files are binary files, you cannot use ASCII file-transfer methods to send the file over a modem. Use XMODEM instead.

To perform compression only on your file, turn off both the Full DES Encryption and the Quick Encryption options.

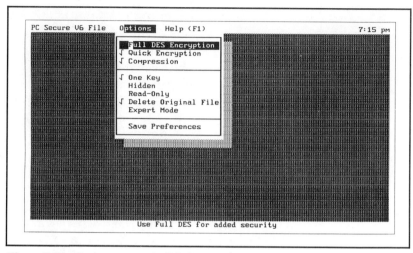

Figure 6.13: Options menu in PC Secure

- Quick Encryption enacts only two encryption rounds, which saves time but is much less secure.

- You can choose compression with or without encryption. PC Secure uses block-adaptive Lempel-Ziv-Welch (LZW) compression, a more advanced method than Huffman coding or Adaptive Huffman coding. Also, LZW compresses the file in one pass and does not require that a translation table be stored with the file. PC Secure compresses most files from 20 to 70 percent.

- With the One Key selection on, PC Secure only asks you to enter the key the first time you work on a file, and continues to use the same key for all following files. With this option off, PC Secure asks you for the key for every file you work with.

- Hidden sets the hidden bit of the file's attribute, making it invisible to the normal DOS commands.

- Read-Only makes the file read-only so that the normal DOS commands cannot access it. If you try to delete a read-only file, DOS responds with the message

    Access Denied.

- With the Delete Original File selection on, PC Secure copies your original file, encrypts the copy, and then destroys the original. There must be enough room on the disk for both files at the same time. This selection provides high security, but remember, you cannot undelete a file that PC Secure has destroyed.

- If this option is off, a copy of your original file is encrypted and the extension .SEC is added. The original file is not affected. Again, you must have enough room on the disk for both files at the same time.

- If you encrypt a file with Expert Mode off and you forget the key used for encryption, you can use the master key that you entered when you started PC Secure for the first time.

- If you encrypt a file with Expert Mode set to on and you lose the key, your master key cannot decrypt the file. In fact, there is no way to decrypt the file. You would have to break DES to do it, and no one has ever done that.

- Save Preferences saves your current settings into a file as the default settings for PC Secure.

COMPLETING THE ENCRYPTION When you have made your choices from the Options menu, move to the File menu, shown in Figure 6.14, and choose Encrypt File or press F4 to start the encryption process.

This brings up the File Selection box, which contains a list of the files in the current directory. Select a file from the list box or type a new name into the text box. Press Enter to proceed. A dialog box requests the key. Enter the key; you are asked to type it again as verification. If you make a mistake entering your key, another dialog box responds with the message

The keys are not equivalent.

PC Secure starts work on the file according to the selections you made from the Options menu. Figure 6.15 shows the encryption Progress screen.

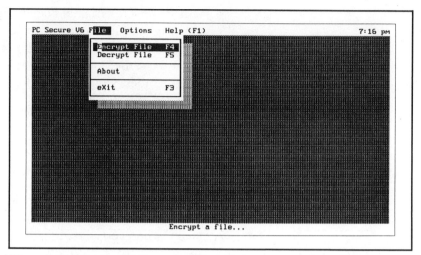

Figure 6.14: Encrypt File from the File pull-down menu starts the encryption process

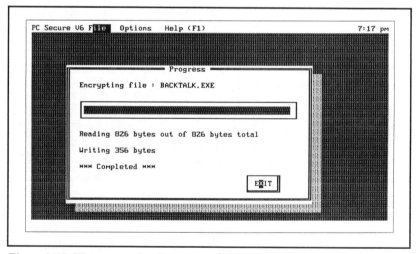

Figure 6.15: The encryption Progress screen

The horizontal bar moves from left to right as the file is encrypted to show the amount of progress made. When PC Secure is finished, you can use the About selection in the File pull-down menu to look at the encrypted file, as shown in Figure 6.16. The About screen shows the file name, the initial and final file size, and the percentage reduction in size.

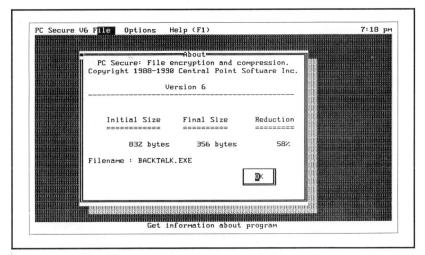

```
  PC Secure V6 File  Options   Help (F1)                         7:18 pm

                         ═══════About═══════
                    PC Secure: File encryption and compression.
                    Copyright 1988-1990 Central Point Software Inc.

                                 Version 6
                    ─────────────────────────────────────────

                Initial Size      Final Size      Reduction
                ============      ==========      =========

                   832 bytes       356 bytes         58%

                Filename : BACKTALK.EXE
                                                ┌──────┐
                                                │  OK  │
                                                └──────┘


                         Get information about program
```

Figure 6.16: The About screen for an encrypted file

To encrypt a whole directory in one pass, select the directory from the File Selection screen. (You can identify a directory because it is contained in square brackets.) This time choose the Directory button. A dialog screen warns you that this option will affect more than one file, and asks for permission to continue. There is a check box if you want to include all subdirectories in the encryption process. After making your choices, you are prompted for your key as before, and the encryption begins.

DECRYPTING YOUR FILES

When you decrypt a file, you restore it to its original condition. Choose Decrypt (F5) from the File pull-down menu to display the File Selection screen shown in Figure 6.17.

Choose the file for decryption and select the Decrypt button. If the One Key choice in the Options menu is on and there is a check mark by the entry, you will not be asked for a key here. Otherwise, enter the key you used to encrypt the file. A second dialog box asks for confirmation of the key. If the keys don't match, a dialog box responds with the message

The keys are not equivalent.

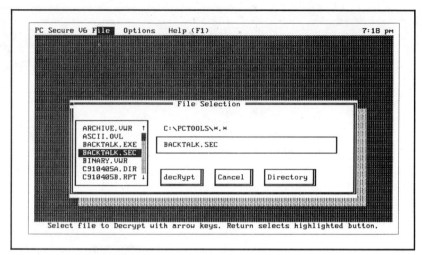

Figure 6.17: File Selection screen for file decryption

Enter the correct key. If you type the wrong key, you'll see a dialog box with the message

Bad password, try again?

If you try to decrypt a file that is not encrypted, you will see the message

This is not a PC Secure file.

As PC Secure decrypts the file, progress is shown on the horizontal bar graph. The message

* * * Completed * * *

is displayed when PC Secure is done.

To decrypt an entire directory, select Decrypt (F5). Then select the directory you wish to decrypt from the File Selection list on the screen. Enter your keys and proceed with the decryption. PC Secure shows its progress with the bar graph as before, and writes the

* * * Completed * * *

message when it is finished.

To exit from PC Secure and return to the DOS prompt, choose Exit (F3) from the File menu.

If you see the message

File already exists. Replace?

when you are decrypting a file, proceed with care. If you encrypted the file with Delete Original File set to off, the original file remains on the disk. When you come to decrypt the file, PC Secure attempts to restore the file to its original name, but finds that the file already exists. If the file has not changed since you encrypted it, you can decrypt the file on top of the original. If you now have two versions of the file—the older one encrypted and the newer one not—be very careful not to destroy the newer file. Copy the file to another directory, or better yet, rename the file before proceeding with the decryption.

If you set the Delete Original File option to off and then encrypt files with the same name but different extensions, files may be overwritten and lost.

You should also be careful if you encrypt files with the same file name but different extensions. For example, if you encrypt the files PCTOOLS.EXE and PCTOOLS.HLP with the Delete Original File option set to off, the first file will be called PCTOOLS.SEC after encryption, and so will the second one. PC Secure sends you the message

File already exits. Replace?

as it processes the second file. If you answer yes to replace the file, the first file is overwritten by the second. If you had encrypted the first file with the Delete Original File option set to on, you could be left without a copy of the file. To avoid this, either rename or move one of the files.

FURTHER PROTECTING DELETED FILES

For a list of the other optional parameters you can use with PC Secure, see Appendix A.

If you start PC Secure by typing

PCSECURE /G

you invoke the Department of Defense standards for file deletion. This parameter is used in conjunction with the Delete Original File selection in PC Secure.

If you use the /G parameter, and Delete Original File is set to on, the original copy of your file is removed according to DOD standards. The deleted file is overwritten seven times and then verified to be sure it can never be recovered. Use this option if you need complete security. This process obviously takes longer than the normal procedures in PC Secure.

Clear File is new for Version 6.0.

If you are using PC Shell to manipulate files, and you decide you want to make a file completely irrecoverable for security reasons, you can use Clear File from the File pull-down menu. First select the file you want to clean in the main PC Shell display, then choose Clear File to open the Clear File dialog box. You can specify the hex character you want to overwrite the file with, or you can use the default F6 character. You can also select the number of times the file should be overwritten, or specify that the U. S. Government standards should be used instead. Remember, none of the file recovery utilities can recover a file after this sort of treatment.

SUMMARY

In this chapter, you learned how to evaluate and improve the performance of your computer. I described the results of file fragmentation and how to use PC Tools to remove these effects. I also examined disk problems and how to deal with them.

System Info makes a report detailing the hardware installed in your PC. Memory Map details memory usage in your computer. Compress reorganizes the files and directories on your disk for optimum performance. It also prepares a report of the fragmentation percentage of a directory or a whole disk, and performs a surface analysis to detect and isolate bad clusters.

PC-Cache increases disk performance by keeping a copy of the most frequently used information in your computer's memory. PC-Cache can also display its own performance statistics and the optional parameters currently in use. PC Secure encrypts or decrypts files, in addition to compressing them to conserve disk space and hiding them to increase security.

7

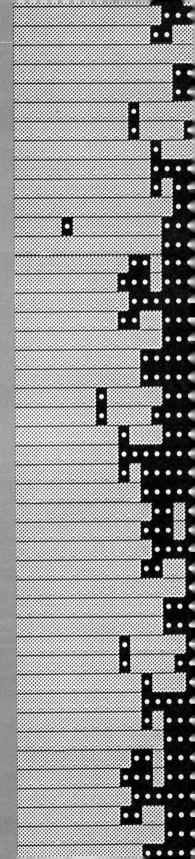

Using the
Desktop Manager
With Words
and Ideas

This first chapter on PC Tools Desktop describes how you can use Desktop with words and ideas. It describes Notepads, Outlines, the Clipboard, and the Macro Editor. Once you can use Notepads to enter and edit text, using Outlines, the Clipboard, and the Macro Editor will be easy, since they all share the same overall interface.

USING NOTEPADS

PC Tools Desktop contains a word processor called Notepads. If you run Desktop in memory-resident mode, you can use Notepads from inside your foreground application. With Notepads, you can cut and paste text to the Clipboard, search for and replace text strings, print your work with headers and footers, and even check your spelling. You can work with ASCII text files or with WordStar-compatible files. In fact, you can have as many as 15 different Notepads open simultaneously.

You can work with files of up to 64K in Notepads. This is equivalent to a file of approximately 64,000 characters, or about 10,000 words (20 single-spaced or 40 double-spaced pages). If you try to load a file of larger than 64K into a Notepad, you will see the message

WARNING: FILE TOO BIG FOR NOTEPAD, IT WILL BE CUT OFF TO FIT.

and you have the option to cancel or to continue. If you choose to continue, the first 64K of the file are loaded but the remainder of the file is discarded. You can edit the file, but first you must delete some of the original text to make room before you can add any new text. The file cannot be larger than 64K at any time.

ENTERING TEXT

There are three ways to enter text into Notepads:

- By typing in new text
- By loading or inserting a file you previously prepared elsewhere
- By cutting and pasting using the Clipboard facilities

This section deals with typing in new text and loading a file. Using the Clipboard to cut and paste with Notepads is described later in this chapter.

When you first select Notepads from the Desktop main menu, you must choose one of three selections:

- You can load an existing file.

- You can make a new document.

- You can cancel this operation.

Select New to make a new document, and the Notepads window will open in the middle of the screen. To make the window as large as possible, choose the Window pull-down menu and select Zoom. This command expands the Notepads window, as shown in Figure 7.1.

The Notepads screen is similar to the screens in other PC Tools programs. The main menu selections are shown along the top line and scroll bars are located on the right side and at the bottom of the screen. The current computer time appears on the upper-right part of the screen, and several function-key shortcuts appear on the message line. In the upper-left corner of the screen, the line and column counters keep track of where you are in your document, and in the upper-right corner of the screen is the name of the file you are working on (in this case, the temporary file WORK.TXT—the name PC

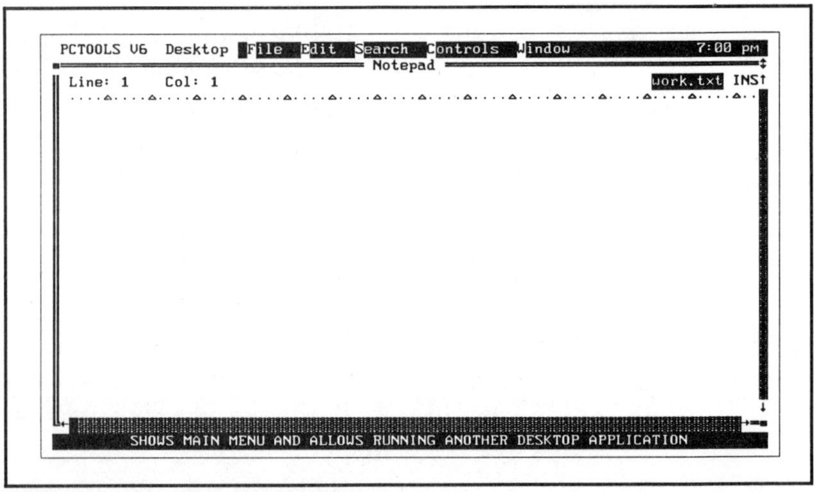

> Remember to use the Alt key before the letter of the pull-down menu you want to use. This tells Desktop that you want to select a menu rather than type the letter into the Notepad. You can also use F10 to get to the menu in PC Tools 6.0.

Figure 7.1: The Notepads opening screen

Tools gives a new file). INS indicates that Notepads is in insert rather than overtype mode. A ruler line is also shown.

To start entering your text, just start typing. You can use the Backspace or Delete keys to edit out any mistakes, and the Enter key to end a paragraph. Use ↑ and ↓ to move around in the screen, and the PgUp and PgDn keys to move the window up and down. Table 7.1 lists the keystrokes you can use in a Notepad. You can do all the major word processing operations you need with key sequences from this list.

Table 7.1: Control Keys Available in a Notepad

KEY	FUNCTION
Delete	Deletes character above the cursor.
Backspace	Deletes character to left of cursor.
Enter	Ends a paragraph.
spacebar	Inserts a space at the cursor.
Tab	Inserts a tab at the cursor.
Alt-*number*	Inserts a character from the extended ASCII character set. Press and hold down the Alt key, then enter the decimal code for the ASCII character you want.
Left Arrow (←)	Moves cursor left one character.
Right Arrow (→)	Moves cursor right one character.
Ctrl-←	Moves cursor left one word.
Ctrl-→	Moves cursor right one word.
Home	Moves to the beginning of the line.
End	Moves to the end of the line.
Up Arrow (↑)	Moves cursor up one line.
Down Arrow (↓)	Moves cursor down one line.
PgUp	Moves text up one window.
PgDn	Moves text down one window.
Ctrl-PgUp	Scrolls display up one line without moving cursor.

Table 7.1: Control Keys Available in a Notepad (Continued)

KEY	FUNCTION
Ctrl-PgDn	Scrolls display down one line without moving cursor.
Home Home	Moves to the beginning of the window.
End End	Moves to the end of the window.
Ctrl-Home	Moves to the beginning of the file.
Ctrl-End	Moves to the end of the file.

You can also enter text into Notepads by loading a file from disk. Start Desktop from inside the \PCTOOLS directory, select Notepads, and you will see the File Load dialog box. From here on, the README.TXT file will be used to illustrate features of Notepads. Either enter the file name README.TXT directly, or choose it from the list of files, and then choose Load to load the file.

As the file is brought into the Notepad, you must choose which format to use for it. Choose WordStar if the file was made with WordStar or is compatible with WordStar. Otherwise, choose ASCII. For README.TXT, choose ASCII; the contents of the file will be displayed on the screen, as shown in Figure 7.2. Once again, you can select Zoom from the Window menu to enlarge the window.

You can also load a file with the Load selection in the File menu. Be careful when you use this selection. If a file is open and you select Load, the file is closed but its contents are not saved. You will lose any changes you made since you last saved the file. This does not affect any files you might have open in other Notepads.

The tab ruler is shown across the top of the text in the Notepads window. Each small triangle indicates a tab. You can turn this ruler on and off with Tab Ruler Display from the Controls pull-down menu. If there is a check mark by this item, the tab ruler display is on. You can toggle it off by selecting it again.

You can add to or replace the original tabs. Choose Tab Ruler Edit from the Controls menu to edit the tabs. You can use ← and → to move the cursor to where you want a new tab, or to an existing tab

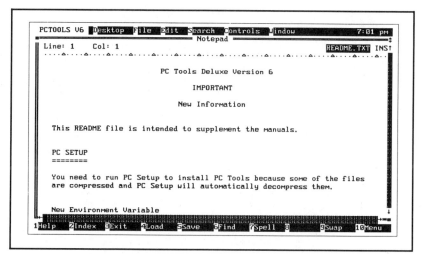

Figure 7.2: The README.TXT file loaded into Notepads

that you want to erase. Press the Insert key to insert a new tab stop or the Delete key to remove an old tab stop.

 Tab Ruler Edit is called Edit Tab Ruler in PC Tools 5.5.

To enter a set of evenly spaced tabs very quickly, choose Tab Ruler Edit and type in the number of spaces you want between tab stops. The numbers you type do not appear anywhere on the screen, but the tab marks will move to the new interval you have chosen.

Another important setting in the Controls menu is the Overtype Mode setting. Usually, you will want to be in Insert mode. In Insert mode, the abbreviation INS appears next to the file name in the upper-right corner of the Notepads screen. As you type in your text, it is inserted at the cursor and all the other text is moved to the right. In Overtype mode, your new text overwrites and replaces the old text. Select Overtype Mode from the Controls menu to set Overtype on, and select it again to toggle Overtype off. A check mark beside the menu entry indicates that it is on.

In Notepads, you can look at the control characters (usually spaces, the tab, and the carriage return characters) embedded in your file to see the exact positioning of each character. Turn this feature on with Control Character Display from the Controls menu. When this setting is turned on, spaces are indicated by dots between words, tabs by small arrows, and carriage return characters by small return symbols. A check mark beside the menu entry indicates that this setting is on.

You do not have to press Enter at the end of a line of text. Notepads automatically moves to the beginning of the next available line when you reach the right margin. This feature is known as word wrap. In Notepads, you toggle it on or off from the Controls menu. Again, a check mark by the menu entry indicates that the setting is on.

You also control the auto-indent feature from the Controls menu. Turn auto-indent on to line up all your text vertically with the first character of the previous line. This is useful for lists or tables. A check mark by the menu entry indicates that the setting is on.

SAVING YOUR WORK

When you click on the close box or press Escape to leave a Notepad, your work is always saved automatically. Additionally, you can save a file any time by using F5 or Save in the File pull-down menu. There are several Save options. You can save the file as a PC Tools format file or as an ASCII file.

- PC Tools Format is the default setting, and saves your text as well as all the page layout commands, headers and footers, tab stop settings, screen colors, and window sizes in the file along with your text.

- ASCII Format saves your work as an ASCII file without any formatting information of any kind (just the text with a carriage return character at the end of each line). If you loaded the file originally as an ASCII file, it will be saved in this format. Use the ASCII format if you want to load this file into a different word processor, since the ASCII format gives you the most flexibility.

You can also back up your file while you save it. The backup file has the same file name as your work file, but has the extension .BAK. In other words, you must make your file names unique without using the extension. For example, don't call separate proposal files SECTION.1, SECTION.2, and so on. At the end of the day, you will only have one backup file called SECTION.BAK—a backup file for the last section you worked on. All the other backup files will have been overwritten. Instead, name your files SECTION1.TXT, SECTION2.TXT, and so on. The backup files will then be called SECTION1.BAK, SEC-TION2.BAK, and so forth.

You can use the Autosave option from the File menu to save your file automatically at a specified time interval. This can be a life-saver if your area is prone to brownouts or power outages. When you select Autosave, a dialog box allows you to set the Autosave feature on or off and to receive the time interval in minutes if you turn it on. Autosave is a global feature of Desktop; it is used in Outlines, the Appointment Scheduler, and the Macro Editor as well as in Notepads. When you turn Autosave on in any of these applications, you turn it on for all of them. Likewise, if you turn it off, you turn it off for all applications.

Finally, you can leave a Notepad without saving your work by selecting Exit Without Saving from the File pull-down menu.

Moving around inside your document is easy. Use ↑ and ↓ to scroll one line at a time, and use PgUp or PgDn to move one window at a time. With a mouse, you can use the scroll bars to scroll through your document. In a Notepad, you can also go directly to a line of text, search for and replace text, and check your spelling.

EDITING TEXT

The Goto selection helps you find a particular line in your file. This is particularly useful if you work with large files. The line and column numbers are shown in the upper-left corner of the Notepad screen, and you can use Goto to move directly to another line in your file. When you choose Goto from the Edit pull-down menu, a dialog box asks you which line number you want to go to. Enter the line number and select OK to continue. The requested line number is moved to the Notepad window and the cursor is positioned at the first character on that line.

At some point, you may want to merge a second file into the body of a file you are working on in a Notepad. You can do this with Insert File from the Edit pull-down menu. Use Goto to position the cursor at the desired location in the file and then choose Insert File. Type the name of the file into the dialog box and select Load. The file is merged with the current file at the cursor location as long as the combined size of the two files is less than 64K. If the combined file size will be more than 64K, you will see the message

**WARNING: FILE TOO BIG FOR NOTEPAD, IT WILL BE CUT
OFF TO FIT.**

You will probably want to choose Cancel in order to abort the merge.

If you started a new document and things are not going as planned, you can start again with the Delete Text selection from the Edit pull-down menu. This command empties the Notepad but keeps the file on the disk open to the Notepad (the file is open but empty). This is a potentially dangerous operation, so Notepads asks you to confirm that you want to erase the document. From the dialog box, select OK to erase the document or Cancel to return to the Notepad and leave its contents intact.

SEARCHING   As you work with a document in a Notepad, you can use the options in the Search menu to search for and replace specified strings of text in your file.

Choose the Find selection from the Search pull-down menu to display the screen shown in Figure 7.3. You can enter a search string of up to 44 characters (including spaces), and you can narrow down the

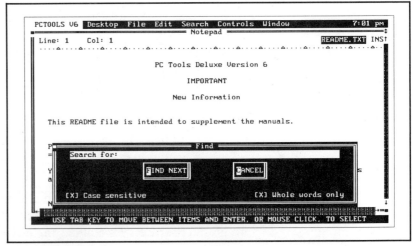

Figure 7.3: The Find selection from the Search pull-down menu

search by using the following options:

- Case Sensitive makes the search sensitive to the case of the text. In this mode, Find considers ''Mother'' and ''mother'' to be two different words. With this option off, case is ignored.

- Whole Words Only finds whole words only. For example, if you search for the word ''moth'' with this selection on, Notepads will find ''moth'' but not ''mother.''

The search starts at the cursor location and continues until a match is found. When Notepads finds a match, it positions the cursor at the beginning of the string and asks if you want to look for the next occurrence of the search string. When there are no more matches, Desktop beeps to indicate that it has finished.

If the text file README.TXT is still loaded in your Notepad, take a moment to experiment here. Enter the text

PCTOOLS

(in uppercase) as the search string, turn on the Case Sensitive and Whole Words Only options, and start the search. Each time the search string is found, the search stops and the match is displayed. Choose Find Next to search for the next occurrence of the string.

When working with text, you often want to do more than find all occurrences of a particular string. You might want to replace one or more of the occurrences of the text. Choose Replace from the Search pull-down menu or press F6 to display the screen shown in Figure 7.4.

The Find and Replace window opens on the Search For box. Enter the string you want to search for. Then Tab down to the Replace With box and enter the new text you want to use in its place. Again, the search string can be up to 44 characters, case sensitive or not, and you can search for whole or partial words. You also have the following options:

- Replace one time finds and replaces only the next occurrence of the search string.

- Replace all automatically finds and replaces all occurrences of the search string from the current cursor location to the end of your file.

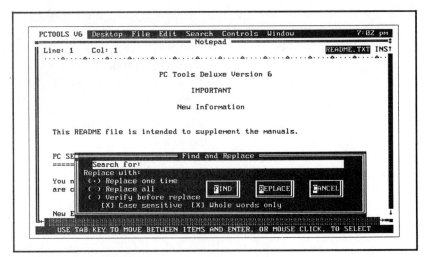

Figure 7.4: The Find and Replace options

- Verify before replace finds the search string and stops for you to verify that you want to replace this particular occurrence of the search string. Press Enter to replace the found text. The search continues to the next occurrence of the search string.

You can use Find and Replace in many ways. For instance, if you change your section numbers in a document, you can easily find all references to Section V and replace them with Section VI. If you have consistently misspelled someone's name (your spelling checker probably won't find this error), you can search the document for the old spelling and replace it with the new.

CHECKING YOUR SPELLING   You can check the spelling in your document over three different ranges in Notepads:

- You can check a single word.
- You can check all the words displayed in a Notepad window.
- You can check all the words in your file.

As Notepads checks your spelling, the message

SPELL CHECKING IN PROGRESS. PLEASE WAIT

is displayed just above the ruler line. Once the spelling checker finds a word that it doesn't understand, the word is highlighted on the screen. You now have the following options:

- Ignore overlooks this word now and for all future occurrences in this document. Use this option to ignore file name extensions, proper names, and other items that the dictionary does not know but are spelled correctly.

- Correct displays the Word Correction dialog box, shows the misspelled word, and waits for you to enter the correction. You can also choose one of the replacement words supplied in the Suggestions box to replace the misspelled word.

- Add accepts the unknown word and then adds it to the Notepads dictionary for future use. Be careful with your spelling, though, because once you add a word to the dictionary you cannot remove it again.

- Quit leaves the word as it is, closes the dialog box, and exits the spelling checker.

Run the spelling checker on the example file README.TXT and notice the kinds of words it flags as misspelled. They are special names (the dictionary does not recognize the name Microsoft), file name extensions, program names, and command-line parameters.

USING THE CLIPBOARD TO CUT AND PASTE Use the Clipboard to cut, copy, or paste text. You cannot add to the text already on the Clipboard. The Clipboard is a temporary area of storage that holds the cut or copied text until you are ready to paste it into a document. If there is already text on the Clipboard and you cut or copy more text, the original text is destroyed. You can paste text from the Clipboard into this or another Notepad, edit it with the Clipboard commands, or transfer it into your foreground application if you are using Desktop in memory-resident mode.

Before you can cut or copy text, you must mark the block you want to work with. Move the cursor to the start of the block and choose Mark Block from the Edit pull-down menu. Use the arrow keys to define the marked block. With the mouse, position the mouse pointer

For a complete discussion of the Clipboard, see "Cut and Paste with the Clipboard" later in this chapter.

The Clipboard in Version 6.0 can hold 80 to 90 lines of text, equivalent to about 4K. The Clipboard in Version 5.5 can hold 40 to 50 lines of text, equivalent to about 2K.

at the start of the text to be marked and hold down the left mouse button as you move the mouse to mark the text. The selected text is highlighted on the screen. You can move out of the current window, marking text as you go.

After the block is marked, you can cut it to the Clipboard, removing it from your document and replacing any text that was already on the Clipboard. Select Cut to Clipboard from the Edit pull-down menu or use the shortcut keys Shift and Delete.

Copy to Clipboard works much like Cut to Clipboard, but the text is not removed from your original file. You must mark the text before choosing Copy to Clipboard from the Edit menu.

When you paste from the Clipboard, the text held on the Clipboard is copied into your Notepad file at the cursor location. Choose Paste from Clipboard from the Edit menu or use the shortcut keys Shift and Insert.

If you decide not to work with the marked text, use Unmark Text from the Edit menu to unmark it. To unmark text, you can also press the Escape key or use the arrow keys to move the cursor. If you are using a mouse, just click the left mouse button anywhere in the window to unmark the text.

FORMATTING PRINTER OUTPUT

Before you print your document, you must make several important decisions about page layout and headers and footers. From the Controls pull-down menu, choose Page Layout to see the display shown in Figure 7.5—the default settings for printing a Notepad document.

If you want to change these settings, select the option to change and enter your new value.

If you have a laser printer, set the top and bottom margins to 2, and the page length to 60 for proper printing.

- Left Margin is the number of spaces in from the left edge of the paper where text begins.

- Top Margin is the number of lines down from the top of the page where text begins.

- Right Margin is the number of spaces in from the left edge where text ends.

- Bottom Margin is the number of lines up from the bottom of the page where text stops.

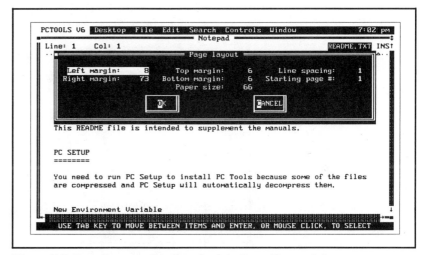

Figure 7.5: Page Layout selections for printing a Notepad document

- Line Spacing lets you select single or double spacing.

- Starting Page # is the number to use for the first page of text. All other pages will be numbered sequentially from this number.

- Paper Size is the number of lines per page for the paper you are printing onto. Normal 8½″ by 11″ paper takes 66 lines, and legal sized paper (8½″ by 14″) takes 84 lines. These lines-per-page numbers assume that your printer is set up for 6 lines per inch.

You can also add headers or footers to your printed document. A header is text that is printed at the top of every page of your document, and a footer is text that is printed at the foot of every page. In Notepads, the headers and footers are restricted to a single line of up to 50 characters, which are centered when they are printed. Choose Header/Footer from the Controls pull-down menu. Figure 7.6 shows the screen used to enter the text for headers and footers.

The # (or pound) symbol at the start of the footer text represents automatic page numbering, starting by default at page 1. Page numbering is controlled by information entered in the Page Layout screen. Delete this character if you do not want your pages numbered at the bottom. Insert the # symbol at the start of the header line if you want page numbers at the top of each page.

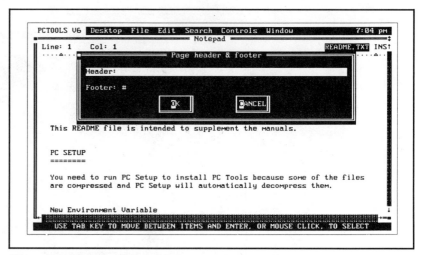

Figure 7.6: The Page header & footer screen

If you will probably have several versions of a document, it is useful to add the file name and today's time and date as headers or footers. This way, you know which version of the document someone is referring to if they call to discuss it.

You can save all your selections from the Controls and Window menus by using Save Setup. This way, the next time you open Notepads, you will have the settings you want.

Now you are ready to print your Notepad document. Choose Print from the File pull-down menu. You can print to one of several devices:

- LPT 1, 2, or 3 selects which parallel printer to send your file to. Printer 1 is the default printer.

- COM 1, 2, 3, or 4 selects which serial printer port to send your file to.

- Disk File formats your file for printing as specified in Page Layout, but writes it to a file so that you can print it later. The file has the same name as the original Notepad file, but has the .PRT extension.

- Number of Copies determines the number of copies of your document to print.

Make your selections from these menus and start printing READ-ME.TXT. The file is divided into neat pages, and is formatted according to your selections. The whole file will take six or seven pages.

You can use advanced formatting commands in your Notepad documents by inserting printer control macros into your text. PC Tools Deluxe contains macro files suitable for the Epson FX-80, the IBM Proprinter, the HP LaserJet, and Panasonic printers. See the section "Making Keyboard Macros" later in this chapter for more details on how to use these macros.

STRUCTURING YOUR IDEAS WITH OUTLINES

You can use Outlines as a tool to help organize your thoughts into a structured list. Each line in the outline represents one point or idea, and its position relative to the other items in the list determines its position in the outline's hierarchy. You can use Outlines whenever you want to make a structured list of items: a meeting agenda, a book proposal, the outline for a class you are going to teach, the outline of a magazine article you plan to write. You can use Outlines to prepare an outline that you can then flesh out in a Notepad. An Outline file can be up to 60K long, which is equivalent to approximately 650 lines of text.

The advantage of using an outliner rather than a word processor is that each level of indentation in the outline represents a different level in the document's hierarchy. Main headings are at one level of indentation, secondary headings are indented one tab, tertiary headings are indented two tabs, and so on. Using Outlines, you can promote or demote headings to different levels as your outline evolves, or you can collapse a portion of the outline to show just the major headings, so you can work on another part of the outline without distractions. If you run Desktop memory-resident, you can open up to 15 different outlines at a time without leaving your main foreground application.

CREATING AN OUTLINE

The main screen in the outliner is similar to the Notepads main screen. Indeed, the File, Edit, Search, and Controls menus are identical and will not be discussed in detail here. To learn more about these menus, refer back to the Notepads section. Just remember that editing text, searching and replacing specific text strings, cutting, and copying and pasting to and from the Clipboard are all available in Outlines.

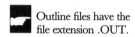 Outline files have the file extension .OUT.

To make a new outline, select Outlines from the Desktop main pull-down menu, and create a new file called TEST.OUT. To have your screen look like the examples in this chapter, choose the Window pull-down menu and select the Zoom option. This makes the outline window occupy all of the computer screen and is convenient when you are dealing with larger outlines.

To start working on your outline, just start typing. The first line you type becomes the first entry in the outline. Use the Tab key to indent lower levels in the list. For example, if you were preparing a meeting agenda, you might enter the main headings first and add the lower level detail later. The first level headings for a meeting agenda are shown in Figure 7.7.

Just type in the text for the item and press Enter at the end of the item. The cursor stays the same number of tab spaces from the margin, so you can enter the next heading at the same level. Once you have established a level, you can edit the text of the entry in the normal way.

Since tabs are used to indicate hierarchy in the structure of the outline, you cannot use them in the body of the text.

Under each of these main headings, you can add detail as you wish. To add an item at a lower level, use the Tab key to indent the right amount. To insert a new entry, position the cursor at the end of the previous line and press Enter. The cursor moves to the beginning of the next line at the same level as the entry above it. After you add second and third level headings, the meeting agenda might now look like Figure 7.8.

You can add detail to the outline until you have the whole meeting sketched out with presentation topics, the names of the presenters, time limits for each presentation, and so on.

EXPANDING AND COLLAPSING THE OUTLINE

The pull-down menus in Outlines are similar to those Notepads. However, there is one new menu item, Headlines, which contains options that allow you to manipulate your outline entries, as shown in Figure 7.9.

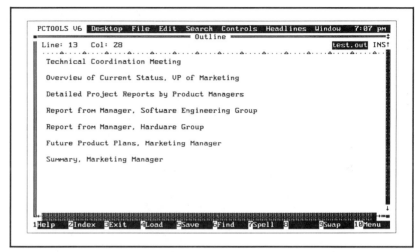

Figure 7.7: First level headings in an outline

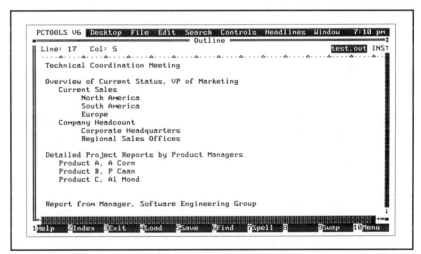

Figure 7.8: Meeting agenda with second and third level headings

As you work on your outline, you may want to hide all but the highest level of entry so that you can work without distractions. You can use Collapse Current or Main Headline Only from the Headings pull-down menu to accomplish this.

- Collapse Current collapses the lines below the current line and displays a small symbol in the left margin next to the main heading to show that there is hidden text below this item.

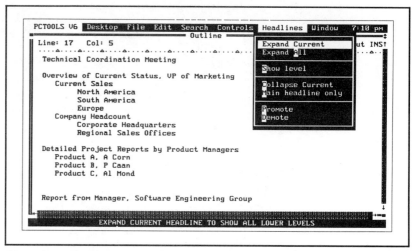

Figure 7.9: The Headlines pull-down menu

- Main headline only hides everything except for the first level headings.

When you want to see the detail of the outline, you need to look at all entries at all levels. Much of this text may be hidden if the outline is collapsed. You can expand just a portion of the outline with Expand Current from the Headlines menu, or you can expand the entire outline with Expand All.

- Expand Current expands all the subentries below the current line, assuming that there are entries to expand.

- Expand All expands the whole outline to show all the previously hidden text.

Since you will inevitably change your mind as you develop your outline, you need to be able to change the level of an entry. This is the feature that really separates an outliner from an ordinary word processor. You can quickly change a heading level with Promote and Demote from the Headlines pull-down menu.

- Promote moves a heading up to the next highest level. All the subheadings in the group below this level are also moved.

- Demote is the reverse of Promote, moving headings to a lower level.

When your outline is complete, you will want to print it. Often you will want to print a simplified version first, to circulate to your colleagues for comment, for example, or to give your supervisor the gist of your proposal. You can use the Show Level option from the Headlines pull-down menu to prepare a simplified outline.

Show Level hides all entries below a certain level. For example, if you position the cursor on a first level heading, all first and second level headings will remain visible, but any level three and lower headings will be hidden. The entries are not deleted from the outline, they are just hidden. To bring back the detail in the current group, use Expand Current. To bring back all headings in the entire document, use the Expand All option.

PRINTING YOUR OUTLINE

Now you are ready to print your outline. As in the Notepads, the Controls pull-down menu contains the entries Page layout and Header/Footer. Use Page layout to establish the margin settings and page length you need. Use Header/Footer to enter header or footer text. Enter the date, time, and file name as headers or footers to help keep track of the evolution of your document.

Use the Print option from the File pull-down menu to print the outline. Your options here are the same as in Notepads: You can print to one of the serial or parallel printers, or to a disk file for printing later if you prefer. You can also specify the number of copies to print.

CUT AND PASTE WITH THE CLIPBOARD

I briefly described parts of the Clipboard during the discussion of Notepads earlier in this chapter. This section is a more in-depth look at all features of the Clipboard.

The Clipboard only handles text, it cannot handle graphics.

If you reboot your computer, the contents of your Clipboard will be lost.

You can leave pieces of text up to 4K (between 80 and 90 lines of text) with Version 6.0, or up to 2K (between 40 and 50 lines of text) with Version 5.5 on the Clipboard, in a kind of temporary storage until you are ready to use them. You can also use the Clipboard as a channel between applications: You can cut and paste from between Outlines, Notepads, the Macro Editor, and your main foreground application if you have Desktop configured as a memory-resident program.

Once you have the correct text on the Clipboard, you can use the Clipboard's editing capabilities to make changes before pasting the text into another application.

OPENING THE CLIPBOARD

Select the Clipboard from the main Desktop menu, choose the Window pull-down menu, and select the Zoom option to make the Clipboard window as large as possible. The opening Clipboard screen is shown in Figure 7.10. The first portion of the meeting agenda prepared with the outliner is shown on the Clipboard.

CUT AND PASTE IN MEMORY-RESIDENT MODE

To take full advantage of features of the Clipboard, you must run Desktop in memory-resident mode. Now you can cut and paste text to the Clipboard using the normal full-screen display, or you can cut

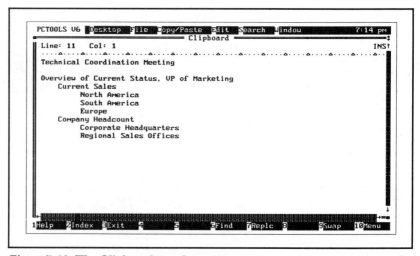

Figure 7.10: The Clipboard opening screen

and paste without opening the Clipboard by using a special hotkey sequence.

To cut and paste using the normal full-screen display and the Clipboard menus, position the cursor in approximately the right place in your application and follow this sequence:

- Use the arrow keys to locate the beginning of the text you want to copy to the Clipboard and press Enter.

- Use the arrow keys to highlight the block of text you want to place on the Clipboard. Press Enter to copy the text to the Clipboard. The Clipboard display reappears, showing the copied text. Since the Clipboard is open, you can edit the text if you want.

If you are using a mouse, just follow these even easier steps:

- Hotkey into Desktop by pressing Ctrl-spacebar.

- Select Clipboard from the main Desktop menu.

- Choose the Copy to Clipboard selection from the Cut/Paste pull-down menu. The Clipboard screen disappears and the previous screen, your original application, reappears.

- Move the mouse to the beginning of the text you want to copy to the Clipboard. Press the left mouse button and hold it down.

- Drag the mouse until the text you want to copy is highlighted; then release the mouse button. The highlighted text is copied to the Clipboard, and you can edit it if you want.

If you have Desktop loaded in memory-resident mode, you can use a different hotkey sequence to copy text to the Clipboard without actually opening Desktop or the Clipboard. This is the fastest way to copy text from your main foreground application onto the Clipboard. Follow these steps:

- Press Ctrl-Delete from inside your main application to start the process. A large cursor appears on the screen. You use this cursor to select the text to copy to the Clipboard.

- Use the arrow keys to position the cursor at the beginning of the text you want to copy, and press the Enter key.

- Now use the arrow keys to mark the block of text you want to copy to the Clipboard.

- Press Enter to copy the text to the Clipboard.

If you want to view or edit the text, hotkey into Desktop and select the Clipboard in the usual way from the main Desktop menu.
If you are using a mouse, this operation is even easier:

- Press Ctrl-Delete from inside your main application to start the process. A large cursor appears on the screen. Use this cursor to select the text you want to copy to the Clipboard.

- Move the mouse to the beginning of the text you want to copy to the Clipboard. Press and hold down the left mouse button.

- Drag the mouse until the text you want to copy is highlighted; then release the mouse button. The highlighted text is copied to the Clipboard.

Hotkey into Desktop and open the Clipboard in the usual way if you want to edit the text.

PASTING   Moving text from the Clipboard to your foreground application is known as pasting. Position the cursor where you want the pasted text to appear and then follow these steps:

- Hotkey into Desktop by pressing Ctrl-spacebar.

- Select Clipboard from the main Desktop menu.

- Choose the Paste from Clipboard selection from the Cut/Paste pull-down menu. As Desktop prepares to close, the message

    RESTORING SYSTEM PLEASE WAIT.

    is displayed on the screen for a moment.

- Your original foreground application reappears, and the Clipboard text is inserted at the cursor position.

There is a special hotkey that you can use to paste the Clipboard text directly into your foreground application without opening the

Clipboard. Position the cursor in your foreground application where you want the pasted text to appear and press Ctrl-Insert. The Clipboard text will be pasted into your application at the cursor location.

If you do not have a foreground application running when you paste the Clipboard text, the text is copied to the DOS command line, which can have unpredictable and sometimes undesirable results. For example, suppose you make a directory listing of your root directory with the DOS DIR command, and copy it to the Clipboard. When you paste that text back to the DOS command line, it is as though you were typing in all those lines by hand. If your root directory contains a file called AUTOEXEC.BAT, which of course it should, pasting the text AUTOEXEC.BAT to the DOS command line actually causes DOS to execute all the commands in the batch file. In other words, proceed with caution when pasting text directly with the Ctrl-Insert key.

SETTING THE PLAYBACK DELAY (VERSION 6.0)

You cannot set the playback delay in PC Tools 5.5.

If you paste text from the Clipboard into another application program, and your computer beeps or not all of the characters are transferred, it may be because the characters are being sent too fast for it to handle. The Set Playback Delay command in the Copy/Paste pulldown menu allows you to insert a short delay between each character to slow down the transfer slightly. The delay time is measured in time periods of $1/18$ of a second, and the number you enter specifies the additional $1/18$ second time periods to insert between characters. A zero value sends a character every $1/18$ of a second.

- Delay (clock ticks) is the number of $1/18$ second time periods you want to insert between each character.

- On turns on the playback delay.

- Off turns off the playback delay.

EDITING TEXT

Once you have copied text to the Clipboard, you can use the editing commands to change the text. These editing commands are the same commands you used in Outlines and Notepads, so I will only discuss them briefly here. Refer to the discussion on Notepads for more detail.

Besides the normal text-editing keystrokes such as Delete, Insert, and Backspace, the Edit pull-down menu provides several important options:

- Erase block deletes a marked block of text from the Clipboard.

- Mark block marks a block of text for deletion.

- Unmark block removes the block marks.

- Delete all text erases all the text from the Clipboard in preparation to receive new text, leaving your original work file open.

- Insert file inserts the contents of a text file at the cursor location. If inserting the file will cause the Clipboard to overflow, a message indicates that the file will be truncated. Only the portion of the file that fits will be loaded into the Clipboard.

- Goto allows you to go directly to a line in the Clipboard that you specify by line number.

You can find or find and replace a specific text string with selections from the Search pull-down menu:

- Find searches for text that you specify. The search string can be case sensitive or not, and can be restricted to whole words rather than word fragments.

- Replace. Enter the text to find in the Search For box, and the replacement text in the Replace With box. You also have the following options:

    Replace one time finds and replaces only the next occurrence of the search string.

    Replace all finds and replaces all occurrences of the search string in your document, from the current cursor location to the end of your file. Replacement is automatic.

    Verify before replace finds the search string and stops for you to verify that you want to replace this particular occurrence of the search string. Press Enter to replace the found text. The search goes on to the next occurrence of the search string.

Finally, if you want to print the text on the Clipboard, choose the Print option from the File pull-down menu. You have the same options that you had in Notepads and Outlines: You can print to one of the serial or parallel printers, or to a disk file for printing later if you prefer. You can also specify the number of copies to print.

MAKING KEYBOARD MACROS

A macro contains a series of commands that are activated by a single keystroke.

A keyboard macro is a convenient way of loading more than the usual single character onto a key on your keyboard. In other words, you can program the keys on your keyboard to perform specific functions. You can use macros as shorthand for long sets of keystrokes that you use frequently, or to simplify complex and repetitive jobs.

DOS itself provides keys on the keyboard with certain editing capabilities. In fact, you can use the DOS PROMPT command to produce the same effect you can achieve with the Macro Editor. However, you can only use the DOS commands at the DOS prompt. In contrast, if you run Desktop in memory-resident mode, the Macro Editor makes your macros available everywhere, even inside other applications. You should avoid key conflicts between macros and foreground applications. Otherwise, you may get unexpected results when you invoke your macro. This section first describes the DOS editing keys and then shows you how to redefine your keyboard with PROMPT. Finally, it explains why the Desktop Macro Editor is more powerful and flexible than these other methods.

If you run the Desktop memory-resident and you have other applications in your path, select your macros carefully. Any applications using the same key combinations can be interfered with.

When you execute a command at the DOS prompt, the command is copied into a special buffer. You can edit the command and reissue it if you want to. This is handy, for example, if you have to deal with many files with similar names. Pressing F1 recalls the last command you entered, one character at a time. Pressing F3 recalls all at once the rest of the line you typed. Using these two keys in combination with the Insert and Delete keys, you can edit simple commands quite effectively. Several of the function keys have a special function, as listed in Table 7.2. F1 and F3 are by far the most useful of these special editing keys.

Table 7.2: Function Keys with Special Functions in DOS

KEY NAME	FUNCTION
F1	Retypes one character at a time from the previous command.
F2	Retypes all the characters from the previous command up to the one identical to your next keystroke.
F3	Retypes all the remaining characters from the last command.
F4	Retypes all the characters in the last command starting with the first character you typed.
F5	Allows direct editing of all the characters in the last command.
F6	Puts a special end-of-file code at the end of the currently open file, sometimes referred to as Ctrl-Z.
Insert	Inserts characters at the cursor.
Delete	Deletes the character to the left of the cursor.
Esc	Abandons the last command without executing it.
Backspace	Deletes the last character on the command line.

If you include the ANSI.SYS driver in your CONFIG.SYS file, you can use the PROMPT command to program virtually any of the keys on your keyboard to type DOS commands. Assigning new meanings to keys requires a special command called an *escape sequence*. In this case, the sequence starts with $e[and continues with the ASCII value of the key you wish to use (if the key is a regular letter or number key), followed by the character p. The p terminates the key-assignment sequence. If you want to assign a command to one of the function keys, you must use a zero followed by a special code to indicate the key. These special function-key redefinition codes are listed in Table 7.3.

Table 7.3: Function-Key Redefinition Codes

FUNCTION KEY	REDEFINITION CODE	FUNCTION KEY	REDEFINITION CODE
F1	59	Shift-F1	84
F2	60	Shift-F2	85
F3	61	Shift-F3	86
F4	62	Shift-F4	87
F5	63	Shift-F5	88
F6	64	Shift-F6	89
F7	65	Shift-F7	90
F8	66	Shift-F8	91
F9	67	Shift-F9	92
F10	68	Shift-F10	93
Ctrl-F1	94	Alt-F1	104
Ctrl-F2	95	Alt-F2	105
Ctrl-F3	96	Alt-F3	106
Ctrl-F4	97	Alt-F4	107
Ctrl-F5	98	Alt-F5	108
Ctrl-F6	99	Alt-F6	109
Ctrl-F7	100	Alt-F7	110
Ctrl-F8	101	Alt-F8	111
Ctrl-F9	102	Alt-F9	112
Ctrl-F10	103	Alt-F10	113

Suppose you want to assign the FORMAT command to a function key, since you use the command frequently. To make the F5 function key automatically type the command

    FORMAT A:

you should add the line

    PROMPT $e[0;63;"FORMAT A:";13p

to your AUTOEXEC.BAT file, or modify your current PROMPT command to include this new statement.

A semicolon separates each statement in the PROMPT command.

The $e[alerts DOS that an ANSI escape sequence is starting, and the 0 indicates that the key to be redefined is on the extended keyboard. Code 63 stands for F5 and "FORMAT A:" is the command to be assigned to the F5 key. Code 13 represents a carriage return character, and p is the terminating character for the whole sequence. Remember that after changing your AUTOEXEC.BAT file you must reboot your computer to load the new commands.

Now, when you want to format a disk, just press F5 to invoke the DOS FORMAT command and then press Enter.

CREATING DESKTOP MACRO FILES

If you do not run Desktop in memory-resident mode, your Desktop macros are only available inside Desktop.

The macros you can assign using DOS and the PROMPT command are limited, since they are only available from the DOS prompt. If you run Desktop in memory-resident mode, you can use your Desktop macros from inside Desktop *and* inside your foreground application.

Among other things, you can design Desktop macros to print text files with custom features, load often-used applications programs, or override other keyboard functions.

You can use macros to start up PC Tools programs such as PC Backup.

Desktop macros are usually compatible with macros made with ProKey version 4 or higher, with only a few exceptions:

- Some key combinations are not supported by the Desktop Macro Editor (see Table 7.4).

- The Desktop Macro Editor does not include support for guarding macros or unique macro names.

- Since the Desktop Macro Editor recognizes the standard IBM BIOS keyboard scan codes, it does not support redefinition of the entire keyboard.

Table 7.4 lists the key combinations *not* supported by the Desktop Macro Editor.

Macros, which are like small programs, have a particular structure that you must observe. Creating a macro involves

- Writing the macro

- Activating the macro

- Testing the macro

Before starting to write a macro, decide what you want it to do. Then be careful to follow the rules for macro creation, which I will explain in a moment.

Table 7.4: Key Combinations Not Supported by the Desktop Macro Editor

CTRL	ALT	SHIFT
Ctrl-c		
Ctrl-q		
Ctrl-s		
Ctrl-1		
Ctrl-2		
Ctrl-3		
Ctrl-4		
Ctrl-5		
Ctrl-6		
Ctrl-7		
Ctrl-8		
Ctrl-9		
Ctrl-0		
Ctrl- –	Alt- –	
Ctrl- =	Alt- =	
Ctrl-[	Alt-[	
Ctrl-]	Alt-]	
Ctrl-;	Alt-;	
Ctrl-'	Alt-'	
Ctrl-\	Alt-\	
Ctrl-,	Alt-,	
Ctrl-.	Alt-.	
Ctrl-/	Alt-/	

Table 7.4: Key Combinations Not Supported by the Desktop Macro Editor (Continued)

CTRL	ALT	SHIFT
Ctrl-Esc	Alt-Esc	Shift-Esc
Ctrl-Tab	Alt-Tab	
	Alt-Backspace	Shift-Backspace
	Alt-Enter	Shift-Enter
	Alt-Prt	Shift-Prt
	Alt-Home	Shift-Home
	Alt-PgUp	Shift-PgUp
	Alt-End	Shift-End
	Alt-PgDn	Shift-PgDn
Ctrl-↑	Alt-↑	Shift-↑
	Alt-←	Shift-←
	Alt-→	Shift-→
Ctrl-↓	Alt-↓	Shift-↓
Ctrl-Insert	Alt-Insert	Shift-Insert
Ctrl-Delete	Alt-Delete	Shift-Delete
Ctrl-keypad 0	Alt-keypad 0	Shift-keypad 0
Ctrl-keypad 1	Alt-keypad 1	Shift-keypad 1
Ctrl-keypad 2	Alt-keypad 2	Shift-keypad 2
Ctrl-keypad 3	Alt-keypad 3	Shift-keypad 3
Ctrl-keypad 4	Alt-keypad 4	Shift-keypad 4
Ctrl-keypad 5	Alt-keypad 5	Shift-keypad 5
Ctrl-keypad 6	Alt-keypad 6	Shift-keypad 6
Ctrl-keypad 7	Alt-keypad 7	Shift-keypad 7
Ctrl-keypad 8	Alt-keypad 8	Shift-keypad 8
Ctrl-keypad 9	Alt-keypad 9	Shift-keypad 9
Ctrl-keypad .	Alt-keypad .	Shift-keypad .
Ctrl-keypad +	Alt-keypad +	Shift-keypad +
Ctrl-keypad −	Alt-keypad −	Shift-keypad −

Once you have written your macro, you have to activate it and specify where it should be active. You can make your macro active only inside Desktop, only outside Desktop, or everywhere. You can also turn your macro off if you don't want to use it anymore. All active macros are saved in a special area of memory and are ready to go to work when you press the correct keystrokes.

When you have written and activated your macro, it is time to test it to make sure it does what you think it should. How you test it really depends on what the macro does. Some can be tested from the DOS prompt; others require you to be inside another application program. If the macro misbehaves, press Escape to stop it from running any further.

Finally, remember to give your macro a descriptive name to help you to remember what it is for. You can also write comments inside your macros as additional reminders.

In PC Tools, the general form of a macro is as follows:

<begdef> *keystrokes script* <enddef>

Macros begin with the statement

<begdef>

which stands for begin definition, and end with the statement

<enddef>

You can use the Alt key with the plus sign key (+) to load the statement <begdef> automatically into your macro. Alt with the minus key (–) loads <enddef> automatically.

which stands for end definition. The body of your macro, the part that actually does the work, must be contained between these two statements. You place the keystrokes for invoking the macro after the <begdef> statement; they must also be contained within angle brackets. The *script* you want the macro to execute—that is, the actual commands you want it to use—come next. These commands are not enclosed in angle brackets unless they are special command words.

You can add comments to a macro. In fact, it is an excellent idea always to add explanatory comments to your macros to help you and others remember what the macro is for and how it works. Place your comments before the <begdef> statement. The Macro Editor ignores anything that is not between the <begdef> and <enddef> statements.

As an example, look at the following macro:

```
<begdef>
  <ctrlf> FORMAT A: <enter>
<enddef>
```

The <begdef> statement starts the macro, and <ctrlf> indicates that you must press Ctrl-f from the keyboard to invoke the macro. FORMAT A: is the command you want to execute, and <enter> is equivalent to pressing the Enter key on the keyboard. The <enddef> statement ends the macro. Now when you want to format a floppy disk in drive A, you just type Ctrl-f.

Macros can be a lot more complex than this simple example. You can use a macro to call your favorite Desktop application. You can also add time delays to your macros, accept fixed-length or variable-length input to a macro, and even add the date and time to a macro. Table 7.5 shows reserved words that have special meanings in the Macro Editor. Some of them have shortcut keystrokes, which are also shown in Table 7.5. For example, when you start a macro, the Macro Editor automatically displays <begdef> if you type Alt-+. Similarly, type Alt-- to end a macro with <enddef>.

Table 7.5: Reserved Words with Special Meanings for the Macro Editor

RESERVED WORD	SHORTCUT	MEANING
begdef	Alt-+	Statement that always begins a macro definition.
cmd		Indicates that the following entries must be treated as commands instead of key entries.
d*n*		Time delay, where d indicates that the number that follows (represented by *n*) is to be treated as the time delay. Always terminate a delay with <enter>.

Table 7.5: Reserved Words with Special Meanings for the Macro Editor (Continued)

RESERVED WORD	SHORTCUT	MEANING
date		Includes the date in a macro.
desk		Shorthand name for Desktop, for use in macros only.
enddef	Alt-–	Statement that always ends a macro definition.
enter		Terminates a delay sequence, or is used to generate carriage return/line feed.
ffld	Ctrl-]	Indicates a fixed field label.
time		Includes the time in a macro.
vfld	Ctrl-–	Indicates a variable field label.

To create a new macro from scratch to automate a complex task, you should write down all the keystrokes you use when you perform the job manually. When you use the Macro Editor, you can construct the macro using your notes. Alternatively, you can use the Learn Mode selection from the Macro Editor, which automatically records all your keystrokes.

EDITING MACRO FILES

Select the Macro Editor from the Desktop menu and then select SAMPLE.PRO from the Macro Files screen to see the opening screen, as shown in Figure 7.11.

The Macro Editor works much like the other text-handling programs in Desktop—the Notepads, Outlines, and Clipboard. However, the Macro Editor has several unique commands, which are covered here. The other commands are discussed only briefly. See the section on Notepads for more details.

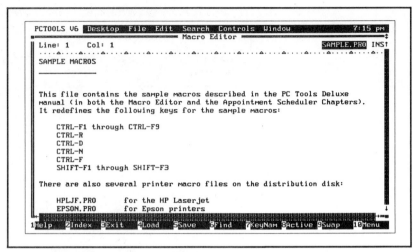

Figure 7.11: Macro Editor opening screen

In the Macro Editor, besides the normal text-editing commands, the Edit pull-down menu contains the following specialized selections:

- Cut to clipboard moves a portion of text from the Macro Editor to the Clipboard.

- Copy to clipboard copies a portion of text to the Clipboard.

- Paste from clipboard moves a portion of text from the Clipboard to the Macro Editor.

- Mark block marks a block of text for deletion.

- Unmark block removes the block marks.

- Delete all text erases all the text from the Macro Editor in preparation to receive new text.

- Insert file inserts the contents of a text file at the cursor. If inserting the file will cause the Macro Editor to overflow, a message indicates that the file will be truncated. Only the part of the file that fits will be loaded into the Macro Editor.

- Goto allows you to go directly to a line in the Macro Editor that you specify by line number.

You can find or find and replace a specific text string with selections from the Search pull-down menu in the Macro Editor.

- Find searches for text that you specify. The search string can be case sensitive or not, and can be restricted to whole words rather than word fragments.

- Replace. Enter the text to find in the Search For box, and the replacement text in the Replace With box. You also have the following options:

     Replace one time finds and replaces only the next occurrence of the search string.

     Replace all finds and replaces all occurrences of the search string in your file, from the current cursor location to the end of your file. Replacement is automatic.

     Verify before replace finds the search string and stops for you to verify that you want to replace this particular occurrence of the search string. Press Enter to replace the found text. The search goes on to the next occurrence of the search string.

The File pull-down menu contains the following selections:

- Load loads another file into the Macro Editor, replacing the current contents.

- Save saves the contents of the Macro Editor to a file. The file can be in ASCII or in PC Tools format, and you can opt to make a backup file at the same time.

- Autosave automatically saves your work periodically at an interval that you set.

The last selection in the File pull-down menu, Macro activation, requires more explanation. With this selection, you can choose which macros are active in your system, and also where in your system they are active. Choose Macro activation from the File pull-down menu to display the screen shown in Figure 7.12.

In Macro Activation, you have the following options:

- Not active. None of the macros in the current file are active.

- Active when in PCTOOLS Desktop. The macros in the

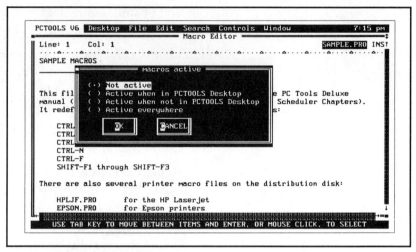

Figure 7.12: Macro Activation screen

current file are active only when you are in Desktop. This is particularly useful for printer macros, which cannot be used outside Desktop.

- Active when not in PCTOOLS Desktop. The macros in the current file can be used anywhere in DOS or in your other applications programs, but not inside Desktop.

- Active everywhere. The macros in the current file can be used anywhere on your system, including inside Desktop.

All your active macro files are kept in a special buffer area, ready for you to invoke with the appropriate key sequence. When you edit a macro file, the system updates existing active macros, so you do not have to reactivate them.

The Controls pull-down menu, shown in Figure 7.13, contains four special commands for use with macros.

- Erase all macros erases your macros from the special buffer area where they are kept once you have activated them. This command does not erase macro files from your disk, nor does it affect the contents of the Macro Editor.

- Playback delay introduces short wait periods between each character in the macro. If you use multiple keystrokes in your

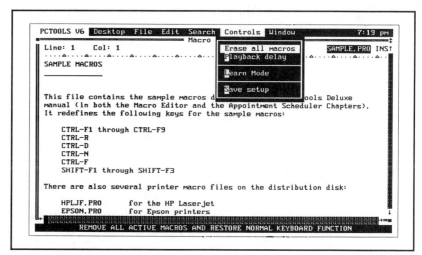

Figure 7.13: The Controls pull-down menu in the Macro Editor

macros, the system may feed them into your application faster than it can process them. You specify this playback delay period in terms of the PC system clock, which ticks at a rate of 18 ticks per second. Enter the number of $1/18$ second time periods you want to wait between keystrokes. A value of zero sends a character every $1/18$ second. The default setting for Playback Delay is off, so you must turn it on if you want to use it.

- Learn Mode records all your keystrokes in a special buffer. This is an easy way to create strong, accurate macros. When you restart the Macro Editor, your macro is saved into a special file called LEARN.PRO. Remember that Learn Mode stays on until you turn if off again.

- Save setup saves the current settings of the Macro Editor Window and Controls settings.

You must run Desktop in memory-resident mode for the Learn Mode command to work.

To use Learn Mode, turn it on inside the Macro Editor and hotkey out of Desktop. When you are ready to record your keystrokes, press Alt-+. This starts the macro and indicates that all subsequent keystrokes will be copied into the Macro Editor. A large square cursor appears. Next, press the keystroke combination you want to use to invoke this macro, and then create the script for the macro by typing

When you make a
macro using Learn
Mode, all the keystrokes
and reserved words are
entered in one long line,
with no formatting.

the keys in your application as you would normally. When you have
finished, close the macro by pressing Alt-− . Your keystrokes are kept
in a file called LEARN.PRO, which is created the next time you
hotkey into the Macro Editor. You can use the Macro Editor to view
or modify the keystrokes in this file.

This is a fast and easy way to make a macro. Be especially careful,
however, if you make a mistake when you are typing the keys that
form the macro script. If you mistype a key and press Backspace to
remove the offending letter, the Backspace keystroke is also copied
into the macro script. If you mistyped the name PCBACKUP as
PCBBACKUP, your macro might look like this:

<begdef><ctrla>CD\PCTOOLS<enter>PCBB<bks>
ACKUP/BW<enddef>

Use the editing features of the Macro Editor to remove the extra B as
well as the unwanted <bks>. This is a good reason for reading your
macros carefully before turning them on for activation.

USING YOUR MACROS

You can use a macro to start Desktop by using the reserved word
<desk>. You must run Desktop in memory-resident mode for this
to work. The following macro opens Desktop at the main startup
menu when you press Shift-Tab:

<begdef>
  <shifttab><desk>
<enddef>

You can be more specific than this: If you use one of the Desktop calculators very often, you can open it directly with the following macro:

<begdef>
  <shifttab><desk>CS
<enddef>

This macro opens the Scientific calculator immediately. In fact, you
can use any of the letters that Desktop uses for menu selections inside
your macros. The example above opens Desktop with the reserved

word <desk> and then uses C to access Calculators from the main Desktop menu and S to select the Scientific calculator. You can set up a macro to open a Notepad and load a specific text file or to start the Database up in a certain way.

Table 7.6 lists some of the codes you can use to open your Desktop applications via macros.

You can invoke other applications programs from macros. The following macro changes to the Lotus directory called \123 and loads Lotus 1-2-3 when you press Shift-Tab:

```
<begdef>
   <shifttab>CD\123<enter>123<enter>
<enddef>
```

Table 7.6: Two-Letter Codes for Opening Specific Desktop Functions via a Macro

CODE	FUNCTION
<desk>	Opens Desktop
<desk>N	Opens a Notepad
<desk>O	Opens an Outline
<desk>D	Opens the Database
<desk>A	Opens the Appointment Scheduler
<desk>T	Opens Telecommunications
<desk>M	Opens the Macro Editor
<desk>b	Opens the Clipboard
<desk>CA	Opens the Algebraic calculator
<desk>CF	Opens the Financial calculator
<desk>CP	Opens the Programmer's calculator
<desk>CS	Opens the Scientific calculator
<desk>U	Opens the Utilities
<desk>P	Opens PC Shell

The next macro changes to the \PCTOOLS directory and loads PCBACKUP in monochrome mode:

```
<begdef>
  <shifttab>CD\PCTOOLS<enter>PCBACKUP/BW<enter>
<enddef>
```

The /BW parameter makes PCBACKUP start up in monochrome.

By introducing a delay into your macro, you can make an event happen at a specific time. For example, you can dial a remote database when rates are lowest. The delay can be from $1/10$ of a second to 256 hours. Delays have the following form in a macro:

```
<begdef>
  <cmd> dn <enter>
<enddef>
```

<cmd> indicates that what follows should be interpreted by the Macro Editor as commands rather than keystrokes. The d indicates that a delay follows, and n defines the length of the delay in the format *hh:mm:ss.tt* (*hours:minutes:seconds.tenths*). For example, 15:0:0 is a 15-hour delay, 15:0 is a 15-minute delay, and 15 is a 15-second delay. All delays in your macros must be followed by the reserved word <enter>.

If you want to use the date and time in a macro, the Macro Editor provides two more reserved words that you can use for this purpose:

```
<begdef>
  <ctrld><date>, <time>
<enddef>
```

Now, if you press Ctrl-d, you will see the date and time displayed as follows:

04-10-91, 5:00

Note that the spacing between the reserved words <date> and <time> in the macro determines the final spacing of the date display on the screen.

You can make macros that wait for you to enter information from the keyboard, and this information can be fixed or variable in length. For example, you can write a macro that makes a directory listing of a disk after asking you for the drive letter. The drive letter always has a fixed length of one character—A, B, or C—so you can use what the Macro Editor calls a fixed field label <ffld>. Pressing Ctrl-] in the Macro Editor generates <ffld>. The final macro looks like this:

```
<begdef>
   <ctrld>DIR <ffld>#<ffld>:<enter>
<enddef>
```

<begdef> starts the macro, and you press Ctrl-d to invoke it. DIR is the DOS directory listing command, and it is followed by a space that separates the command from the drive letter you enter when the macro is running. The first <ffld> indicates the start of the fixed-length label; you can press Ctrl-] from the Macro Editor to display it. The # character indicates the length of the label. You can use any character you like; you don't have to use #. Just remember that # means that you enter one character, ## means that you enter two characters, and so on. The second <ffld> terminates the fixed-length label. The macro provides the colon character after you enter the drive letter to complete the entry.

To run this macro, escape from Desktop back to the DOS prompt and press Ctrl-d. The macro generates DIR, leaves a space, and waits for you to enter the drive letter. After you enter a drive letter, the macro adds the colon and DOS generates a listing for the appropriate drive.

If the input to your macro is not always the same length or the same number of characters, you must use a variable field label <vfld> instead of a fixed field label <ffld>. In this case, the Macro Editor always requires two placeholder characters between the <vfld> statements in the macro (for example, <vfld>##<vfld>) to hold the variable-length input. Using this technique, you can enter file names and other variable-length input into your macros.

The final type of macro described in this section is the printer macro. These are special macros for use in text files in Notepads,

You can only use printer macros inside Desktop Notepads, Outlines, and Database forms.

Outlines, and Database forms. You cannot use them outside Desktop.

Printer macros are commands that you insert into the body of your text. When you print the file, they create special formatting effects such as italics or superscripts. These commands never appear in the printed text. Instead, they are sent to the printer to make it do something specific. Since printers from different manufacturers observe different conventions, you need a special file for each different type of printer. PC Tools is shipped with files tailored to common printers like the Epson FX-80, the HP LaserJet, the IBM Proprinter, and Panasonic printers.

An example printer macro that turns on near letter quality mode looks like this:

```
<begdef>
  <ctrlf1>¦NLQON¦<esc>x1
<enddef>
```

The <begdef> statement starts the macro, which you invoke by typing Ctrl-F1. The ¦NLQON¦ statement appears in the body of your document to show where in the text the macro takes effect. The <esc>x1 statement turns on near letter quality mode for Epson printers, and is the sequence that is actually sent to your printer by the macro. The <enddef> ends the macro. To turn near letter quality mode off again, write another macro such as:

```
<begdef>
  <ctrlf2>¦NLQOFF¦<esc>x0
<enddef>
```

■ Use Macro Activation from the File pull-down menu in the Macro Editor and turn your printer macro on by choosing the option Active when in PC Tools.

This time, the label ¦NLQOFF¦ appears in your text file where you turn the near letter quality mode off.

You can use macros like these to turn boldface on or off, turn subscript or superscript on or off, or change anything that is controllable by a character sequence. See the appendices of your printer manual for specific details on which features you can control on your printer.

SUMMARY

In this chapter, I described the different ways you can use the Desktop applications with words. Use Notepads as your text editor, Outlines to organize and develop your ideas, the Clipboard as a convenient channel for passing text between programs, and the Macro Editor to automate commonly used key sequences.

8

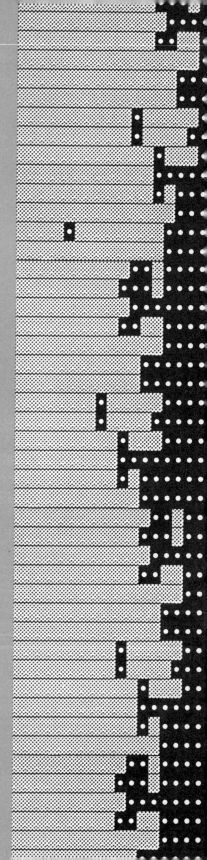

Figuring with the Four Calculators

8

How often do you use your pocket calculator for figures in a report that you are writing with a word processor, even though you could perform the calculations with your computer? With PC Tools, those days are gone.

FOUR CALCULATORS

PC Tools Desktop includes four different calculators: the Algebraic calculator, the Financial calculator, the Programmer's calculator, and the Scientific calculator. If you are running Desktop memory resident, you can use any of the calculators from within your foreground application.

THE ALGEBRAIC CALCULATOR

Before you use the numbers on your ten-key pad, check the status of the Num Lock key.

Using the Algebraic calculator is like using an adding machine with a paper tape printout. To enter numbers, use the keys on the ten-key pad or the keys along the top of your keyboard. Use the usual keys to represent addition (+), subtraction (−), multiplication (*), and division (/). If you use a mouse, you can click on the screen keys instead. As you make calculations, the numbers, the operations, and the results are recorded on the tape. The current operation is shown in the single display line at the bottom of the tape window. Figure 8.1 shows the main screen for the Algebraic calculator.

To make a calculation, type the numbers and keys that correspond to the operation you want to perform. For example, to add 50 to 75, type

50 + 75 =

You press Enter or type the equal sign to see the result, 125.

To subtract 39 from 1989, type

1989 − 39 =

to see the result of 1950.

Similarly, to multiply 12 by 20, type

12 * 20 =

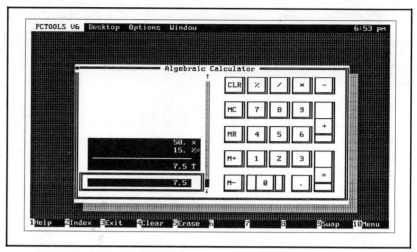

Figure 8.1: The main screen for the Algebraic calculator

The result is 240.

Finally, to divide 160 by 8, type

160 / 8 =

The answer is 20.

You probably think of percentages in terms of whole numbers rather than decimal fractions—6 percent rather than 0.06, for instance. You can use whole numbers in the calculator if you follow them with the % symbol. To work out a 15 percent tip on a restaurant bill of $50, multiply 50 by 15 percent by typing

50 * 15 % =

The result is 7.5 or a tip of $7.50. You can even add or subtract a percentage of a number. To work out the sales tax on a $200 item, type

200 + 6.5 % =

The answer is 213, or a total of $213.

The tape is 1000 lines long. If you fill it, the entries at the top are removed to make room for the new ones.

The calculator tape can hold up to 1000 lines, the last 12 of which you can see in the calculator window. You can scroll through the tape to check your earlier entries with the arrow keys, or with the scroll bar

Remember to turn Num Lock off or hold down the Shift key when you use the arrow keys.

Numbers are displayed with a comma between each group of three digits and a period as the decimal point. Toggle the comma on and off by typing a comma from the keyboard.

Set the number of decimal places by typing D followed by the desired number of decimal places.

If you set the number of decimals in the display to zero and you calculate with fractions, the display may not look right. The answers will always be correct unless they, too, contain fractions.

if you use a mouse. You can correct mistakes by editing the number and rerunning the calculation.

Use the arrow keys to move the number to be corrected into the calculator display and enter the correct number. When you have corrected the error, press the End key to rerun the calculation. The new values appear on the tape and in the display. Calculated results themselves are not editable. You have to edit the input data.

Table 8.1 summarizes the functions of the Algebraic calculator.

The Algebraic calculator has one memory register, which you can use to collect the totals from a series of calculations when you only care about the combined total. If you use the memory register, an "M" in the lower-left corner of the tape reminds you that the memory register is nonzero. There are four memory functions:

- Add a number to the total in memory
- Subtract a number from the total

Table 8.1: Algebraic Calculator Functions

FUNCTION	KEYBOARD	MOUSE
Add	+	+
Subtract	–	–
Multiply	*	*
Divide	/	/
Total	Enter or =	=
Clear	C	CLR
Calculate percentage	%	%
Add to the memory register	M and +	M +
Subtract from the memory register	M and –	M –
Erase the memory register	M and C	MC
Recall the memory register	M and R	MR
Toggle the separator character	,	,
Set number of decimals (0 through 9)	D followed by the number	D followed by the number

- Clear the memory register

- Recall a number from memory

The Options pull-down menu contains two entries to help you use the calculator: Clear Display and Erase Tape. These are duplicated in the message line with the function keys F4 for Clear Display and F5 for Erase Tape. Figure 8.2 shows the Options menu.

If you want to move calculations into a document you are working on, you can use Copy to Clipboard from the Options menu to copy the last 100 lines of the tape into a file called CALC.TMP. You can even open a Clipboard window on top of the calculator if you want to edit the data.

To print the results of your calculations with Version 6.0 of PC Tools, choose Print Tape from the Options pull-down menu. You can send the output directly to your printer or to a disk file so that you can work on it later. The disk file is called CALC.PRT and is saved in the current directory.

Wide Display toggles the wide and narrow displays; your current choice is indicated by a checkmark to the left of the selection. The wide display includes the mouse keys, while the narrow display is the width of the tape.

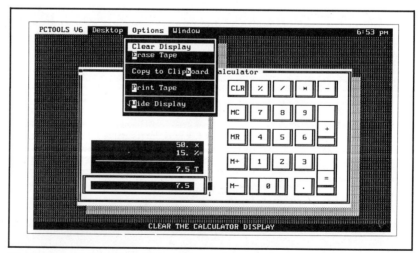

Figure 8.2: Options pull-down menu in the Algebraic calculator

THE FINANCIAL CALCULATOR

This section is only a brief introduction to the Financial calculator.

The Financial calculator is based on Hewlett-Packard's HP-12C calculator. You can use it to perform simple or compound interest calculations, to solve five-key problems and mortgage calculations, discounted cash flow analysis, depreciation and appreciation problems, and statistical calculations. As with most advanced HP calculators (including the Scientific calculator modeled after the HP-11C, and the Programmer's (hex) calculator modeled after the HP-16C, which are both described later in this chapter), the Financial calculator uses reverse polish notation to enter numbers and operations.

If you are familiar with the HP-12C calculator, the Financial calculator will be easy to use. If you have not used the HP-12C, don't worry; reverse polish notation is quite straightforward. When making a one-number operation like finding the square root of a number, you enter the number followed by the square root operator. For example, to find the square root of 81, type

    81
    Enter
    F8 √

and you will see the result, 9, in the calculator's display. In a two-number calculation, enter the numbers for the calculation, followed by the operator. For example, to add 50 to 75, type

    50
    Enter
    75
    +

You will see 125 in the calculator's display.

Your calculations can obviously get much more complex than this, especially when you consider that most of the keys on the calculator keyboard can have several functions. The keyboard layout is shown in Figure 8.3.

The main function of each key on the calculator is indicated in white (reverse video if you have a monochrome monitor) at the top of the key. If the key has secondary functions, these are shown above the key (in red on color monitors) or on the key itself below the main function (in blue if you have a color monitor). To use these secondary functions, first use

To access the secondary function on a key, click on either the F or G prefix key or press F7 or F8 before selecting the function key.

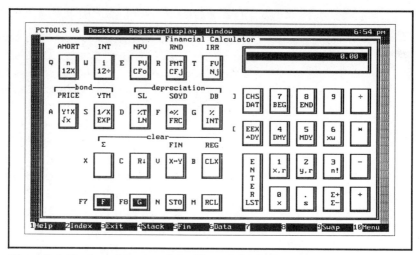

Figure 8.3: Keyboard layout of the Financial calculator

the F prefix key if the function you want is above the key or use the G prefix key if the secondary function is located on the lower part of the key. You can also use the F7 or F8 function key in place of the F or G prefix key. Finally, if you are using your keyboard rather than a mouse, a shortcut character you can type from the computer keyboard to access the function is shown to the left of some of the keys on the calculator.

For example, the key at the top left of the calculator is the n key used in five-key problems to represent the number of identical time periods in an analysis. To use it, click on the key with the mouse or press Q from your computer keyboard. A secondary function of this key is AMORT, used in calculating amortization schedules. To access AMORT with a mouse, first click on the F prefix key and then click on n. To do the same thing from the keyboard, press F7 followed by Q. The other secondary function for this key is the annualizer, 12X. To access this with a mouse, first click on the G prefix key and then click on n. From the keyboard, press F8 followed by Q.

Table 8.2 lists the financial, mathematical, and statistical functions available on the Financial calculator.

Several of the keys on the calculator are devoted to keystroke and internal register management. These keys are listed in Table 8.3.

Table 8.2: Financial Calculator's Financial and Mathematical Functions

KEY	FUNCTION
Financial Functions	
n	Number of identical sequential time periods.
i	Interest rate accruing over each n period.
PV	Present value.
PMT	Payment, or the once per period cash flow.
FV	Future value.
AMORT	Computes amortization schedule over a given number of periods.
NPV	Computes net present value.
PRICE	Computes a bond's PRICE for a desired YTM.
YTM	Computes a bond's yield to maturity given the PRICE.
SL	Computes straight line depreciation.
SOYD	Computes sum-of-the-year's-digits depreciation.
DB	Computes declining balance depreciation.
DAT	Computes the new date by adding a number of days to an old date.
ΔDY	Computes the number of days between two dates.
DMY	Sets calendar date entry mode to Day.MonthYear format and displays ''d.my'' in the calculator's display.
MDY	Resets calendar date entry mode to Month.DayYear format. Nothing is shown in the display.
BEG	Payment is due at the beginning of the payment period.
END	Payment is due at the end of the payment period.
IRR	Computes internal rate of return.
12X	Multiply by 12 to calculate an annualized total.
12 ÷	Divide by 12 to calculate a monthly total.

Table 8.2: Financial Calculator's Financial and Mathematical Functions (Continued)

KEY	FUNCTION
Mathematical Functions	
CFo	Amount of cash flow in the first group.
CFj	Subsequent cash flow amounts.
Nj	Number of periods CFo or CFj amounts apply to.
INT	Computes partial interest over a short period.
Y↑X	Exponent. Raises Y to the X power.
$\sqrt{X}$	Computes the square root of the number in the display.
1/X	Computes the reciprocal, or multiplicative inverse, of the number in the display.
LN	Computes the natural logarithm, the logarithm to the base e.
FRC	Returns the fractional part of a number.
INT	Returns the integer portion of a number.
RND	Rounds the internal 12-digit mantissa of the value in the display to match the number of digits specified by the current fixed or scientific specification.
CHS	Changes the sign of the number in the display, or the sign of the exponent of 10 in the display.
%T	Computes the percentage of the total.
Δ%	Computes the percentage difference.
%	Computes percentage.
Statistical Functions	
Σ+	Accumulates a series of data points into the statistical storage registers for statistical analysis.
Σ–	Removes a data point from the statistical storage registers to correct an error in data entry.

Table 8.2: Financial Calculator's Financial and Mathematical Functions (Continued)

KEY	FUNCTION
Statistical Functions	
x,r	Computes a linear projection for x, based on the rate of change of y.
y,r	Computes a linear projection for y, based on the rate of change of x.
x	Computes the arithmetic mean from the data points in the statistical storage registers.
s	Computes standard deviation.
xw	Computes a weighted mean from data entered into the statistical storage registers.

Table 8.3: Financial Calculator's Key and Register Management Functions

KEY	FUNCTION
Key Manipulation	
F	When selected before a function key, performs the function above the key. The display shows the "f" character.
G	When selected before a function key, performs the function below the key. The display shows the "g" character.
ENT	Enters a copy of the number displayed in the X register into the Y register.
LST	Recalls the display before the last function was executed.
EEX	Indicates that the next numbers entered are to be used as the exponent of a number.

Table 8.3: Financial Calculator's Key and Register Management Functions (Continued)

KEY	FUNCTION
Register Management	
Σ	Clears all the statistical storage registers.
FIN	Clears the financial registers.
REG	Sets all the storage registers to zero. To clear an individual register, store zero into the register.
R↓	Rolls down the contents of the stack.
X↔Y	Swaps the contents of the X and Y registers.
CLX	Sets to zero the value of the displayed X register.
STO	Stores a number into the R.0 to R.9 and R0 to R9 data registers, or into the financial registers.
RCL	Recalls a stored number. Follow the RCL key with the register number to recall.

The Financial calculator uses several different sets of registers to store the results of different types of calculations.

- The five financial registers are used by the Financial calculator to solve five-key problems. These are common financial calculations used to solve problems relating to different kinds of mortgages, interest rates, and so on. You can use the data in any four of the registers to solve for the unknown fifth. The registers are

n	Number of identical sequential time periods.
i	Interest rate accruing over each of these n periods. i and n always apply to the same period of time.
PV	Present value.
PMT	Payment, or the consistent, once in the period cash flow.
FV	Future value.

To perform five-key calculations properly, observe the sign conventions carefully.

You can look at the contents of the financial registers by selecting Financial Registers from the Register Display pull-down menu or by choosing F5 from the main calculator display.

- Stack Registers store the intermediate results of your calculations, and are labeled T, Z, Y, X, and LSTX. The number in the calculator display is stored in the X register. If you enter another number or perform an operation, the numbers already on the stack are moved up or down one place.

  Use R↓ to roll the contents of the stack down one register at a time. X↔Y swaps the values contained in the X and Y registers.

  When you perform a calculation, the number that was in the X register before the calculation is moved into a special register called LAST X. You can recall this number into the X register by clicking on G (or pressing F8) followed by LST. This way, you don't have to reenter the number into the next calculation.

  You can look at the contents of all the stack registers by selecting the Stack Registers option in the Register Display pull-down menu, or by choosing F4 from the main calculator screen.

- Data Registers are 20 general-purpose registers called R0 to R9 and R.0 to R.9. Use STO and RCL to store or recall numbers from these registers. STO copies the number in the X register into the data register that you designate by number. RCL performs the reverse operation, copying a number from a data register into the X register. To clear all data storage registers, click on F (or press F7) followed by REG. This also clears the statistical storage registers.

  You can look at the contents of all the data registers with the Data Registers option in the Register Display pull-down menu, or by pressing F6 from the main calculator screen.

- Statistical Storage Registers. The results of statistical calculations are stored in another set of registers, R1 to R5. These special registers are handled automatically by the calculator. They cannot be inspected from the Register Display menu. You can clear these registers by clicking on F (or pressing F7) followed by Σ. This also clears all stack registers.

The calculator normally uses a fixed notation to display the results of your calculations. You can change the number of decimal places shown in the display by clicking on F (or pressing F7) followed by the desired new number of decimal places. You can select from 0 to 9 decimal places for the display, but internal calculations are still performed to the full 12 digits.

Alternatively, you can select scientific notation by clicking on F (or pressing F7) followed by a period. Now if you enter 45,678 in fixed format with six places of decimals and then select scientific notation, the number is displayed as

4.567800 E + 4

This number is equivalent to 4.5678 times 10 raised to the fourth power. (The E stands for exponent.) If you select two decimal places, the number looks like this:

4.57 E + 4

In the Financial calculator, if you calculate an extremely large number that will not fit into the display, the calculator automatically changes from fixed to scientific notation.

There are three other calculator settings that affect the way calculations are performed:

- You can calculate compound interest in two ways: straight line or continuous. Both give the same result at the end of the period, but different results during the period. Select STO followed by EEX to turn continuous compounding on. A "c" appears in the display to confirm your setting. Press STO and EEX again to return to straight line. Notice that the "c" disappears from the display.

- The calculator supports calculations based on payment at the beginning or at the end of the payment period. To indicate payment at the beginning of the period, click on G (or press F8) followed by the BEG key. The abbreviation ''beg'' appears in the display, and all loan and annuity calculations are performed assuming that payment is made at the beginning of the period. To indicate payment at the end of the period, click on G (or press F8) followed by the END key. In this case, the word ''end'' appears in the display.

- Normal entry of dates is in the format Month.DayYear. To enter dates in the Day.MonthYear format, click on G (or press F8) followed by the D.MY key. The characters ''d.my'' appear in the display as a reminder. To revert to the normal method of entry, click on G (or press F8) followed by the M.DY key. Now nothing is shown in the display.

Finally, the Financial calculator can display four error messages:

- ERROR 0. You have attempted an impossible operation, such as division by zero.

- ERROR 1. You have tried to enter too many values into the storage registers.

- ERROR 2. You have tried to enter an improper statistical operation, such as performing a linear regression before you have entered any data points.

- ERROR. You have pressed two unsuitable keys in sequence.

Press a key from the keyboard or click the mouse to clear any one of these errors.

THE PROGRAMMER'S (HEX) CALCULATOR (VERSION 6.0)

The Programmer's calculator is based on Hewlett-Packard's HP-16C calculator, but it is not programmable. You can use it to convert values into different numbering schemes, perform arithmetic in 1's or 2's complement or in unsigned mode, and look at the results of using the logical operators and the shift left and shift right operators.

The calculator works with words from 1 to 64 bits in size, but the default word size is 16 bits. This means you can enter up to 64 bits in

See Appendix B for a complete discussion of computer numbering schemes.

binary or up to 1,844,674,407,370,955,161 in decimal. The current word size setting is shown on the right side of the calculator display. To change the word size, enter a number between 1 and 64 and press the F7 function key followed by the WSZ key.

Use the mouse or ↑ and ↓ to select the numbering scheme you want to use. Choose HEX to calculate in hexadecimal, OCTAL to calculate in octal, BINARY to calculate in binary, or DECIMAL to calculate in decimal. When the calculation is complete, the result is shown in all four numbering systems.

To convert a number from one system to another, just select the starting numbering scheme and key in the number. The calculator automatically converts the number into the other numbering systems and displays the result.

For example, to convert FB in hexadecimal notation into all the other systems, select the HEX system for entry, and type

FB

The results—373 in octal, 251 in decimal and 11111011 in binary—are shown in the display. Figure 8.4 shows this calculation.

The CHAR display shows the ASCII character corresponding to the low order hex byte, which in this case is the √ character. If the

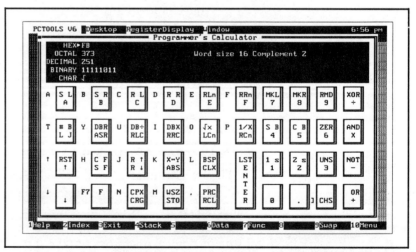

Figure 8.4: Sample operations using the Programmer's calculator (Version 6.0)

number is less than 32 in decimal, the normal abbreviation for the ASCII control character is displayed. If the decimal number is 32, then the word SPACE is shown in the CHAR display. If the decimal number is greater than 32, the normal ASCII character is displayed. See Appendix B for a list of all the ASCII control characters.

The main function of each key on the calculator is shown in bright white on the lower part of the key. Most of the keys have secondary functions, and these are shown in gray on the key above the main function. To use these secondary functions, first use the F prefix key just like you would use the shift key on your computer keyboard. A shortcut character you can type from the computer keyboard to access the function is shown to the left of some of the keys on the calculator. As an example, the key at the top left of the calculator keyboard is the A key. To use it click on the key with the mouse or press A from your computer keyboard. The secondary function of this key is S L (shift left), which moves all the bits in a word one place to the left and replaces the empty one on the right with a zero. To access S L with the mouse, first click on the F prefix key and then on S L. To do the same thing from the keyboard, press F7 followed by A. The letters to the left of the calculator keys indicate the keys on your computer keyboard that are equivalent to the keys on the calculator. For example, type K when you want to compute the absolute value of a number in the display, or type] when you want to change the sign of the number. If you use a mouse, just click on the keys you want to use in the correct sequence.

To perform calculations with the Programmer's calculator, you must use reverse polish notation once again. To perform the calculation

F + 3

type F and press Enter, then press 3 and press the + key. The solution—12 in hex, 22 in octal, 18 in decimal, and 10010 in binary—is shown in the display. The CHAR line in the display shows the ASCII control character equivalent, DC2.

Table 8.4 lists the arithmetic, logical, and register manipulation functions of the Programmer's calculator.

The Programmer's calculator works in three different modes: 1's complement mode, 2's complement mode, and unsigned mode.

Table 8.4: Functions Included in the Programmer's (Hex) Calculator

KEY NAME	FUNCTION
Math Functions	
√X	Computes the square root of the number in the X register.
1/X	Computes the reciprocal, or multiplicative inverse, of the number in the display.
CHS	Changes the sign of the number in the display.
ABS	Computes the absolute value of the number in the display.
RMD	Remainder from a division.
Key Manipulation	
F	When selected before a function key, performs the function above the key. The display shows f.
ENTER	Enter key.
LST	Recalls the number displayed before the last function was executed.
BSP	Backspaces one character.
S F	Sets a flag when followed by the flag number.
C F	Clears a flag when followed by the flag number.
CPX	Clears a prefix (f, C, G or P).
ZER	Allows the display of leading zeros.
Calculator Register Manipulation	
STO	Stores a value into the R0 to R9 and R.0 to R.9 data registers.
RCL	Recalls a stored number when followed with the register number to recall.

Table 8.4: Functions Included in the Programmer's (Hex) Calculator (Continued)

KEY NAME	FUNCTION
Calculator Register Manipulation	
X↔Y	Swaps the contents of the X and Y stack registers.
R↓	Rolls down the contents of the stack.
R↑	Rolls up the contents of the stack.
CLX	Sets the value of the displayed X register to zero.
CRG	Clears a register when followed by the register number.
Mode Selection	
↑	Select numbering scheme.
↓	Select numbering scheme.
PRC	Sets precision for floating point operations.
WSZ	Sets word size.
RST	Restores the calculator's start-up state.
1 s	Selects 1's complement mode.
2 s	Selects 2's complement mode.
UNS	Selects unsigned mode.
Logical Operators	
AND	Compares bits in two words and returns a 1 at that location if both bits are ones.
OR	Compares bits in two words and returns a 0 at that location if both bits are zeros.
NOT	Inverts the value of all the bits in the X register.
XOR	Compares bits in two words and returns a 1 at that position if the two bits are different.

Table 8.4: Functions Included in the Programmer's (Hex) Calculator (Continued)

KEY NAME	FUNCTION
Masking Operations	
MKL	Mask left.
MKR	Mask right.
Bit Operations	
B#	Counts the number of bits in the X register.
CB	Clear bit.
SB	Set bit.
LJ	Left justify.
SL	Shift left.
SR	Shift right.
RL	Rotate left.
RR	Rotate right.
RLC	Rotate left through carry.
RRC	Rotate right through carry.
RLn	Rotate left n bits.
RRn	Rotate right n bits.
LCn	Rotate left through carry n bits.
RCn	Rotate right through carry n bits.
ASR	Arithmetic shift right.
Double Functions	
DBX	Double multiply.
DB +	Double divide.
DBR	Double remainder.

These are three different ways of representing numbers. 1's complement was used in early computers but is not often used these days. 2's complement is much more common now. The current mode is shown to the right of the word size in the calculator display.

The Programmer's calculator has three system flags to control leading zeros, number carry-over, and number overflow, and it has an indicator for further input. You can set these flags by pressing the S F (set flag) key, followed by the number. To clear a flag, press the C F (clear flag) key followed by the number.

- Flag 3 manages the display of leading zeros. They are suppressed if this flag is not set. Z appears in the calculator display to indicate that this flag is set.

- Flag 4 is set if an arithmetic operation results in a remainder. C appears in the calculator display to indicate that this flag is set.

- Flag 5 is set whenever a calculation result cannot be expressed in the current word size. G appears in the calculator display to indicate that this flag is set.

- P appears in the display to indicate that an operation is incomplete, and requires more input. Operations like STO, RCL, and CF all generate a P if incomplete.

The Programmer's calculator uses two sets of registers to store the results of different kinds of calculations.

- Stack Registers store intermediate results from your calculations, and are labeled T, Z, Y, X, and LSTX. The number in the calculator display is stored in the X register. If you enter another calculation, the values on the stack are moved one place.

    You can use R↑ or R↓ to roll the contents of the stack up or down one register at a time. X ←→ Y swaps the values contained in the X and Y registers.

    You can look at the contents of all the Stack Registers with the Stack Registers option from the Register Display pulldown menu, or by pressing F4 from the calculator main screen.

- Data Registers are 20 general-purpose registers called R0 to R9 and R.0 to R.9. Use STO and RCL to store numbers in or recall numbers from these registers.

  You can view the contents of the Data Registers with the Data Registers option from the Register Display pull-down menu, or by typing F6 from the main calculator display.

If you enter a number containing a decimal, the Programmer's calculator switches into floating point mode automatically, and the default word size changes to 64 bits. Decimals are not shown in the hex, octal, or binary numbering schemes.

The Programmer's calculator can display several error messages:

- ERROR 1. You have attempted an improper mathematical operation, such as dividing a number by zero, or trying to calculate the square root of a negative number.

- ERROR 2. You have entered an illegal digit for this number base, such as 8 or 9 as an octal number, A, B, C, D, E, or F as a decimal number, or anything other than 0 or 1 as a binary number.

- ERROR 3. You have already entered the decimal point and you tried to enter another.

- ERROR 4. You attempted to set or clear a flag using the wrong index number.

- ERROR 5. You have entered an improper register number, such as a nonexistent register number.

- ERROR 6. You tried to recall the contents of a register originally stored using a larger word size.

In PC Tools 5.5, the Programmer's (hex) calculator is much less powerful than the HP 16C emulation in Version 6.0.

THE PROGRAMMER'S (HEX) CALCULATOR (VERSION 5.5)

See Appendix B for a complete discussion of computer numbering schemes.

The Programmer's calculator performs basic arithmetic functions as well as conversions between different numbering systems. It is a full 32-bit calculator, which means that you can enter up to 32 bits in the binary system or up to 4,294,967,295 in decimal.

Use the mouse or ↑ and ↓ to select the numbering system you want to use. Choose HEX to calculate in hexadecimal, OCTAL to calculate in octal, BINARY to calculate in binary, or DECIMAL to calculate in decimal. When the calculation is complete, the result is displayed in all four numbering systems.

To convert a number from one system to another, just select the starting numbering system, key in the number, and press Enter. The calculator automatically converts the number into the other numbering systems and displays the result. For example, to convert FF in hexadecimal notation into all the other systems, select the HEX system for entry, type

FF

and press Enter. The results—377 in octal, 11111111 in binary, and 255 in decimal—are shown in the display. The ASCII character corresponding to the decimal value is also displayed on the right, opposite the decimal line. In this case, the character represented by 255 decimal is a blank. If the decimal number is less than 32, the normal abbreviation for the ASCII control character is also displayed. See Appendix B for a list of the ASCII control characters.

To perform calculations with the Programmer's calculator, enter numbers in the usual way; you do not need reverse polish notation. For example, select DECIMAL from the list of numbering schemes and, to add 32 to 32, type

32 + 32

and press Enter. The result, 64 in decimal, is displayed as 40 in hex, 100 in octal, and 1000000 in binary. Figure 8.5 shows the results of this calculation. The ASCII character represented by the value 64 (the @ character) is shown to the right of the decimal line.

THE SCIENTIFIC CALCULATOR

The section is just a brief introduction to the Scientific calculator.

PC Tools includes an immensely powerful Scientific calculator. You can use it to perform mathematical functions, probability and statistical

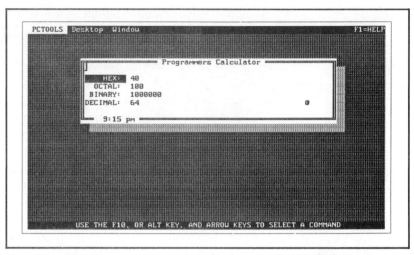

Figure 8.5: Sample operations using the Programmer's calculator (Version 5.5)

functions, and the usual set of transcendental functions. Several sets of internal registers are available for use in complex calculations.

The Scientific calculator emulates the functions of the HP-11C calculator, except that it is not programmable. As with other Hewlett-Packard calculators, it uses reverse polish notation for the entry of numbers and operations, rather than the infix notation used by most other calculators (including the PC Tools Algebraic calculator). The keyboard layout is shown in Figure 8.6.

The main function of each key on the calculator is indicated in white (reverse video if you have a monochrome monitor) at the top of the key. If the key has secondary functions, these are shown above the key (in red on color monitors) or on the key itself below the main function (in blue if you have a color monitor). To use these secondary functions, first use the F prefix key if the function you want is above the key or use the G prefix key if the secondary function is located on the lower part of the key. These prefix keys act like the shift keys on your computer keyboard. You can also use the F7 or F8 function key in place of the F or G prefix key. If you are using your keyboard rather than a mouse, a shortcut character you can type from the computer keyboard to access the function is shown to the left of some of the keys on the calculator.

For example, the key at the top left of the calculator is the e↑x key, which raises e to the power of the number in the display. To use it,

See the section "The Financial Calculator" for a description of how to use reverse polish notation for data entry.

To access the secondary function on a key, click on either the F or G prefix key or press F7 or F8 before selecting the function key.

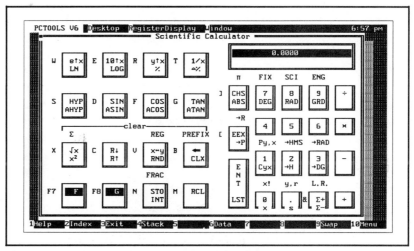

Figure 8.6: Scientific calculator keyboard layout

click on the key with the mouse or press W from your computer keyboard. A secondary function of this key is LN, which calculates the natural logarithm of the number in the display. To access LN with a mouse, first click on the G prefix key and then on e↑x. To do the same thing from the keyboard, press F8 followed by W.

Other keys have two secondary functions rather than just one. For example, to access π, FIX, SCI, or ENG, click on F (or press F7) followed by], 7, 8, or 9. To access ABS, DEG, RAD, or GRD, click on G (or press F8), followed by], 7, 8, or 9. The middle row of number keys on the keypad, 4, 5, 6, the division, multiplication, addition, and subtraction keys, and RCL do not have shifted functions. So for example, to obtain the fractional part of a number, type

RCL, ÷, *, −, +, and the numbers 4, 5, and 6 do not have additional shifted functions.

F
FRAC

or to see the integer part, type

G
INT

You can also use the function keys F7 and F8 in place of the F and G shift keys. Now to obtain the fractional part of a number, type

F7
FRAC

or to see the integer portion of a number, type

F8
INT

The letters to the left of the keys indicate the keys on your computer keyboard that are equivalent to keys on the calculator. For example, type M when you want to use RCL (recall a stored number) or X when you want to obtain the square root of a number. If you use a mouse, just click on the keys you want to use in the correct sequence.

Table 8.5 lists the math, transcendental, statistical, and probability functions available on the Scientific calculator.

Table 8.5: Mathematical Functions Included in the Scientific Calculator

KEY	FUNCTION
Math Functions	
LN	Computes the natural logarithm, the logarithm to the base e.
$e{\uparrow}x$	Computes the natural antilogarithm. Raises e to the power of the number in the display.
LOG	Computes the common logarithm (base 10) of a positive number.
$10{\uparrow}x$	Computes the common antilogarithm. Raises 10 to the power of the number in the display.
$y{\uparrow}x$	Exponent. Raises the number in the Y register to the power of the value in the display.
%	Computes X percent of the value in the Y register.
$1/x$	Computes the reciprocal or multiplicative inverse of the number in the display.
$\sqrt{}$	Computes the square root of the number in the X register.

Table 8.5: Mathematical Functions Included in the Scientific Calculator (Continued)

KEY	FUNCTION
Math Functions	
x^2	Computes the square of the number in the X register.
x!	Computes the factorial of an integer. To compute the gamma function, Γ, subtract 1 from the number and then calculate x!.
$\Delta\%$	Computes the percent change between the number in the Y register and the number in the X register.
π	The constant 3.141592654.
CHS	Changes the sign of the number or the sign of the exponent of 10 in the display.
ABS	Computes the absolute value of the number in the display.
INT	Returns the integer portion of a number.
FRAC	Returns the fractional portion of a number.
RND	Rounds the internal ten-digit mantissa of the value in the display to match the number of digits specified by the current FIX, SCI, or ENG specification.
Trigonometric Functions	
SIN	Sine of X.
COS	Cosine of X.
TAN	Tangent of X.
ASIN	Arc sine of X.
ACOS	Arc cosine of X.
ATAN	Arc tangent of X.

Table 8.5: Mathematical Functions Included in the Scientific Calculator (Continued)

KEY	FUNCTION
Hyperbolic Functions	
HYP	Hyperbolic sine (sinh), cosine (cosh), or tangent (tanh), using SIN, COS, or TAN of X.
AHYP	Inverse hyperbolic sine ($\sinh^{-1}$), cosine ($\cosh^{-1}$), or tangent ($\tanh^{-1}$), using SIN, COS, or TAN of X.
Probability Functions	
Py,x	Permutation. Computes the number of permutations of y taken x at a time, without repetitions. Must be a positive integer.
Cy,x	Combination. Computes the number of combinations of y taken x at a time, without repetitions or order. Must be a positive integer.
Statistical Functions	
Σ +	Collects information from numbers in the X and Y registers into the statistics storage registers R0 through R5 as follows:
	R0: The number of data points collected.
	R1: The sum of the x values, Σx.
	R2: The sum of the squares of the x values, Σx^2.
	R3: The sum of the y values, Σy.
	R4: The sum of the squares of the y values, Σy^2.
	R5: The sum of the products of the x and y values, Σxy.
Σ –	Subtracts information from the statistics storage registers to correct data collection. Delete and reenter both x and y in the correct sequence, even if only one value is incorrect.

Table 8.5: Mathematical Functions Included in the Scientific Calculator (Continued)

KEY	FUNCTION
Statistical Functions	
Σ	Clears the statistics storage registers and the stack registers, but leaves the LAST X register intact, removing data from previous calculations.
x	Computes the arithmetic mean of the x and y values in the R1 and R3 registers.
s	Computes the standard deviation of the x and y values collected using Σ +. R0, R1, and R2 values are used to calculate the standard deviation of the x values, and R0, R3, and R4 values are used for the standard deviation of the y values.
L.R.	Computes linear regression using the linear equation y = Ax + B, placing the slope (A) in the Y register, and the intercept (B) in the X register.
y,r	Computes the linear estimate and correlation coefficient. Assuming the x and y values approximate a straight line, the linear estimate is placed in the X register and the correlation coefficient in the Y register.

Table 8.6 lists all display and unit conversions available on the Scientific calculator.

The Scientific calculator can display information in fixed format, in scientific (or exponential) notation, and in engineering format.

- In fixed format, numbers in the display are always shown with the same number of digits after the decimal point. You can set the number of decimal places from 0 to 9, by selecting F (or F7), the FIX key, and entering a number for the number of decimal places to show. The calculator initially starts with four decimal places.

Table 8.6: Display and Unit Conversions Available on the Scientific Calculator

KEY	FUNCTION
Display Conversions	
FIX n	Fixes the number of decimal places for the display, where n is between 0 and 9.
SCI n	Sets the display to scientific notation.
ENG n	Sets the display to engineering notation.
DEG	Sets the display mode to degrees for trigonometric functions.
RAD	Sets the display mode to radians for trigonometric functions.
GRD	Sets the display mode to gradians for trigonometric functions.
Units Conversions	
→HMS	Converts decimal hours to hours, minutes, seconds, or decimal degrees to degrees, minutes, seconds.
→H	Converts hours, minutes, seconds to decimal hours, or degrees, minutes, seconds to decimal degrees.
→DG	Converts radians to degrees.
→RAD	Converts degrees to radians.
Polar-Rectangular Coordinate Conversions	
→R	Converts the polar coordinates in the X and Y registers (magnitude r, angle φ) to rectangular coordinates (x,y)
→P	Converts the rectangular coordinates in the X and Y registers (x,y) to polar coordinates (magnitude r, angle φ).

- In scientific notation, you can display a very large or very small number easily with the minimum of digits. Numbers are shown as a multiple of 10 raised to a power. For example, 45,678 is displayed as 4.5678 04 (consider this 4.5678 times 10 raised to the fourth power). −45,678 is displayed as −4.5678 04. To select the number of decimal places, select F (or F7), the SCI key, followed by the number of decimal places to display. If you chose SCI 3, the number 4.5678 will be shown as 4.568 04.

- Engineering notation is similar to scientific notation, but the exponent (the power of 10) is always a multiple of 3, so any number in the display can be read easily in units of K (kilo, or 10^3), or m (milli, or 10^{-3}) commonly found in engineering. The digit following the selected number of places is automatically rounded off. Select F (or F7) and the ENG key followed by the number of digits to display after first significant figure.

Managing the keystrokes and internal registers on the calculator can become quite complicated. Table 8.7 lists all calculator key and internal register management functions available on the Scientific calculator.

Table 8.7: Calculator Key and Internal Register Management Functions Available on the Scientific Calculator

KEY	FUNCTION
Key Manipulation	
F	When selected before a function key, performs the function above the key. The display shows the "f" character.
G	When selected before a function key, performs the function below the key. The display shows the "g" character.
PREFIX	Cancels the F (F7) or G (F8) prefixes for partially entered functions.

Table 8.7: Calculator Key and Internal Register Management Functions Available on the Scientific Calculator (Continued)

KEY	FUNCTION
Key Manipulation	
ENT	Enters a copy of the number displayed into the Y register.
LST	Recalls the number displayed before the last function was executed.
EEX	Indicates that the next numbers entered are to be used as the exponent of a number.
Calculator Register Manipulation	
STO	Stores a number in the R0 to R9 and R.0 to R.9 data registers.
RCL	Recalls a stored number. Follow RCL with the register number to recall.
X←→Y	Swaps the contents of the X and Y stack registers.
R↓	Rolls down the contents of the stack.
R↑	Rolls up the contents of the stack.
REG	Sets all the storage registers to zero. To clear an individual register, store zero into the register.
CLX	Sets the value of the displayed X register to zero.

The Scientific calculator uses several different sets of registers to store the results of different kinds of calculations.

- Stack Registers store the intermediate results of your calculations, and are labeled T, Z, Y, X, and LSTX. The number in the calculator display is stored in the X register. If you enter another number or perform an operation, the numbers already on the stack are moved up or down one place.

Use R↑ or R↓ to roll the contents of the stack up or down one register at a time. X↔Y swaps the values contained in the X and Y registers. When you perform a calculation, the number that was in the X register before the calculation is moved into a special register called LAST X. You can recall this number into the X register with G LST or F8 Enter, so you don't have to reenter the number in the next calculation.

You can look at the contents of all stack registers with the Stack Registers option in the Register Display pull-down menu, or by pressing F4 from the main calculator screen.

To ensure that no results from previous calculations remain, clear the stack registers by clicking on F (or pressing F7) followed by Σ. This does not clear LAST X.

- Data Registers are 20 general-purpose registers called R0 to R9 and R.0 to R.9. Use STO and RCL to store or recall numbers from these registers. STO copies the number in the X register into the data register you designate by number. RCL performs the reverse operation, copying a number from a data register into the X register. To clear all the data storage registers, click on F (or press F7) followed by REG. This also clears the statistical storage registers.

    You can view the contents of all data registers with the Data Registers option in the Register Display pull-down menu, or by pressing F6 from the main calculator screen.

- Statistical Storage Registers. The results of statistical calculations are stored in another set of registers, R1 to R5. These are special registers, handled automatically by the calculator. They cannot be inspected from the Registers Display menu.

    These registers are used as follows:

R0	The number of data points collected
R1	The sum of the x values, Σx
R2	The sum of the squares of the x values, Σx^2
R3	The sum of the y values, Σy
R4	The sum of the squares of the y values, Σy^2
R5	The sum of the products of the x and y values, Σxy

When you start a new calculation, make sure no old values remain in these registers. You can clear them by clicking on F (or pressing F7) followed by Σ. This also clears all the stack registers.

Finally, the Scientific calculator can display three error messages:

- ERROR 0. You have attempted an impossible operation, such as division by zero.

- ERROR 1. You have tried to enter too many values into the storage registers.

- ERROR 2. You have tried to enter an improper statistical operation, such as performing a linear regression before you have entered any data points.

Press a key from the keyboard or click the mouse to clear any one of these errors.

SUMMARY

In this chapter, you learned about the four powerful calculators contained in PC Tools Desktop. The Algebraic calculator is for general-purpose use at home or in business. The other three calculators, the Financial calculator, the Programmer's (hex) calculator, and the Scientific calculator are very powerful emulations of Hewlett-Packard calculators designed to perform very specific functions.

9

Using the
Desktop Manager
for Appointments

This chapter concentrates on the Desktop Appointment Scheduler. It shows how to use the Appointment Scheduler to organize your time. You will learn how to make a to-do list, how to automatically load your schedule, and how to customize the Appointment Scheduler. You'll also learn how to print an appointment schedule and run a program at a time that you specify.

USING THE APPOINTMENT SCHEDULER

Desktop's Appointment Scheduler consists of three separate parts for organizing your time: a monthly calendar, a time planner, and a to-do list. When you enter appointments into the time planner, you specify the time and duration of the appointment and can also attach a reminder. You can set an alarm that sounds just before your next appointment. You can also search for a particular appointment or find the next block of free time. You can make a to-do list with different priorities attached to the items in the list. Finally, you can use macros with the Appointment Scheduler to pop up notes before a meeting, run a program when you are away from your computer, or dial a phone number.

You are not restricted to making appointments or scheduling meetings with the Appointment Scheduler. You can use it to remind you of birthdays, anniversaries, or other special regularly occurring dates. You can also use it to track your own time-management activities, to track consulting work you do for different clients, or even to track the time you spend working on different projects.

The Appointment Scheduler creates files with .TM extensions. When you start the Appointment Scheduler from the Desktop main menu, the File Load dialog box lists any files with this extension in the current directory. If several different people use the computer, you can create individual Appointment Scheduler files, each with a different name.

When you start the Appointment Scheduler from the main Desktop menu, you will see the screen shown in Figure 9.1 after you specify which file to load.

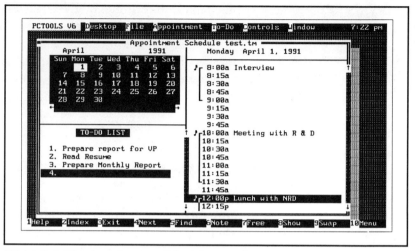

Figure 9.1: The Appointment Scheduler opening screen

Use the Tab key to move from the monthly calendar window to the time planner window or the to-do list window, or click the mouse in the window you want to make active. The shortcut function keys are shown on the message line at the bottom of the screen.

This month's calendar is shown in the upper-left corner of the screen with today's date highlighted. This is a perpetual calendar: there is no end date. To select a new date using the keyboard, use the left or right arrow keys. If you move past the beginning or end of the month, the calendar scrolls to show the previous or next month. Use Tab to activate/highlight Calendar and PgUp or PgDn to change to another month. Use the Ctrl key with PgUp or PgDn to change the year.

To change to another date using the mouse, just click on the new date. To display a different month with the mouse, click on either of the two small arrow characters at the bottom corners of the calendar box. Press the Home key to return to today's date.

The time planner display on the right side of the screen shows today's appointments listed by their scheduled time. The default business day runs from 8:00 A.M. to 5:00 P.M. and is divided into 15-minute intervals. However, you can change this interval using the Controls menu commands. The highlighted bar shows the current time. To select a time from the keyboard, use the Tab key to select the daily schedule and the up or down arrow keys, or page through the list with PgUp or PgDn. Home selects the earliest appointment time and End selects the latest.

If you use a mouse, just click on the time you want to select or use the scroll bars to move through the list.

Once you have selected a time, press Enter to make an appointment for that time. If you already have an appointment at the highlighted time, press Enter to edit or delete the entry. If you have attached a Notepad to the appointment, you can pop up the note by pressing F6.

Today's to-do list is displayed below the calendar in the lower-left corner of the screen, arranged in order of priority. You can move through the list one line at a time with the up or down arrow keys, or you can page through the list using PgUp or PgDn. Home selects the first entry in the list and End selects the last. You can enter as many as 80 items in this list, although the screen can only show eight entries at once. The to-do list is independent of the calendar and the list of appointments on the time planner.

The Appointment Scheduler uses your computer's internal clock. Always make sure that the clock is set correctly after you turn on your computer.

MAKING APPOINTMENTS

All the selections you need to make, delete, or edit appointments are contained in the Appointment pull-down menu, shown in Figure 9.2.

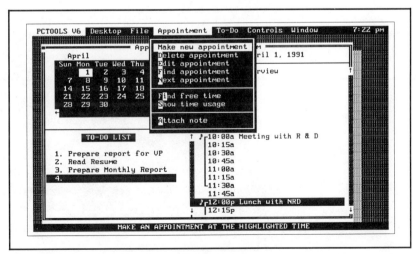

Figure 9.2: The Appointment pull-down menu

To make a new appointment, you can use several shortcuts as alternatives to the Appointment menu. You have the following choices:

- Select the appropriate time on today's time planner display and either press the Enter key or click on it with the mouse.

- Select the appropriate month from the monthly calendar and then choose the correct day for the appointment. Now move to the time planner display and select the time for the appointment.

Whichever method you use, the Make Appointment screen appears, as shown in Figure 9.3.

The selections in the Make Appointment screen are as follows:

- Start Date. Enter the start date for recurring appointments or the appointment date for single appointments.

- End Date. Enter the end date for a series of recurring appointments or leave the field blank for a single appointment.

- Time. Enter the appointment time.

- Note. Enter a message of up to 24 characters to remind you of the purpose of the appointment. This text is displayed opposite

If you try to make an appointment for a date that has passed, or try to make a recurring appointment that has an end date prior to today's date, you will receive a warning message.

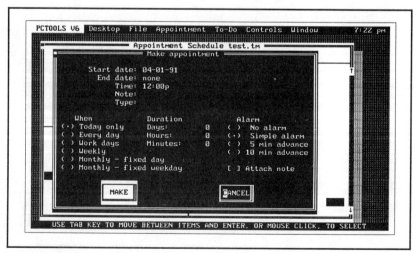

Figure 9.3: The Make Appointment screen

the appointment time in the time planner display when you return to the main Appointment Scheduler display.

- Type. Enter a single character to classify your appointments. This is especially useful if you categorize your activities. If you are a consultant, use this field to differentiate between clients by giving each client a unique code. If you use modern time-management techniques, assign a different code to each activity that you want to track or to each of the different projects that you work on.

- When. Allows you to specify when the event will take place. Use Today Only for a one-time appointment. Use the other choices to schedule regular activities. You can schedule lunchtime each day by selecting Work days. Schedule regular weekly meetings with Weekly. If you want an appointment to repeat each month on the same day, select Monthly - Fixed Day, or if you want the appointment on the same day of the week each month, choose Monthly - fixed weekday.

- Duration. Enter the length of time you expect the appointment to take in Days, Hours, or Minutes. If this conflicts with an existing appointment, the Appointment Scheduler displays a message to this effect when you select MAKE to save the appointment.

- Alarm. You can set an alarm to go off at the time of the appointment, or five or ten minutes before the time. If you set an alarm, the Appointment Scheduler will interrupt your foreground application program with a message and beep when the alarm goes off. You can acknowledge the alarm or select the SNOOZE button, which reactivates the alarm after five more minutes. You can also select No Alarm.

- Attach note. Place a mark in the box by pressing Enter or clicking if you want to attach a Desktop Notepad to the appointment. Among other things, this is useful for meeting agenda or notes for a presentation. If you choose Attach note, a Desktop Notepad file opens on top of the Appointment Scheduler screen when you select the MAKE button to save the appointment. The top line of the Notepad displays the appointment reminder note along with the date and time; the rest of the file is empty and ready for text. All the usual Notepad features are available. The Notepad file will have the same name as the current appointment file, but with a file name extension based on the internal identification number of the selected appointment. The file is created in the same directory as the appointment file. Press Escape or click on the close box with the mouse to return to the Appointment Scheduler when you have finished your note.

Select the MAKE button when you have entered all the information for the appointment. You will return to the main display, which now shows the appointment you have just entered. The duration of the appointment is shown as a vertical bar down the left side of the time planner display. If appointments overlap, the overlapping times are indicated on the duration bar.

If you set an alarm, a musical note symbol is also shown opposite the appointment. A double musical note indicates a recurring appointment with alarm. If you attached a note to the appointment, the letter "N" appears to the left of the musical note.

If you want to delete an appointment, move the highlight to the appointment and press the Enter key. A dialog box opens with the following options:

- DELETE deletes the appointment.

- Select EDIT to edit the appointment. This opens the Make appointment box so you can enter your changes.

- Use ALTER NOTE if you want to alter the information in the Notepad file.

- CANCEL cancels the appointment deletion.

Alternatively, choose the Delete appointment option from the Appointment pull-down menu and select OK from the dialog box when asked to confirm the deletion.

If the appointment you delete is a recurring appointment, the Appointment Scheduler asks if you want to delete this particular appointment for today only or if you want to delete all occurrences of the appointment.

To edit an appointment, place the highlight on the entry you want to edit, press the Enter key, and choose from Delete, Edit, Alter note, or Cancel, or choose Edit appointment from the Appointment pull-down menu. Either way, the Make appointment screen appears, displaying the current appointment for you to enter your changes.

You can search for a particular appointment with the Find appointment option from the Appointment pull-down menu. You can search by text (the text that you originally entered in the note box in the Make appointment screen), appointment type, appointment time, or appointment date. Select Find appointment from the Appointment menu or press the FIND button to start the search. Starting the search without a text entry finds all appointments after the current time and date.

Use Next appointment from the Appointment pull-down menu, or press F4 to find the next appointment scheduled for today. If you are free for the rest of the day, the cursor moves to the current time.

To find your next available period of free time, use Find free time from the Appointment pull-down menu or press F7. You will see the screen shown in Figure 9.4.

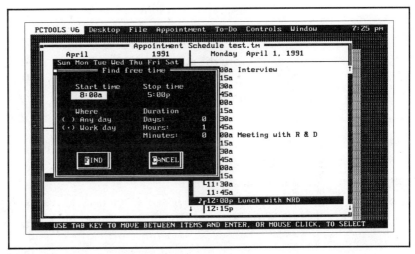

Figure 9.4: Find free time screen

When searching for the next available period of free time, you can establish the following criteria:

- Start time. Enter the time of day you want the search to start.

- Stop time. Enter the time of day you want the search to stop.

- Where. Choose between Any day or Work day.

- Duration. Enter the length of the free period you are looking for in days, hours, and minutes.

Start the search by choosing the FIND button. The Appointment Scheduler moves the cursor through the time planner as it searches for the first block of free time to match the search criteria. Find Free Time can search up to a year ahead to find the block of time you need.

For example, suppose you have to interview a candidate for a position and you want to hold the interview during normal business hours on a work day sometime this week. You estimate that the interview will last for 90 minutes. Using Find free time, set the Start time to 8:00 A.M. and the Stop time to 3:30 P.M. If you search any later than 3:30 P.M., you may not complete the interview inside normal business hours. Choose Work day from the Where column and enter the Duration as 1 hour and 30 minutes. Choose the FIND button to start the search for the next free period that matches these criteria.

To see how you are using your time, the Show time usage selection from the Appointment pull-down menu displays five days' schedule on the screen, as shown in Figure 9.5. The solid dots represent appointments, the shaded areas represent free time, and the transparent dots are scheduling conflicts. All days in the week are shown, not just work days. You can use the arrow keys or the mouse to move through the five-day window one day at a time, or the PgUp or PgDn keys to move five days at a time. Press the Home key to return to today's date.

An appointment must exist before you can attach a Notepad to it.

You can attach a Notepad to an appointment when you create it. If you decide to add a Notepad after you have made the appointment, however, you must use Attach note from the Appointment pull-down menu, or press F6. You enter the actual text as described earlier in the "Making Appointments" section.

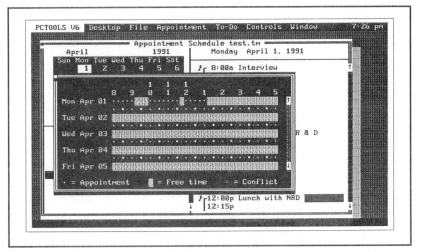

Figure 9.5: Show time usage display

MAKING A TO-DO LIST

The to-do list is completely independent of the time planner and the monthly calendar. You can enter up to 80 items in your to-do list, although only eight can be displayed on the screen at one time. You can attach a priority to each entry—from 1 for the highest priority to 10 for the lowest—and the list will be displayed in priority order. You can also attach a Notepad to each item if you wish. The items in the to-do list are displayed only for as long as you specify when you create each item. Then they are removed from the list.

There are several ways you can create a new entry in the list:

- Position the cursor on a blank line in the to-do list, enter the name of the item, and press the Enter key.

- Position the cursor on a blank line in the to-do list and press the Enter key.

- Click the mouse on a blank line in the to-do list.

- Choose the New to-do entry from the To-Do pull-down menu.

Using any of these methods opens the New to-do entry box on the screen, as shown in Figure 9.6.

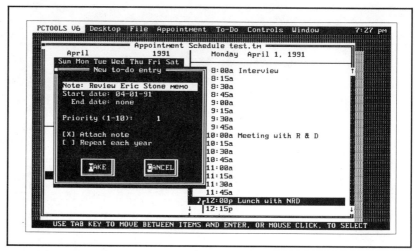

Figure 9.6: New To-Do item entry box

Enter the information into the screen as follows:

- Note. Enter the name of the item in less than 24 characters. This is the text that appears in the to-do list shown on the main Appointment Scheduler screen.

- Start date. This is normally filled automatically with today's date.

- End date. Enter the last date you want this item to be active. If you do not specify an end date, the item stays on the list until you delete it manually.

- Priority. Assign a priority from 1 to 10. Items in the list are displayed in this priority order. Most people find a three- or four-level priority sufficient; more levels than this tends to confuse things. Try categorizing your to-do list into the four categories of vital, important, useful, and wasteful.

- Attach note. Press Enter or click to mark this box if you want to attach a note to the entry. A Notepad will open when you select the MAKE button to save the entry. The letter ''N'' beside the item in the to-do list indicates that a note is attached.

- Repeat Each Year. Mark this box to display the reminder note for the same time interval next year. This is especially useful for birthday or anniversary reminders.

Select the MAKE button to confirm your entry. If you selected Attach Note to add a note to your item, a Notepad opens, ready to receive your text.

When you return to the main Appointment Scheduler screen, your entry will be displayed in the to-do list according to the priority you selected.

If you want to delete an item from your to-do list, position the cursor over the item in the to-do list in the main Appointment Scheduler screen and press the Enter key, or click on the item with the mouse. Alternatively, position the cursor over the entry and choose Delete To-Do Entry from the To-Do pull-down menu. In either case, you will see a dialog box containing the following options:

- DELETE deletes the item from your to-do list.

- EDIT opens the New To-Do entry box so you can edit your entry.

- Use ALTER NOTE if you want to keep the to-do item intact but want to change or review the contents of the Notepad.

- CANCEL cancels and closes the dialog box and returns you to the main Appointment Scheduler screen.

If you forgot to attach a Notepad to your to-do list item when you created it, you can add one now by positioning the cursor on the item and selecting Attach note from the To-Do pull-down menu, or by pressing the F6 key. A Notepad window opens on top of the Appointment Scheduler. The top line of the Notepad contains the text of the to-do item, the date and the time, and the priority you assigned to the item. The rest of the screen is blank for you to add your text. All the usual Notepad text-editing features are available. The Notepad file is created in the same directory as the Appointment Scheduler file with the same file name. The file name extension is a number based on an internal Appointment Scheduler counter. Press the Escape key to return to the Appointment Scheduler.

AUTOMATICALLY LOADING YOUR SCHEDULE

If you run Desktop in memory-resident mode, you can add a parameter to your AUTOEXEC.BAT file to open the Appointment Scheduler and display the day's time planner and to-do list every time you boot up your system. Add the following line to your AUTOEXEC.BAT file to make the Appointment Scheduler open when you boot up your system:

DESKTOP /RA

The /R parameter loads Desktop in memory-resident mode, and the A parameter automatically opens the Appointment Scheduler. All the other parts of Desktop are also fully functional at this point.

If you do not have an active Appointment Scheduler file containing appointments, Desktop comes up in the main screen as if you had loaded it with the

DESKTOP /R

parameter in your AUTOEXEC.BAT file.

Make sure that the DESKTOP entry is the last entry in your AUTOEXEC.BAT file, because any commands that come after it will not be executed until after you leave Desktop.

CUSTOMIZING THE APPOINTMENT SCHEDULER

There are several options in the Controls pull-down menu that you can use to personalize the Appointment Scheduler. Figure 9.7 shows the Controls pull-down menu.

To change the work days, method of date entry, or the start and stop time for your work day, select the Appointment Settings option from the Controls menu. A dialog box opens, as shown in Figure 9.8.

You can change any of the following settings:

- Work days. Select which days of the week are your work days. If you free-lance or do consulting work, all the days may be work days.

Figure 9.7: The Controls pull-down menu

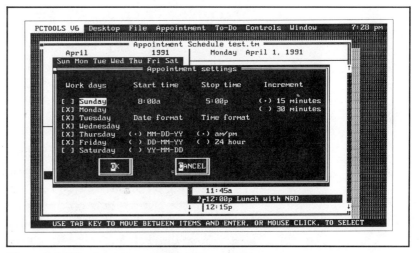

Figure 9.8: The Appointment Settings screen

- Start time. Specify the time you want your work day to begin. This is normally 8:00 A.M., but if you do shift work you can select a different start time.

- Stop time. This is the time you want your work day to end, and is normally 5:00 P.M. If you do shift work, or if you make evening appointments, change the stop time to suit your needs.

- Increment. Choose between a 15- or 30-minute increment for the time planner, depending on the degree of accuracy you require.

- Date format. The Appointment Scheduler offers three different date formats. You can use MM-DD-YY if you work in the United States, DD-MM-YY if you work in Europe, or YY-MM-DD if you work in an area using the metric system or for the military.

- Time format. Similarly, you can choose between two different time formats: am/pm or 24 hour.

When you are satisfied with your choices, select the OK button to save them and return to the main Appointment Scheduler screen. Your new settings are now in effect.

To avoid scheduling appointments on holidays, you can designate which holidays you want to observe by using the Holiday settings selection from the Controls pull-down menu. The Appointment Scheduler has the main United States holidays already built in, but allows you to designate ten additional holidays. Any day designated as a holiday is shown on the time planner screen with an asterisk beside it. Figure 9.9 shows the Holiday settings screen.

If there is a mark in the box opposite the holiday, it is turned on. To change the setting, select the holiday and use the Enter key to toggle the setting on or off. You can also add new holidays by entering them into the Date column on the right side of the display. Remember to use the format you chose in Appointment Settings for the date entry. Use the Tab key to move between the two columns in this screen. Recurring appointments are not made on holidays.

To prevent your appointments file from growing too large, delete old appointments from the file. Choose Delete old entries from the Controls pull-down menu; a dialog box opens, asking you for a cutoff date. All appointments with dates before this cutoff date are deleted when you choose the DELETE button. Use the CANCEL button if you do not want to delete old appointments.

Figure 9.9: The Holiday Settings screen from the Controls pull-down menu

Finally, if you do not use the monthly calendar or the to-do list, you can use the Wide display option from the Controls pull-down menu to suppress them. If the Wide display selection has a mark in front of it, all three elements of the display are shown: the monthly calendar, the to-do list, and the time planner. If there is no mark, only the time planner is displayed.

WORKING WITH APPOINTMENT SCHEDULER FILES

To load an existing Appointment Scheduler file, use the Load option in the File pull-down menu. The File Load dialog box opens, listing all the files in the current directory that have the .TM file name extension. Select the desired file from the list and load it. When you load a file in this way, the Appointment Scheduler file you were working with is saved before the new file is loaded.

Files in the Appointment Scheduler are saved when you click on the close box with the mouse or when you exit the Appointment Scheduler. You can also save your file using Save from the File menu. If you want to save your appointments in a file with a different name, specify the new name in the Save file to disk dialog box. You can also use Autosave to save your files at intervals that you specify. Remember, Autosave is global to the Appointment Scheduler, Notepads, Outlines, and the Macro Editor. That is, when you turn Autosave on in one of these applications, you turn it on in all of them. Likewise, if you turn it off in one of them you turn it off in all of them. To use Autosave, first turn it on and then specify the time interval in minutes.

You can use the final option in the File menu—Exit Without Saving—if you have been demonstrating the Appointment Scheduler and don't want to save your entries.

PRINTING AN APPOINTMENT SCHEDULE

The Appointment Scheduler has several different printing options, shown in Figure 9.10.

You can print today's appointment schedule and to-do list together, or the schedule or to-do list for the whole week. You can also print your monthly appointment list or your monthly to-do list.

Several graphics characters are used in the time planner to indicate alarm settings and the duration of an appointment. Many printers cannot print these characters, so the Appointment Scheduler lets you translate them into printable characters, as shown in Table 9.1.

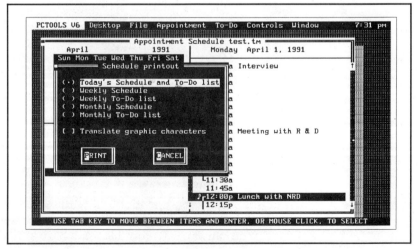

Figure 9.10: Appointment Scheduler printing options

Table 9.1: Graphics Characters Used in Time Planner

SYMBOL	EXPLANATION
/	Top of the appointment duration bracket
¦	Center of the appointment duration bracket
\	Bottom of the appointment duration bracket
#	Single musical note
%	Double musical note

Choose the PRINT button to start the printout or the CANCEL button to return to the Appointment Scheduler. Choose from the usual Desktop print device options or send the printout to a file for later printing. An example printout with today's schedule and to-do list is shown in Figure 9.11.

RUNNING A PROGRAM AT A SPECIFIC TIME

You can use the Appointment Scheduler to run a program at a specific time if you use a special character in the Note text box in the Make Appointment dialog box. The broken vertical bar (¦) character has a special meaning when you use it in this way. The general form of the entry is

note¦file name

where *note* is any text you want to associate with the alarm and *file name* is the name of the file you want to run. For example, use this feature when you want to start programs that take a long time to load or programs that can run without any operator interaction, such as backup programs backing up to tape. You can schedule the program for lunchtime or after work.

If you want to load WordStar at 1:00 P.M., enter

Run WordStar¦WS.EXE

Include the file name extension of .BAT, .COM, or .EXE when specifying program names.

opposite the 1:00 P.M. time slot in the time planner display, or enter it into the Note text box in the Make appointment screen. At 1:00 P.M., a

```
.--------------------------------------------------------------------------.
|                                    |                                      |
|   August              1990         |   Thursday  August 30, 1990          |
|                                    |                                      |
| Sun Mon Tue Wed Thu Fri Sat        | N#/ 8:00a Interview                  |
|                 1   2   3   4      |  |  8:15a                            |
|                                    |  |  8:30a                            |
|   5   6   7   8   9  10  11        |  |  8:45a                            |
|                                    |  \  9:00a                            |
|  12  13  14  15  16  17  18        |     9:15a                            |
|                                    |     9:30a                            |
|  19  20  21  22  23  24  25        |     9:45a                            |
|                                    | #/10:00a Meeting with R & D          |
|  26  27  28  29  30  31            |  |10:15a                             |
|                                    |  |10:30a                             |
|                                    |  |10:45a                             |
|------------------------------------|  |11:00a                             |
|             TO-DO LIST             |  |11:15a                             |
|                                    |  \11:30a                             |
| 1. Prepare report for VP           |    11:45a                            |
| 2. Read Resume                     | #/12:00p Lunch with NRD              |
| 3. Prepare Monthly Report          |  |12:15p                             |
| 4.                                 |  |12:30p                             |
|                                    |  |12:45p                             |
|                                    |  \  1:00p                            |
|                                    |     1:15p                            |
|                                    |     1:30p                            |
|                                    |     1:45p                            |
|                                    |     2:00p                            |
|                                    |     2:15p                            |
|                                    |     2:30p                            |
|                                    |     2:45p                            |
|                                    |     3:00p                            |
|                                    |     3:15p                            |
|                                    |     3:30p                            |
|                                    |     3:45p                            |
|                                    |     4:00p                            |
|                                    |     4:15p                            |
|                                    |     4:30p                            |
|                                    |     4:45p                            |
|                                    |     5:00p                            |
|                                    |                                      |
'--------------------------------------------------------------------------'
```

Figure 9.11: Example printout with today's schedule and to-do list

If the program you want to run is in a different directory, you must enter the whole path name unless it is already included in your path statement.

window will open, asking if you want to run the program. If you select the OK button, WordStar runs just as though you had entered the name from the DOS command line.

To make WordStar run without asking your permission, enter

WS.EXE

without any text in front of the file name. When the alarm goes off, DOS issues the program name and the program loads automatically.

If you want to load a program that needs a large number of command-line parameters, there may not be room for all of them in the small text entry box. If so, create a batch file that contains the parameters in the correct sequence and enter the name of this batch file into the text box instead. The batch file runs at the specified time, loading the application program and passing all the parameters to it as though you had entered them from the DOS command line.

Similarly, you can load a Notepad file automatically. Enter

¦STAFFMTG.TXT

into the text box opposite 2:00 P.M. in the time planner, and select a ten-minute advance alarm in the Make Appointment screen. When the alarm goes off, the file STAFFMTG.TXT containing your notes from last week's meeting is loaded into a Notepad. You now have ten minutes to review your notes before the meeting starts.

Remember to select the Activate Everywhere option from Macro Activation in the File pull-down menu before using macros in your appointments.

Finally, you can use macros with appointments if you include the macro name in the Note box after the broken vertical bar symbol. The macro name must be enclosed in angle brackets. To run a macro called <CTRLF1> at a specific time, enter

¦<CTRLF1>

into the Note box in the Make Appointment screen. Macros are not just restricted to the Appointment Scheduler. You can use them from other places in DOS and you don't need to create many batch files to do the job.

SUMMARY

This chapter covered the Desktop Manager's Appointment Scheduler. You learned a variety of ways to plot your schedule and manage your time.

10

Using the
Built-In
Database

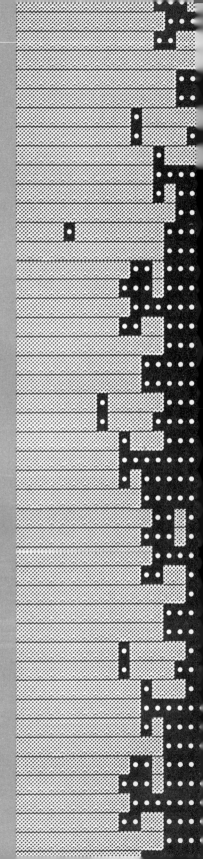

10

The Database in Desktop can stand alone. You can use it for any database purpose, ranging from a patient address list to a catalog of your stock photography slides. You can prepare the text of a form letter in a Notepad and then merge that letter with the addresses in your database to produce personalized letters. You can also use files originally made with dBASE (or any program that makes a dBASE-compatible file) because the Desktop Database file format is completely compatible with dBASE. This compatibility lets you make ad hoc queries against a dBASE file from Desktop without having to load all of dBASE. Later in this chapter, you will learn how to build a Desktop Database.

WHAT IS A DATABASE?

A database is any organized collection of information. Common examples are the patient record cards at your dentist or the personnel files at work. When this collection grows too large and cumbersome for a person to manage, the system is often computerized. A computerized database consists of two main parts:

- The database software. This is the program that organizes the data. It usually allows you to add, delete, sort, and update the information in the database. A large computerized database is often referred to as a database management system or DBMS.

- Data. The actual information contained in the database. A database can contain information on just about anything that is useful to you or your company. A database usually consists of items that contain similar elements, for example, addresses that include street names and numbers, cities, and states. Databases often contain tax records, club membership lists, company financial records, personnel data, and so forth.

Here are some of the advantages of a computerized rather than a manual database system:

- Manual, paper-based systems occupy lots of space. Computerized systems are typically much smaller.

- Accurate, up-to-date information is available at all times in a computerized database.

- Speed is one of the primary advantages of a computerized database. The computer can search the database much faster than a human.

- Using a computer to maintain the data removes the need for a human to update all the paper records.

There are many different database models but most systems developed recently tend to be relational or to have a large component of the relational model. In such databases, the data appears to the user as a set of tables.

DESKTOP DATABASE FILES

Before you learn more about the Desktop Database, you need to understand the basic components of the Desktop Database system, including the different file types and some of the limitations on data storage.

- A database *file* is a group of records. A file may contain a list of the names, addresses, and telephone numbers of a number of people. We'll use photographers as an example.

- A database *record* is a collection of fields. For example, one database record would contain all the details for one of the photographers.

- A database *field* is one of the pieces of information in the record, such as the photographer's first name, street address, or work phone number.

Desktop Databases have three different types of files associated with them: database files, record files, and form files.

In PC Tools 5.5 the limit is 3500 records per database. In Version 6.0 the limit is 10,000 records per database.

- *Database files* contain the actual data. They have a file name extension of .DBF and are compatible with dBASE files. If you try to load a dBASE file that contains more than 10,000 records, the file is truncated to fit: you can perform all the usual Database functions on these records except add new records or *pack* the database. (Since packing the database permanently erases specific records, it is not allowed.)

- *Record files* have a file name extension of .REC and contain information on various Desktop Database settings like sort settings, display options, and so on. These files are specific to Desktop Database and have nothing to do with dBASE. For your Desktop Database to work properly, your database files and your record files must have the same file name and either the .DBF or the .REC extension.

- *Form files* have a file name extension of .FOR. They are standard Notepad files that allow you to view the data in a particular way. For example, one might contain the text of a letter you want to send to all the photographers in your database. You can make your own form files or, if you prefer, Desktop Database will make one for you with the same file name as the database and record files but with the .FOR extension.

These limits only apply to files inside Desktop, they do not apply to dBASE files used in dBASE.

There are several limitations on the amount of data you can maintain in a Desktop Database:

- There is a maximum of 10,000 records per database. You could expand your photographer's database to include up to 10,000 photographers.

- There is a maximum of 4000 characters per record. That is, you can keep up to 4000 characters of information on each of the photographers.

- There is a maximum of 128 fields per record. You can keep up to 128 different pieces of information on each photographer as long as you stay below the limit of 4000 characters per record.

- There is a maximum of 70 characters in each character field. You can keep up to 70 characters in each character field for each photographer in the database.

- There is a maximum of 19 digits in each numeric field. The size of the entry is determined by the size of the field and the number of decimal places you specify.

Before you start working with your database, you must make several important decisions on record structure, field size and type, and field names. Desktop Database supports several different data types.

The memo field type is supported in dBASE but is not supported in Desktop Database. If your dBASE file contains memo fields, they will be ignored in Desktop Database.

- Character data are any data consisting of letters or numbers that are not used in calculations in dBASE. For example, in addition to names and addresses, you could enter social security numbers, phone numbers, and zip codes as character data. If you enter zip codes as numeric data, the beginning zero will always be suppressed. You can have up to 70 characters in any field in Desktop Database, but dBASE supports up to 254. If you are working with dBASE files, remember that any fields with more than 70 characters will be truncated. The default field size for character data is one character.

- Numeric data are values used in calculations. Desktop Database does not perform any calculations on the data, but dBASE does.

- Logical data represent the condition of true or false. True is represented by T, t, Y, or y, and false by F, f, N, or n. You can use an entry in a logical field to divide your database into two parts. If you want to differentiate between people who have and have not renewed their subscription to your newsletter, use a logical field. The default for a logical field is F for false. Logical fields are always one character long.

- Date fields are eight-character fields that can only contain dates in the form *mm/dd/yy,* where *yy* is assumed to be in this century. The default date field contains 00/00/00. You can use dates for sorting data, but you cannot use them in dBASE formulae.

The other two criteria you must define are the field name and the field size.

- Field Name is the name of the item in the database. For example, for an address list you will need to enter the first name, last name, street address, city, state, and zip code. It makes sense to call the fields by very obvious names like FIRST NAME, LAST NAME, ADDRESS, CITY, STATE, and ZIP. For a horticultural database, you would need fields such as PLANT NAME, LATIN NAME, CLIMATE, SOIL TYPE, as well as logical fields for DECIDUOUS, EVERGREEN, SUN, SHADE, and so on. The field name must be no longer than ten characters and cannot begin with a number. All lowercase letters are converted into uppercase, and the Desktop database automatically replaces spaces between words by underscore characters. Blank names are not allowed.

dBASE and other databases do not allow spaces in field names; you must type in underscores. In the Desktop Database, you must type in the underscores when specifying fields that have already been named.

- Field Size is the size of the field in characters. It reserves space in the database for future additions. To select the right field size, find the length of the longest item you anticipate including in your database and then add a few more characters for good measure. For example, if the longest city name you can think of is Sacramento at ten letters, make the field length 20 so that it can include Lake of the Woods (17 letters) in Minnesota. Seventy characters is the maximum size for any character field in a Desktop Database. If you need more space, consider breaking the entry into two sections. For example, if you need to include extensive comments in an entry, call the first field COMMENTS1 and the next COMMENTS2 to create enough space. A numeric field can be up to 19 characters, but the size is really defined by the number of digits in the field and the number of digits after the decimal. The decimal point counts as one character. The default is one digit with no decimals. Date fields are always limited to eight characters, and logical fields are limited to one character.

Once you have entered a field type and field size into the Database, you cannot change them without creating another database. However, you can edit the field name if you have made a spelling mistake.

CREATING A DATABASE FROM SCRATCH

For the example database, you will make a mailing list for a photographic newsletter. The database will maintain accurate, up-to-date mailing addresses for the newsletter, make address labels for the mailing, record which subscribers have paid the yearly subscription, and send out renewal reminder letters to subscribers in arrears. You can use many of the items in this example database as the basis for your own database.

DEFINING THE DATABASE STRUCTURE

Now that you know what the database is for, you can define its structure. Information on each subscriber will include first name, last name, address, city, state, zip code, and subscription status information.

Select Databases from the Desktop main menu and enter a new file name into the File Load dialog box. Call the file PHOTO.DBF. The next screen to appear is the Field Editor, shown in Figure 10.1, which is used to establish all the fields in the database.

To create the fields needed in the PHOTO database:

1. Enter the name of each field into the Field Name box. You can use upper- or lowercase letters because all names are automatically converted into uppercase, with the underscore character representing spaces. Since the field name length is restricted to ten characters, the name of the last field, subscription status, must be abbreviated to SUB_STATUS.

2. Select the type of data the field will contain from Character, Numeric, Logical, or Date. All the fields in the PHOTO database except one will be character data; SUB_STATUS is a logical field.

3. Select the size of the field in characters. This will vary from field to field.

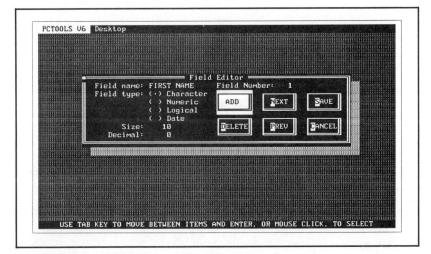

Figure 10.1: The Field Editor screen

4. Select the number of decimal places for numeric data. This does not apply to the PHOTO database, since it does not contain any numeric data.

5. Select the Add button to add the field to the database. The field is created and the screen clears, ready to accept input of the next field. Each field is numbered automatically by Desktop Database.

When you have added all the fields needed for the PHOTO database, select the Save button to save all the entries in the PHOTO.DBF file. The field names, sizes, and types for the PHOTO database are summarized in Table 10.1.

After you save the fields, the dialog box is replaced by the form file, which displays an empty record. A line of dots corresponding to the size of the field is displayed opposite each field name. This is a useful guide when you start entering the data for the database, since it shows the maximum length for each field. The default F (false) is shown opposite the logical field SUB_STATUS.

The other options on the Field Editor screen are

- Next selects the next field, if there is one.

- Delete deletes the selected field.

- Previous selects the previous field, if there is one.

If you want to use the Autodialer to dial phone numbers from the database, make sure that you position the phone number field before any other fields likely to contain groups of numbers. If you put the zip code before the phone number, the Autodialer will try to dial the zip code.

Table 10.1: Field Names, Types, and Sizes for the PHOTO Database

FIELD NAME	FIELD TYPE	FIELD SIZE
FIRST_NAME	Character	10
LAST_NAME	Character	20
ADDRESS	Character	50
CITY	Character	25
STATE	Character	2
ZIP	Character	10
SUB_STATUS	Logical	1

- Cancel cancels the database creation and exits Desktop Database without saving the database.

Now you should be ready to enter the subscriber data into the database, one record at a time. For your convenience, these data are summarized in Table 10.2.

To keep things simple, there are only seven subscribers in this example. Ideally, a real photographic newsletter would have many more subscribers.

Type in the data for the first field on Don Hegbert and press Enter. If you make a mistake, just use the Backspace key to remove it and then retype the information. Table 10.3 shows the other keys you can use to edit your entries. When you have entered all the information on Don, press F8 or choose the Add New Record option from the Edit pull-down menu to add the next new record. Continue adding records until you have entered the data for all seven subscribers.

Several shortcut function keys are available on the message line as you enter this data. Use F8 to add another record to the database. You use the other function keys to move around in the data. F6 loads and displays the next record if there is one, and F5 loads and displays the previous record. Use F4 to go from the first record to the last

Table 10.2: Example Data from the PHOTO Database

FIRST NAME	LAST NAME	ADDRESS	CITY	STATE	ZIP	SUB_STATUS
Don	Hegbert	879 Back Lane	Todmorden	MA	07381	F
Jim	Jones	123 Canal Street	Rochdale	MN	09876	T
Al	Smith	475 Gasworks Alley	Cleckheaton	PA	13254	T
Allen	Shute	7788 Bradford Road	Macclesfield	IA	50312	F
Pete	Pedersen	4 Northern Way	Huddersfield	MA	71542	F
Sue	Susan	673A Hightofts Road	Giggleswick	CA	95819	T
Abe	Riley	Mill Lane	Golcar	CA	96678	T

Table 10.3: Editing Keys in Desktop Database

KEY	FUNCTION
Backspace	Deletes character to left of cursor.
Enter	Ends a field entry.
Tab	Moves to the next field.
Shift-Tab	Moves to the previous field.
Alt-*number*	Inserts a character from the extended ASCII character set. Press and hold the Alt key and then enter the decimal code for the ASCII character you want.
Left arrow (←)	Moves cursor left one character.
Right arrow (→)	Moves cursor right one character.
Ctrl-←	Moves cursor left one word.
Ctrl-→	Moves cursor right one word.
Home	Moves to the beginning of the line.
End	Moves to the end of the line.
Up arrow (↑)	Moves cursor up one line.
Down arrow (↓)	Moves cursor down one line.
PgUp	Moves text up one window.
PgDn	Moves text down one window.
Ctrl-PgUp	Scrolls display up one line without moving cursor.
Ctrl-PgDn	Scrolls display down one line without moving cursor.
Home Home	Moves to the beginning of the window.
End End	Moves to the end of the window.
Ctrl-Home	Moves to the beginning of the form.
Ctrl-End	Moves to the end of the form.

record. The F7 shortcut key provides direct access to the search facilities in Desktop Database (discussed in full later in this chapter).

EDITING EXISTING RECORDS

As subscribers to the newsletter change their addresses or as you add and remove subscribers, you will need to edit or update the information in the database. To edit an existing record, first locate and display the record on the screen using the shortcut function keys shown on the message line: First/Last Record, Next Record, or Previous Record. Alternatively, you can use the Goto Record option from the Search pull-down menu to go directly to a record. The number of the record being displayed is always shown at the top of the main Desktop Database screen. With Goto Record, you access the record by number. Once you have located the right record, move to the field you want to change and type in the new information.

You edit the database in overstrike rather than insert mode—that is, the characters you type replace the previous entry. If you want to edit in insert mode, press the Insert key on your keyboard. This way, existing text will be pushed to the right as you insert text in front of it. When you have finished editing the data, press the Enter key to add the new information to the field. The data is automatically updated and saved and the cursor moves to the next field.

To add a new subscriber, you must add a new record to the database. Select the Edit pull-down menu and choose Add New Record, or use the F8 function key. The screen shows an empty record at the end of the database, ready to accept your input. Enter the new subscriber information and the new record is added to the database when you press Enter after the last field. The new record may be added at any point in the database.

To delete a record from the database, select the Edit pull-down menu and choose Delete Record. Delete Record does not immediately erase the record. Instead, the record is marked for deletion and is deleted the next time you pack the database, which permanently deletes marked records from the database. Until you pack the database, the records are still in the database and you can use the Undelete Records option in the Edit menu to bring them back into view.

Use the Pack Database option when you want to remove records from the database permanently. As your database grows, you may approach the maximum record limit. If you have a large number of deleted records, you can pack the database to recover space.

At times, you may not want all the records in the database to be viewable. You can hide records from view. A hidden record is still part of the database but will not be displayed or printed and cannot be deleted. To hide a record, choose Hide Current Record from the Edit pull-down menu. The record displayed on the screen is hidden and the next record is displayed.

To restore any hidden records, use the Select All Records option from the Edit menu. All previously hidden records will be restored to view.

You can change the name of any field but you cannot change its size or type. Nor can you add new fields to the database.

If you want to look at all the fields in many records at the same time and you are using Version 6.0, select the Browse mode from the File pull-down menu. All the fields in each record in your database are displayed on the same line on your screen. A check mark appears next to Browse in the menu to show that it is selected. Choose Browse again to return to the single record display. All Database functions including editing and printing are available in Browse mode. Figure 10.2 shows the PHOTO database displayed in Browse mode.

With a large database, some fields will run off the right side of the screen. To see these fields, use the Tab key to move across the screen, and Shift-Tab to move back again. If you are using a mouse, just click on the scroll bars to move horizontally or vertically.

If you print your database while you are in Browse mode, the field names are printed across the top of each page followed by the data in the records, one on each line of the printout.

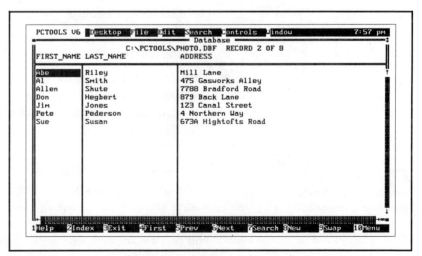

Figure 10.2: The PHOTO database shown in Browse mode

Finally, you may decide to change the name of one or more of the fields in your database. To do this, choose Edit Field Names from the Edit menu. This brings up the Field Editor that you used to create the fields when you first created the database. Enter the new field name and select Save to record the changes into the .DBF file. Remember that you can only change the field name; you cannot change its size or type or add new fields to the database. Editing the field name takes care of the changes to the .DBF file. However, since the field now has a new name you must also use Notepads to make a corresponding change to the form file.

TRANSFERRING AND APPENDING RECORDS

You may want to create a new database that contains a specific group of records in an existing database. One way to do this is to reenter all the data into the new database by hand. A better way is to use the Transfer function from the File pull-down menu to do it automatically. Transfer allows you to move records from one database to another. To transfer a group of records from the original database to the destination database, follow these steps:

> Version 6.0 contains two new Database features for transferring and appending records. These commands are not found in PC Tools 5.5.

1. Start Desktop Database, and open the database that contains the records you want to transfer.

2. Choose the records you want to transfer with Select Record or Hide Current Record from the Edit pull-down menu.

3. Choose Transfer from the File pull-down menu. This opens the Transfer dialog box. Enter the name of the destination database you want to move the selected records into. This database must already exist, as Transfer cannot create a database.

> If the original database contains fields not found in the destination database, they will not be transferred.

If the destination database contains a field that does not exist in the original database, the Field Defaults dialog box opens asking you to enter a default value for this field. Type in the value you want to be used for this field, or leave it empty if you don't want anything in the field.

4. When you have confirmed the last default entry, the transfer is made. The records are sorted according to the order in the Sort Database selection in the Edit pull-down menu.

The Append command from the File pull-down menu allows you to add all the records in a database to the current database. For example, if you buy a mailing list from a photography magazine, you can add it to your newsletter mailing list with the Append command. To join two databases together, follow these steps:

1. Start Desktop Database and load the file containing the database you want to add records to.

2. Choose Append from the File pull-down menu. This opens the Append dialog box. Enter the name of the database you want to append to your original database and choose the SELECT button.

   If your original database contains fields not found in the database you are appending, the Field Defaults dialog box opens so you can enter a value for that field.

3. When you have confirmed the last entry, the new database is appended to your original database. The new records are sorted according to the order in the Sort Database selection in the Edit pull-down menu.

If the database you are appending contains a field that your original database does not, it is ignored and not appended.

You now know how to select a set of records in a database and transfer them to another database, and also how to join two databases together. In the next section you will learn about sorting and searching in your database.

SORTING AND SEARCHING

You can use the Desktop Database ability to reorganize your data using a particular field. For example, if you have a bulk mailing permit, the post office accepts mail sorted into groups of zip codes. With Database, you can easily arrange your mailing labels into zip code order.

To sort into zip code order the address list for the photography newsletter, select Sort Database from the Edit pull-down menu. You will see the screen shown in Figure 10.3. The screen displays the name of the current sort field and contains several options:

- Next selects the next field as the sort field.

- Prev selects the previous field as the sort field.

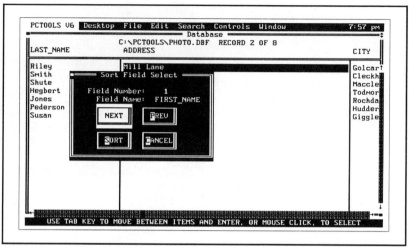

Figure 10.3: Sort Field Select screen

- Sort performs the sort using the selected field.

- Cancel cancels the sort and closes the dialog box.

As the database records are sorted into the requested order, a message asks you to wait for the sort to finish. Desktop Database can only sort on one field at a time, using the first 12 characters in the field.

You can also use Desktop Database, for example, to determine how many subscribers you have in the 95819 zip code area. Choose Select Record from the Edit pull-down menu; you will see the screen shown in Figure 10.4. You can specify up to eight fields for the selection process. Record selection is made as follows:

- Field Name. Enter the name of the field or fields you want to use as the basis for the selection.

- Field Criteria. Enter the actual criteria you want to use as the match for the field you selected.

You must type in any underscores. Spaces are not allowed in select or search field names.

To find out how many subscribers you have in the 95819 zip code area, enter ZIP as the Field Name and 95819 as the Field Criteria. Choose Select to search the database for all the fields that match the Field Criteria. All the records that do not match the criteria are hidden. You can now use this information to make a direct mailing to this specific zip code.

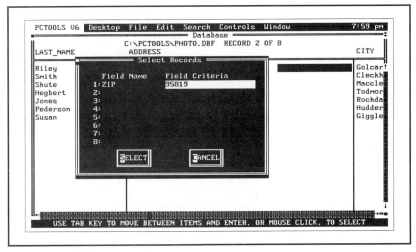

Figure 10.4: Select Records screen

Since you can specify up to eight field names as selectors, your selection criteria can grow quite complex. Additionally, Desktop Database allows you to enter wildcards that match with any character in that position. For example, you can use the question mark character to represent a single character. For instance, a zip code of 9581? matches all zip codes from 95810 to 95819. You can also specify ranges. For example, you can enter

95000..95999

to match all zip codes from 95000 to 95999. Similarly, you can select zip codes greater than a particular number by entering

95..

which selects all zip codes whose first two digits are greater than or equal to 95. Also, you can select zip codes that are smaller than a particular number by entering

..19

which selects all zip codes with the first two digits less than or equal to 19.

You can also specify a range with letters, which is useful for names, cities, and states. To select all last names from A to C, enter

A..C

To make the selection more specific, enter

A..CAT

which matches fields from A to CAT. In these range selections, the case of the letters is ignored.

You can view the data in your database in other ways by using the commands in the Search pull-down menu, which is shown in Figure 10.5. These commands search through your database, looking for particular text:

- Find text in all fields searches all the fields in your database for the search string.

- Find text in sort field restricts the search to the field that was last used as a sort field. In many situations, Find Text in Sort Field will be faster since the search is restricted to the sort field. Use the Sort Database command in the Edit pull-down menu to change to different sort criteria.

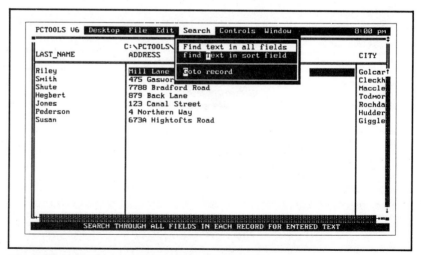

Figure 10.5: Search menu selections

Both options—Find Text in All Fields and Final Text in Sort Field—have the following options:

- Search All Records starts the search at the beginning of the database and includes all records, even hidden and deleted records.

- Search Selected Records searches for the specified text in previously selected records.

- Search from Current Record begins the search with the current record.

You now know how to sort your database by any given field and how to search for specific occurrences of text.

The next section shows how to make address labels from your subscriber database. Then you will learn how to make form letters for people whose subscriptions have not been renewed.

CUSTOMIZING THE FORM FILE

The form file used for data entry into your database must contain an entry for each of the fields in your database. The same is not true of other form files, however. You can make as many form files as you want for your database. Each can present a different view of your data, and some can take advantage of just a portion of the data. When you design the form, remember to enclose the field names in square brackets. For example, to insert a person's name into the form file, type

[FIRST_NAME] [LAST_NAME]

When you load your database, the information from the database replaces the field names in the form. An example will make this clearer.

You can make a form file in a Notepad that will produce address labels for your newsletter, assuming that your printer can handle adhesive address labels. First, open a Notepad and create a new file called ADDRESS.FOR. Then enter the field names into the Notepad, as shown in Figure 10.6. In this example, the only field from

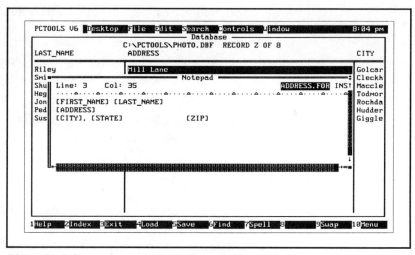

Figure 10.6: Enter the field names for an address label

the database that you are not using is the subscription status field, SUB_STATUS. Be sure that the entries in the Notepad file match the field names in the database exactly; otherwise, no records will be retrieved from the database and nothing will appear on the form.

You must provide any punctuation required in the address, including underscores, because the Desktop Database only provides the data itself and the rest must come from the Notepad. Leave a space between [FIRST_NAME] and [LAST_NAME] in the Notepad so that the names are written with a space between them. Also add a comma and a space between [CITY] and [STATE]. The position of the abbreviation for the state on this line of the label will change depending on the length of the city name, as you can see here:

Todmorden, MA

Rochdale, MN

Cleckheaton, PA

Macclesfield, IA

Huddersfield, MA

Giggleswick, CA

Golcar, CA

To see this, choose Select Load Form from the File menu and ADDRESS.FOR from the Load Form menu. If you want to fix the position of a field, place a tab where you want the field. Open ADDRESS.FOR in the Notepad and use a tab with the [ZIP] field. The example addresses just shown will look like this, with the zip codes aligned:

Todmorden, MA	07381
Rochdale, MN	09876
Cleckheaton, PA	13254
Macclesfield, IA	50312
Huddersfield, MA	71542
Giggleswick, CA	95819
Golcar, CA	96678

As you leave the Notepad where you made the change, the results are reflected on the screen.

To print the database onto small adhesive address labels, you must first define the size of the page with Page Layout from the Controls pull-down menu. Set the page size to a length suitable for your labels (say six lines), set the left margin to an appropriate setting, and set the top and bottom margins to zero. Finally, choose the Save Settings option in Notepads so that you can use these settings when you print the data in your database the next time you use Desktop.

To print the address labels, return to Desktop Database, load the PHOTO.DBF database file, and then choose Load Form from the File pull-down menu. Load the form file you have just created in the Notepad, ADDRESS.FOR, and you will see the record on the screen displayed in the new format. Now just load the labels into your printer and choose one of the following print options from the File menu:

- Print Selected Records prints only the records previously selected.

- Print Current Record prints only the current record.

- Print Field Names prints the field names used in the database.

You are then asked to choose which device you want to print to from the usual Desktop list of device names:

- LPT1, LPT2, or LPT3 selects one of the parallel printer ports.
- COM1 or COM2 selects one of the serial printer ports.
- Disk File formats the file for printing and saves it in a disk file with the same file name and the extension .PRT.

Make the appropriate choices from the lists and start printing the address labels.

If you want to enter more data into your database or edit existing data, first make sure that you reload the original form file from the Notepad. This lets you see all the data in your database as well as all the field names. The form file used for data entry has the same name as the database file but has the .FOR file name extension.

PRINTING FORM LETTERS

In the next example, you will write a form letter reminding subscribers that you have not received their dues. Then you will merge the names and addresses from the database into the form letter based on the setting of the logical field SUB_STATUS.

First, prepare the text of the letter in a Notepad, as shown in Figure 10.7, and call the file LETTER.FOR.

The letter is a short reminder that $17 is due for subscription renewal. Remember to use square brackets around the database field names and to add any necessary punctuation between fields. Now open Desktop Database and load the form file LETTER.FOR. Your screen will look like Figure 10.8, where the data from the database replaces the field names.

Next, divide the database into two parts based on SUB_STATUS. Choose Select Records from the Edit pull-down menu and enter SUB_STATUS into Field Name and F (for false) into Field Criteria. In other words, use Sort Records to find all subscribers who have not renewed their subscriptions by finding records in which the subscription status field is set to false. In the example database, this sort option isolates three subscribers—Pedersen, Shute, and Hegbert—who will all receive copies of the form letter. Next, choose Print from

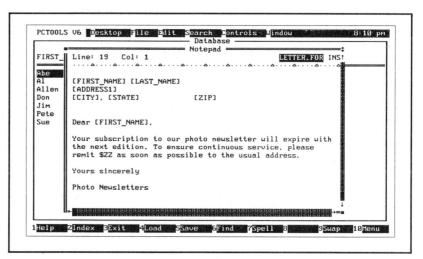

Figure 10.7: Form letter prepared in a Notepad

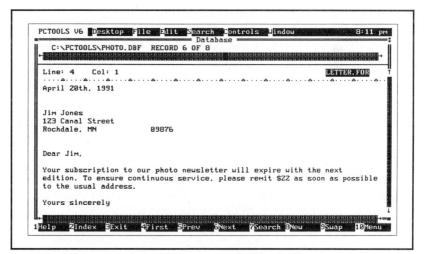

Figure 10.8: LETTER.FOR loaded into the Desktop Database

the File menu and run out the three form letters. Change the page layout information since the reminder letter is going out on regular computer paper with 66 lines per page.

You might also load the ADDRESS.FOR form file into Desktop Database and run off a set of address labels for these subscribers. Both form files LETTER.FOR and ADDRESS.FOR use data from the same PHOTO.DBF database file, but they use different fields from the database and present the data in very different ways.

USING THE AUTODIALER

The Autodialer is a flexible Desktop Database feature that enables you to make automatic phone calls using a Hayes-compatible modem. You can make the call based on a Desktop Database record or according to a macro run by the Appointment Scheduler. If you have difficulty remembering certain telephone numbers, use the Autodialer. This way, you just have to remember the name of the person or company you want to call.

The Autodialer scans all the fields in a Desktop Database record for groups of numbers. It recognizes any group of three or more numbers as a valid telephone number, and can accept spaces, dashes, parentheses, or hyphens as delimiters within the number, as well as an x to signify an extension number.

If you want to use the Autodialer to dial a number from your Desktop Database, remember that the phone number field must be the first field in the record to contain numbers. If you place the address or zip code field before the phone number field, the Autodialer may begin to dial those numbers rather than the phone number you wanted.

AUTODIALER PHONE NUMBERS

The Autodialer recognizes the following characters when used in a phone number:

- P indicates that you are using a pulse phone.

- T indicates that you are using a Touch-Tone phone.

- , (comma) inserts a two-second delay in dialing. This is very useful when dialing out through a switchboard. Use groups of commas to make longer delays.

- *, #, or x can be used to set off telephone extension numbers.

- W waits for a dial tone before continuing. This is useful with long distance services.

- K delays dialing until after you press another key from the keyboard. This is useful with certain on-line services such as banking where you select the service you want directly from your phone. When you use K in a number, the Autodial Pause dialog box appears with two more options:

  Resume Dialing dials the remaining digits in the phone number.

  Cancel cancels the call.

- @ waits for a dial tone.

MODEM SETTINGS FOR THE AUTODIALER

Before you can use Autodial, you must set the transmission parameters for your computer and modem. Once set, these parameters remain constant until you change your modem. Choose the Configure Autodial selection from the Controls pull-down menu in Desktop Database to enter your modem parameters. The data entry screen is shown in Figure 10.9.

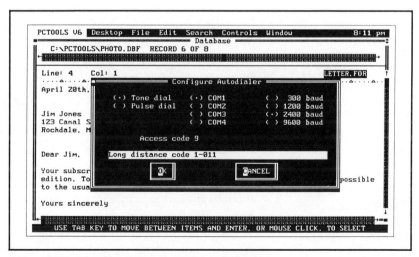

Figure 10.9: The Configure Autodialer screen

Select from the following configuration settings:

- Tone dial selects the dialing procedure for Touch-Tone phones. If you use a T in the phone number, it will override this setting.

- Pulse dial selects the dialing procedure for pulse phones. If you use a P in the phone number, it will override this setting.

- COM Port Number indicates the number of the serial port your modem is attached to.

- Set the Baud Rate according to the speed of your modem.

In PC Tools 6.0 two additional Autodialer settings are available.

The Access and Long Distance Codes are applied for all numbers you dial.

- Access code indicates the number you dial to get an outside line. The Autodialer recognizes this number and dials it for you. If you are working from home you probably don't need an Access code and so you can leave this entry blank.

- Long distance code indicates the long distance code you use when making long distance calls. The Autodialer dials this number after dialing the Access Code.

The settings made when you configure the Autodialer are saved in the DESKTOP.CFG file. Once you have chosen your settings from the screen, select OK to set these new transmission parameters.

AUTOMATIC DIALING WITH THE AUTODIALER

To make a call using the Autodialer, select the Desktop Database record containing the phone number you want to call and choose Autodial from the Controls pull-down menu. The Database scans the record to find the phone number. When the number is found, the modem dials the number and a message is displayed, as shown in Figure 10.10.

You must wait for the number to ring before disconnecting the modem. You cannot cancel an Autodial before the modem has dialed the number.

When the modem finishes dialing the number and the number is ringing, pick up the phone handset and disconnect from the modem by pressing Escape or the Enter key, or click on the Disconnect Modem button with the mouse. You can now talk to the person on

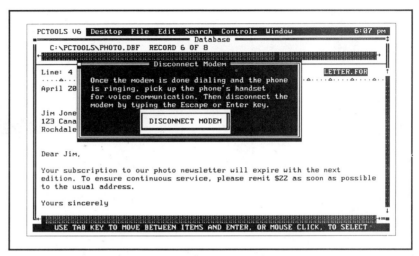

Figure 10.10: The Autodialer message

the other end of the line; you have used the Autodialer to complete your first automatic call.

When you are happy with the selections that you have made in the Desktop Database Controls and Window menus, you can save them for future use with the Save Setup option in the Controls pull-down menu.

USING THE AUTODIALER WITH DESKTOP IN MEMORY-RESIDENT MODE

When you use Desktop in memory-resident mode, you can hotkey directly into the Autodialer by pressing Ctrl-O. Now you can automatically dial any number appearing anywhere on the screen with the Autodialer, provided that you have previously configured the Autodialer modem settings. The phone number can be in any Desktop document, in a word processed document, in a spreadsheet, or even at the DOS prompt.

Enter the number to dial at the DOS prompt and use the Ctrl-O hotkey to access the Autodialer directly. Do not press the Enter key after typing the number, since a number is not a valid DOS command. The Autodialer opens a dialog box, as shown in Figure 10.11.

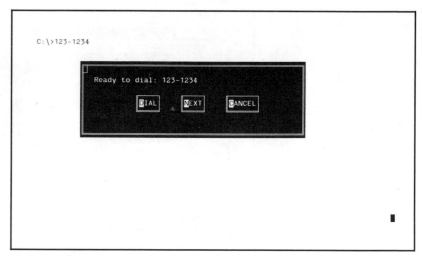

Figure 10.11: Autodialer dialog box

At the top of the dialog box you can see the number that the Auto-dialer is about to dial. If you choose the DIAL button, the Autodialer will use the modem to dial the number. Use the NEXT button if the number is not the one you want, and the Autodialer will search for another number. If there is no number on the screen, the Autodialer beeps. Finally, you can use the CANCEL button to return to your application program. Remember that you must let the modem dial the number and the number must be ringing before you can disconnect the modem and pick up the telephone handset.

SUMMARY

This chapter explained the built-in Desktop Database. You learned how to create a database from scratch, including how to define the database structure. You also learned how to edit existing records, how to search through and sort the database, and how to create and print customized form letters. Finally, the chapter described how to use the Autodialer.

11

Telecommunications
Made Easy

11

A modem is a device that allows computers to communicate over telephone lines. The modem generates an audible tone over which it superimposes the digital information from your computer.

Telecommunications allows you to connect your computer via a modem (or a null-modem cable) to almost any other computer capable of serial communications. You can transfer files between computers of the same or different types, or between micros and mainframes. If you have a Hayes-compatible modem, you can dial bulletin boards or the large commercial services like CompuServe. Telecommunications supports up to four serial ports on your computer at baud rates from 300 to 9600 baud. You can transfer files in ASCII or with the popular XMODEM error-correcting protocol. You can automate your sessions by using script files and you can use Telecommunications in background mode while you continue to work with your main application in the foreground.

If you have a fax card in your computer, you can send files directly from your computer to a facsimile machine or to another computer with a fax card. You can tell Telecommunications who you want to send the fax to, and also at what time of day you want it to be sent. Telecommunications supports the following fax cards:

- Connection CoProcessor from Intel Corporation

- SpectraFax from the SpectraFax Corporation

If you work on a Novell network, and have a fax card installed in one of the computers on the net, you can use it to send faxes, as well as use the fax log to check which files have been sent or received.

When you choose Telecommunications from the main Desktop menu, you will see a small submenu containing three entries:

- Modem Telecommunications

- Send a Fax

- Check the Fax Log

PC Tools 5.5 does not support fax cards. Selecting Telecommunications will put you into Modem Telecommunications.

I will describe how to use Modem Telecommunications first, and then deal with facsimile transmissions later in this chapter.

When you choose Modem Telecommunications from the main Telecommunications submenu, you will see a screen like the one in Figure 11.1. The default phone directory file, PHONE.TEL, is displayed on the screen.

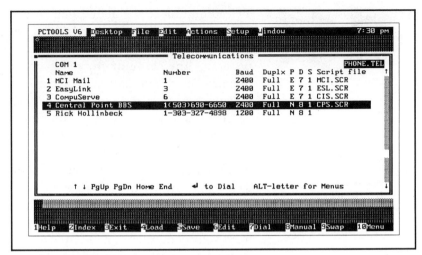

Figure 11.1: Telecommunications main display

The main parts of the display are as follows:

- COM port. The number of the communications port your modem is connected to is shown in the upper-left corner of the display.

- File name. The name of the current phone directory file is shown in the upper-right corner of the screen.

- Name. The name of the person or service to dial is shown in the far left column.

- Number. The telephone number of the person or service to dial. If you leave this item blank, Telecommunications will ask you for the number when you try to dial out.

- Baud. The baud rate for this entry, usually 1200, 2400, or 9600.

- Duplex. Defines whether the computers communicate as full duplex or half duplex.

- P D S. Defines the character format for communications, and is an abbreviation for Parity, Data bits, and Stop bits. See Appendix C for a full discussion of these items.

- Script file. In the far left column is the name of the script file you want to use with this entry. Script files automate certain repetitive functions like entering your log-on sequence.

WORKING WITH PHONE DIRECTORY FILES

When you start Modem Telecommunications from the Telecommunications submenu, the program loads the default phone directory file called PHONE.TEL. This file contains the names, numbers, and communications settings for the people and for the services you want to use. The file can hold up to 200 entries. If you need more entries, you can create an additional file.

Instead of one large file, you might have several smaller files: one for work numbers, another for home numbers, and perhaps a third for bulletin board numbers. Use the file name extension .TEL for Telecommunications configuration files.

To load a different phone directory file, select the Load option in the File pull-down menu and enter the file name and extension into the File Load dialog box. Telecommunications loads the file, replacing the original phone directory information with information from the new file.

To change the information for a particular entry in the phone directory file, place the highlighted bar over the entry you want to change and select Edit Entry (F6) from the Edit pull-down menu. Click on the entry if you use a mouse. You will see the screen shown in Figure 11.2. You can change any of the entries on this screen.

Data communications can sometimes be difficult if the number you call is routed through an office PBX system. If a dedicated data line goes directly into the building, use it instead.

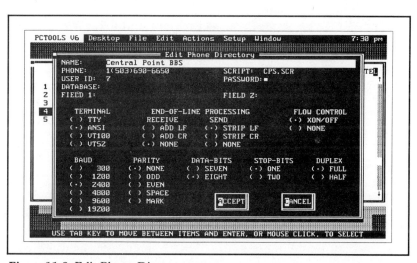

Figure 11.2: Edit Phone Directory screen

- NAME is the name of the person, company, or bulletin board. This entry can be as long as 50 characters.

- PHONE is the phone number that goes with the name you entered in the NAME line. This entry can be up to 50 characters, the first 25 of which you can see in this screen. You can enter the phone number as you would normally because Telecommunications ignores spaces, dashes, and parentheses. (This is not true in most telecommunications software, which require pure number entries.)

- SCRIPT is the file name of the script file you want to use with this entry. Script files are described in detail later in this chapter.

- USER ID. Your user ID identifies you when you log on to an on-line service like CompuServe or MCI Mail. The user ID can be up to 25 characters long, and can contain upper- and lowercase letters.

USER ID, PASSWORD, DATABASE, and FIELD 2 are new to the Edit Phone Directory screen in PC Tools 6.0.

- PASSWORD. This is a code known only to you that you enter when you access a bulletin board or other on-line service. The password can be up to 21 characters long, and again it can contain upper- or lowercase letters.

- DATABASE. Enter the path and file name of a database file that has fields containing phone numbers or fax numbers.

- FIELD 1 and FIELD 2. These are the fields in the database that actually contain the phone numbers or fax numbers you want to use.

- TERMINAL. Telecommunications can emulate several different terminal types found on mainframe computers. Choose from TTY (teletype, often used by computer services and bulletin boards), ANSI (American National Standards Institute), VT100, or VT52. If you are going to log on to a remote computer that requires terminal emulation, choose from one of these terminal types.

- END-OF-LINE PROCESSING, RECEIVE selects the characters used to mark the end of a line when receiving an ASCII file transfer or when you press the Enter key during an on-line communications session.

ADD LF. If the remote computer only uses a carriage return character to mark the end of a line, use ADD LF to add a line feed during the incoming transmission, giving a carriage return/line feed pair at the end of each line.

ADD CR. If the remote computer only uses a line feed character to mark the end of a line, use ADD CR to add a carriage return during the incoming transmission, giving a carriage return/line feed pair at the end of each line.

NONE. The remote computer expects a carriage return/line feed pair at the end of each line. Since this is what Telecommunications uses, there is no need to modify the data.

- END-OF-LINE PROCESSING, SEND selects the characters used to mark the end of the line in an outgoing ASCII file transfer.

    STRIP LF. The receiving computer only expects a carriage return at the end of the line, so Telecommunications removes all line feed characters.

    STRIP CR. The receiving computer only expects a line feed character at the end of the line, so Telecommunications removes all carriage return characters. The Enter key sends a line feed character.

    NONE. The receiving computer expects a carriage return/line feed at the end of each line. Since this is what Telecommunications sends, there is no need to modify the data. The Enter key sends a carriage return.

- FLOW CONTROL is used to prevent information from being transmitted faster than it can be received, which can sometimes result in data loss.

    XON/XOFF. With XON/XOFF flow control, the receiving computer sends an XOFF to temporarily stop the sending computer from transmitting. This gives the receiving computer time to catch up. When the receiving computer is ready to start again it sends an XON, and the transmission resumes. Most systems use

XON/XOFF, but the settings must match on both computers.

NONE. With Flow Control set to NONE, there is no flow control of any kind.

Mismatched baud rates are often the cause of communications errors.

- BAUD is the speed of data transmission, usually the number of bits per second (bps). The higher the number, the faster the data transmission rate. Baud rates of up to 9600 bps are supported in all versions of DOS, and baud rates of up to 19,200 bps are supported in DOS 3.3 or later. This setting must match the setting on the remote computer. Modern modems can often operate at several different rates. They detect the speed of the transmission and change their baud rate setting as required to match.

- PARITY is used to help achieve correct communications. The sending computer adds an extra bit to the end of each data byte transmitted. You can set parity to NONE, ODD, EVEN, MARK, or SPACE. NONE indicates that no parity checking will be done; indeed, there is no parity bit. ODD indicates that the sum of all the 1 bits in the byte plus the parity bit must be odd. That is, if the total is already odd, the parity bit is set to 0. If it is even, the parity bit must be set to 1. In EVEN parity, if the sum of the 1 bits is even the parity bit must be set to 0. If it is odd, the parity bit must be 1. ODD and EVEN are the most common settings. In MARK parity, the parity bit is always set to 1 and is used as the eighth bit. In SPACE parity, it is set to 0 and used as the eighth bit. The parity setting must match the parity setting on the remote computer for successful communications.

- DATA-BITS. Select SEVEN or EIGHT data bits for the number of bits in the transmitted character. Most systems use 8 data bits.

- STOP-BITS. Select ONE or TWO stop bits to indicate the end of the transmitted character. Most systems use 1 stop bit.

- DUPLEX. Select FULL for simultaneous two-way transmission or HALF for transmission of data one way at a time.

If you cannot see what you are typing, change to half duplex, or if you see two of every character, change to full. Most systems use full duplex.

If you want to create a new entry in your phone directory, choose Create New Entry from the Edit pull-down menu. The screen used for creating new entries is identical to the one just described for editing entries. Choose the ACCEPT button to save the information you have just entered or edited.

To remove an entry from your phone directory, place the highlighted bar over the entry and select Remove Entry from the Edit pull-down menu. Be careful with this selection because it does not ask you to confirm your choice and deletes the entry immediately.

When you have finished entering your data, you can save your work by clicking on the close box or selecting the ACCEPT button. If you want to keep your entries in a different file, select Save from the File pull-down menu and specify the new file name.

SETTING MODEM PARAMETERS

See Appendix C for more on modem setup parameters.

The final step you must complete before transferring files is to check the modem parameters in Modem Setup from the Setup pull-down menu. When you select Modem Setup, you will see the screen shown in Figure 11.3.

Figure 11.3 shows the modem initialization sequence for 300/1200, 1200/4800, and 9600/19,200 baud modems. The Hayes-compatible modem command set is described in Appendix C. You can also consult your modem reference manual for more information.

Hayes-compatible modems issue the string

CONNECT

to inform your communications program that a connection has been established. If your modem is not Hayes-compatible, you may need to use a different connect string; enter the correct string into the Connect string text box. Consult your modem manual for more information.

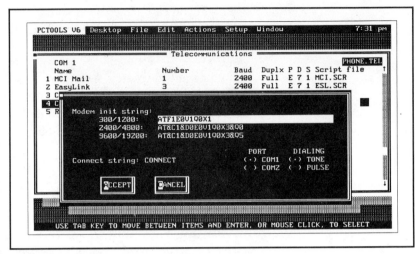

Figure 11.3: Modem Setup screen

The remaining items on this screen are PORT and DIALING.

- PORT. This is the serial port you want to use with your modem.

- DIALING. Select either Touch-Tone or pulse dialing.

DIALING A NUMBER WITH TELECOMMUNICATIONS

Before you can send or receive files, you must know how to use Telecommunications to dial a number. The simplest way is to position the highlighted bar over the entry you want to dial and press the Enter key. If you use a mouse, just double click on the entry to dial the number. If your modem can make dialing and ringing sounds, you will hear the number being dialed. If the entry you selected did not contain a phone number, a dialog box opens for you to input the number to dial.

Alternatively, you can dial the number by selecting the Manual option from the Actions pull-down menu. Use this method if you want to use a different phone number without changing the other parameters you have already selected.

Make sure that your modem is attached and turned on before dialing a number, especially if your modem is external.

The options available in the Actions pull-down menu change when you are connected to a remote computer.

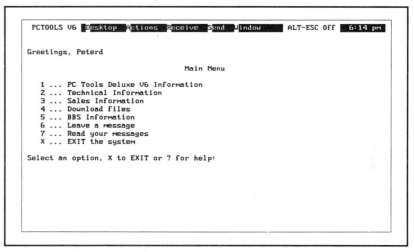

Figure 11.4: Telecommunications on-line window

In either case, once a link has been established to the remote computer the screen displays the on-line window shown in Figure 11.4.

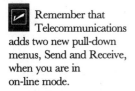 Remember that Telecommunications adds two new pull-down menus, Send and Receive, when you are in on-line mode.

Note that several other things also change in the on-line mode. The options available in the Actions pull-down menu change, and two new menus appear: Send and Receive. The communications settings in use are shown on the right side of the message line. In Figure 11.4, the baud rate is 1200, parity is set to none, there are 8 data bits and 1 stop bit. Duplex is set to FULL and the computer is in ANSI terminal-emulation mode. The shortcut function keys are shown on the next line. When sending a file, choose F4 to send the file in ASCII or F5 to send it using the XMODEM protocol. When receiving a file, choose F6 to receive it in ASCII or F7 to receive it in XMODEM. Use F8 to hang up the phone at the end of your session. If you press the Escape key from the on-line window, you will return to the Telecommunications window inside Desktop. Sometimes you need to send an escape character to the remote computer. To do this, press Shift and Escape simultaneously.

HOW TO RECEIVE FILES

Using Telecommunications, you can receive (download) files from a remote computer. For example, you can download a program file from a service like CompuServe or from your local PC user group's

Remember that
Telecommunications
changes the entries in the
Actions pull-down menu
when you are on-line.

When you register
with a computer
service, you will receive
an explanation of how to
use the service.

If you use the
ASCII file-transfer
protocol, you must use
the End Transfer option
in the Actions menu to let
Telecommunications
know that the transfer is
complete.

bulletin board. You can even download files from the office computer to work on at home. To receive a file, select the communications protocol that the computers in the transfer must both use. Telecommunications offers two choices:

- The ASCII file-transfer protocol does not check for errors caused by interference on the phone lines. However, you can use it to transfer text files if you have no other choice. If the remote computer supports the XMODEM protocol, use it rather than ASCII.

- XMODEM is probably the most well-known microcomputer file-transfer protocol. It checks for and corrects transmission errors, so you should use it for all file transfers even though it is slower than ASCII.

To transfer a file, call the number and establish a connection. The remote computer will ask you questions or give you a menu from which to select. Answer the questions or enter the commands. Make your choice of protocol from the options in the Receive pull-down menu. You can also use the Receive shortcut function keys on the keyboard: F6 for ASCII or F7 for XMODEM. Be sure that your choice matches the protocol in use on the remote computer. The Save dialog box appears. Enter the file name you want to use with the file and select the Save button to capture the file. If you selected the ASCII protocol, the contents of the file are shown on your screen as the transfer takes place. If you chose XMODEM as the file-transfer protocol, the Receive box opens, as shown in Figure 11.5.

The Receive box contains the following information

- Protocol is the name of the communications protocol in use.
- Filename is the name you gave to the file.
- Elapsed time is the time the transfer has taken so far.
- Bytes transferred is the number of bytes transferred so far.
- Error checking is the error-checking method. XMODEM uses a checksum or a cyclical redundancy check to detect communications errors during the transmission. Telecommunications automatically selects the method that the remote computer is using.

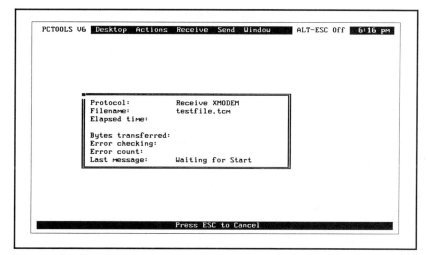

Figure 11.5: The Receive box

- Error count is the number of errors encountered on a block of data. If there are more than ten errors on one block of data, Telecommunications stops the file transfer. If this happens, or if you see a large number of errors, try dialing the number at a different time of day or even at night to get a ''cleaner'' phone line for the transfer.

- Last message shows the text of the last message.

You can use End Transfer from the Actions pull-down menu to stop a transfer if you are seeing too many errors or decide that you do not want the file you are downloading. Finally, you should log off the remote computer before choosing the Hangup Phone selection (F8) from the Actions pull-down menu to end your session.

HOW TO SEND FILES

Sending files is easy once you know how to use Telecommunications to receive files. Sending a file to a remote computer is often called uploading, and you must dial, establish the link, and communicate with the remote computer, as you did to receive files. Again, the choice of file-transfer protocol is important: the selection must be the same on both computers. This time, make your choice from the Send pull-down menu or use F4 for ASCII or F5 for XMODEM. Next, the File Load dialog box appears. Select the file you want to send and choose Load to send the file to the remote computer. A Send box, identical to the Receive box, appears on the screen to show the progress of the transfer.

COMMUNICATING BETWEEN YOUR PC AND AN APPLE MACINTOSH

PC Tools is available for the Apple Macintosh as well as for the PC.

You can use Telecommunications to transfer files from your PC to an Apple Macintosh, either via a modem as already described or by using a null-modem cable. (A *null-modem cable* is a short length of serial cable with the appropriate connectors on either end to take the place of the two modems.) Several of the individual wires inside this special cable are changed from their normal pin connections in order to convince the two computers to communicate with each other properly. The two computers must be physically close together for this to work because if the cable is too long, voltage levels may fall below the accepted levels.

TRANSFERRING ENCRYPTED FILES

If you have encrypted a file using PC Secure, you can send the file to another computer running PC Tools for decryption. Remember that you cannot decrypt the file without knowing the key, so you must arrange a safe method for transferring the key before the file can be used. You should not give your key to the recipient over an ordinary phone line. Consider using a trusted courier or a scrambled phone to transfer the key. Once you have solved this part of the problem, the transfer proceeds like any other file transfer.

1. Use PC Secure to encrypt the file using the agreed key. All of the PC Secure parameters are stored in a special location in the file header.

2. Dial the number, establish a link, and transfer the file using the XMODEM file-transfer protocol.

3. End the Telecommunications program and decrypt the file using the prearranged key. PC Secure uses information

encoded in the file header to recreate all the original program settings.

You can now use the file at both ends of the communications link.

USING AUTOMATIC COMMUNICATIONS

If you use on-line services regularly, you will enter the same information—your log-on information, for example—each time you link up with a bulletin board. You can automate this process if you use a script file containing this information. Script files use a simple programming language to start or stop a file transfer, to send comments to the remote computer, or to hang up the phone.

HOW TO WRITE A SCRIPT FILE

Telecommunications script files are text files, so you create them in a Notepad in Desktop. Several script files, all with the .SCR extension, are provided on the PC Tools Deluxe distribution disks. The commands in a script file perform actions after you have made a connection with the other computer. Script files are not case sensitive. The commands you can use in your script files are as follows:

- * indicates that what follows will be treated as comments and will not be used as commands. It is a good idea to include comments in your script files to remind you what the script is doing.

- :*label*. A label is the destination for the GOTO command. Only the first eight characters in a label are used.

The BACKTALK and DATABASE commands are not available in PC Tools Desktop 5.5.

- BACKTALK tells Telecommunications to run the rest of the script file in background mode. This allows your computer to run an application program while continuing with the communications in the background. BACKTALK must be loaded memory-resident before this command will work. Remember, if you do run your script file in the background, commands that require input like INPUT or DATABASE will be ignored if they occur after the BACKTALK command. Be sure that they occur before BACKTALK in your script file.

- DATABASE combined with one or two of the variables (v1, v2, or v3) allows you to send the contents of up to two fields in a PC Tools Desktop database. The DATABASE command is used with the Database and Field 1 and Field 2 entries in the Edit Phone Directory screen. The contents of Field 1 are stored in v1, and the contents of Field 2 are stored in v2; if you only want to send one field, just use one of the variables.

- DOWNLOAD *protocol variable* or "*file name*" initiates a file transfer from the remote computer. The remote computer must be ready to send the file using the ASCII or XMODEM protocol.

- ECHO displays the characters received from the remote computer during a WAITFOR command. The first ECHO command in a script file turns on the display for all subsequent WAITFOR commands. This command is very useful if you are troubleshooting a new script file, but you should remove it once the script is working correctly.

- GOTO *label* transfers execution of the script to the commands following the label. Only the first eight characters of a label are used.

- HANGUP hangs up the phone.

- IF *variable* = < >CONTAINS "*string*" provides the means for a conditional branch in your script when used with the GOTO command. The contents of *variable* are evaluated against "*string*" and may be equal to (=) or not equal to (< >) "*string*". Also, you can use CONTAINS to see if the variable contains "*string*".

- INPUT *variable* allows entry of up to 80 characters from the keyboard, ending in carriage return or line feed, into one of the three named variables: v1, v2, or v3.

- PAUSE *number* pauses the script for a specified number of seconds. PAUSE without a number pauses the script file for one second.

- PRINT *variable* or *"string"* prints the contents of a named variable or the contents of the string on the screen. Use a semicolon to suppress the return character at the end of the line for continuous printing. Does not send anything to your printer.

- RECEIVE *variable* captures up to 80 characters from the remote computer into one of the three named variables: v1, v2, or v3. The character string is terminated by the first carriage return or line feed sent by the remote computer. If nothing is received within ten seconds, the variable is set to null.

The USER ID and PASSWORD options are not available in PC Tools Desktop 5.5.

- SEND *variable* or *"string"* or USER ID or PASSWORD allows you to send a message to the remote computer. The message can be contained in one of the named variables or in a *"string"*. Use a ^ to indicate a control character (as in ^M for carriage return) and use a semicolon at the end of the sequence to suppress the return character at the end of the message.

  The SEND command has two other parameters, USER ID and PASSWORD. You can add USER ID or PASSWORD to your script file rather than having to put your bulletin board user identification or password into a variable or quote string. These entries are used with the corresponding entries of USER ID and PASSWORD in the Edit Phone Directory screen, and they are used when the script file is processed.

- TRON turns on trace mode, which displays the commands in your script file in the message line at the bottom of the screen. When the command is displayed, the script stops executing until you press the spacebar. This is especially useful if you are troubleshooting a new script. However, you should remove the command once the script is running correctly. Press the Escape key to terminate the script.

- TROFF turns trace mode off and execution of the script file continues normally.

- UPLOAD *protocol variable* or *"file name"* initiates a file upload from your computer to the remote computer, using either the ASCII or XMODEM protocol. The remote system must be ready to receive the file.

- VARIABLES allows you to use up to three named variables in your script: v1, v2, and v3.
- WAITFOR "*string*" compares the characters coming from the remote computer with the characters in "*string.*" Script execution is paused until a match for "*string*" is found. The case of all characters is ignored.

To use a script file in your communications, first make sure that it is in the PC Tools directory. Otherwise, Desktop will not be able to find the file and you will see the message

Unable to open file

Then choose the phone number entry you want to use the script file with and select Edit Entry from the Edit pull-down menu. The Edit Phone Directory screen opens and you can add the name (and extension) of the script file into the SCRIPT FILE box at the top of the screen, as shown in Figure 11.6.

Make sure that all the other information on the screen is correct and select the ACCEPT button to confirm your entries. To run the script, call the number. When the remote computer answers, the script will run. Figure 11.7 shows a simple script file for logging on to an imaginary system. You can make script files that are much more complex

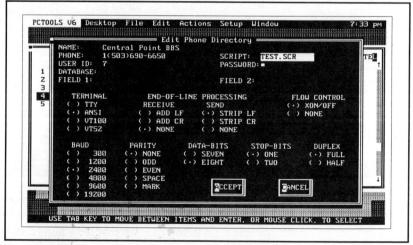

Figure 11.6: The SCRIPT FILE box in the Edit Phone Directory screen

```
*comment: My user id number is 123456
*comment: My password is UNKNOWN
*
WAITFOR "ENTER USER ID"
SEND    "123456"
WAITFOR "ENTER PASSWORD"
SEND    "UNKNOWN"
*
*4 APRIL 1991
```

Figure 11.7: A script file for logging on to an imaginary bulletin board

than this simple example. Be careful, however, not to make them too long in case something unexpected happens, such as the sysop changing the start-up procedures.

USING BACKGROUND TELECOMMUNICATIONS

Do not use the COM port selected for background communications from your foreground application program when a file transfer is taking place. You will interrupt the transfer.

If you use Desktop in memory-resident mode, you can make file transfers in background mode. In other words, you can start a file transfer, load an application like Lotus 1-2-3, and work with Lotus while the transfer continues unattended in the background.

If you selected background communications when you installed PC Tools with PC Setup, you are already configured for background communications. If you did not, add the line

BACKTALK /2

Backtalk occupies approximately 64K of memory.

to your AUTOEXEC.BAT file before the line that loads Desktop. This designates COM2 as the serial port for background communications. You can choose any COM port (COM1 to COM4).

Computer-to-computer links are prone to interruption, and if you use background mode you will not see any of the communications error

If your phone has call waiting, you should disable it by dialing *70 before starting an important communications session. Otherwise, your session may be interrupted by the noise that signals an incoming call.

messages that may be generated during a transfer. To overcome this problem, Telecommunications creates a file called TRANSFER.LOG when you start a background file transfer using the XMODEM protocol. Any communications errors reported during the transfer are stored in this file. The first line of TRANSFER.LOG contains the name of the file you sent or received and the last line contains the word "COMPLETED" if the transfer was successful. If the transfer was not successful, the last line contains an error message such as "Time Out," "CRC Error," or "Too Many Retries."

Telecommunications creates a TRANSFER.LOG file each time you start a background session using the XMODEM protocol, so you can delete the file if you want to save space once the file transfer has been successfully completed. You can look at TRANSFER.LOG with Notepads.

Start the file transfer as you would start a normal transfer, and then press Alt-B to invoke the background mode. Once you are in background mode, you can return to the main Desktop menu or go back to your foreground application program to continue working. A blinking B is displayed in the upper-right corner of your screen as the transfer proceeds. When the transfer is complete, you will hear a beep. If you are using a script file, however, you must stay in Telecommunications until the script file has executed.

USING YOUR FAX CARD WITH TELECOMMUNICATIONS

PC Tools Desktop 5.5 does not support fax cards.

For a more detailed discussion of how fax cards and fax machines work, see Appendix C.

A fax card is an add-in board that allows you to perform many of the functions of a facsimile machine right from your computer. You can send files to any remote facsimile machine, or to other computers that have fax cards installed. If you work on a Novell network and you have a fax board, anyone on the network can send or receive faxes.

There are two entries from the Telecommunications menu concerned with fax transmissions:

- Send a Fax allows you to send faxes, and to add, edit, or delete fax entries.

- Check the Fax Log allows you to look at the fax transmission you have set up, and review fax statistics.

You can review information on up to 99 faxes; you can even keep them and reuse them at a later time.

SENDING A FAX

From the Telecommunications menu, select Send a Fax, and you will see the Send FAX Directory screen shown in Figure 11.8.

Before seeing how the Send FAX Directory screen works, you should take a moment to look at the selections in the Configure pull-down menu. This is where you set up some of the basic information for your fax transmissions. The Configure pull-down menu contains FAX Drive, Page Length, Cover Page, Time Format, and Sent From.

- FAX Drive. Enter the path and directory name you specified when you installed Fax Telecommunications with PC Setup. See Chapter 1 for a complete description of PC Setup.

- Page Length. Enter the length of the page you want to use in inches. Normally this will be set to 11 inches to represent a normal 8½ by 11 inch page. If you will be sending very short faxes, you might consider making this entry smaller to save paper.

- Cover Page. Select Cover Page if you plan to use a cover page for your faxes. If you don't want to use a cover page,

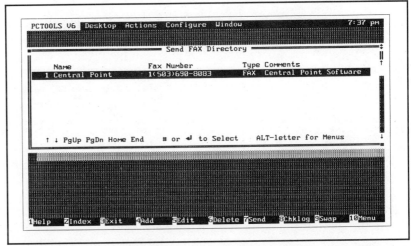

Figure 11.8: The Send FAX Directory screen from the Telecommunications menu

you can set this entry to No. You can include a personal or company logo at the top of your cover page if you wish. The logo is kept in a file called PCTOOLS.PCX. You can customize this file with a graphics editor like PC Paintbrush, Corel DRAW!, or any other graphics program that supports the .PCX file format. If you make a new logo file, be sure to name it PCTOOLS.PCX and copy it into your PC Tools directory; otherwise it will never be used.

- Time Format. Select the time format you prefer from the 24 hour clock or the AM/PM setting.

- Sent From. Enter your name or company name here, and the information will be used whenever you create a new fax.

Now that you have configured your system, we can look at how to send a fax. The Send FAX Directory screen is divided into four columns of Name, Fax Number, Type, and Comments:

- Name. This is the name of the person or organization you want to send the fax to. The entry also has a sequence number that allows up to 99 entries.

- Fax Number. This is the number of the phone line to the fax machine.

- Type. You can send a file in fax or in nonfax mode.

  In fax mode, the file you send is translated into a form that all group 3 fax machines and fax cards can understand.

  If you send the file in nonfax mode, the file is not converted, but is sent in much the same way a normal modem would send the file. You can send any type of file by this method, including .EXE files, but the files can only be received by another fax card supported by PC Tools. They cannot be received by stand-alone group 3 fax machines.

- Comments. You can add information about a given fax entry.

To add a fax, select Add a New Entry from the Actions pull-down menu (F4), or click on Add in the message bar, and the FAX Details dialog box opens as shown in Figure 11.9.

You can edit or change all the entries in this screen:

- Date. Enter the date you want your fax sent. Usually today's date appears in this box, but if you want to delay sending your fax until a future date, enter the new date into this box.

- Time. Enter the time you want your fax sent. The current time usually appears in this box, but you can use a later time if you want to delay the fax transmission until the rates are cheaper.

    If you enter the current date and time into these two boxes, the fax will be sent immediately.

- From. Enter your name or company name here. If you have already entered this information into the Sent From dialog box in the Configure pull-down menu, there is no need to enter the information again.

- To. Enter the name of the person or company you are sending the fax to.

- FAX Number. Enter the phone number of the fax machine you are transmitting your fax to.

Figure 11.9: The FAX Details dialog box

- Comments. You can add descriptive comments to the fax entry to remind you of the fax contents.

- Normal Resolution. Select this setting if you are sending a text fax. This mode is faster than the Fine Resolution mode, so it is cheaper too.

- Fine Resolution. Use this setting if you want your fax to appear especially sharp, or if you are sending a fax containing graphics. This mode is slower than the Normal Resolution mode because more information is actually sent. Thus it is slightly more expensive.

- FAX Board to FAX Board. Use this mode if you want to send binary files to another computer with a PC Tools-supported fax card installed. You cannot send binary files to a facsimile machine. In this mode you are actually using the high-speed modem on the fax card to transfer your files from your computer to another identical modem in the receiving computer.

- Select Files and Send. Use this choice to open the Files to Select dialog box, and choose the files you want to send as faxes. Use the Add button to add these files to the list of files to be sent. When you have finished your selection, use the Send button to actually send the files you selected. You can use the Cancel or Delete buttons at any time to stop selecting files or to remove a file you have added to the list.

  A new dialog box opens to ask if you want to include a cover page with your fax, or send it without one. If you requested a cover page in the Configure pull-down menu, you can select the OK button to open a Notepad, and create your cover page. Choose No Cover Page This Time to send the fax without a cover page. The same Notepad file, COVER.TXT, is always used for the fax cover page. The file contents are automatically erased each time you send a fax. Press the Escape key or click on the close box to save the cover page, and a dialog box appears telling you that your fax has been sent. Select the OK button, and you return to the Send FAX Directory screen where you will see the fax you just created.

- Create a new File and Send. Use this selection if you want to open a new fax file now using a Notepad. The Create A File dialog box opens for you to enter a new file name, and then a Notepad opens for you to type in the text of your fax. The next screen you see is the Cover Page Selection dialog box, and the procedure for creating the cover page is exactly as I just described above. Finally, when you return to the Send FAX Directory screen, you will see all your faxes listed in order.

CHANGING AND DELETING FAX ENTRIES

After you have set up and sent a fax, you can use several of the selections in the Actions pull-down menu to edit the fax control information.

For example, if you want to send the same fax to several different people, just select the appropriate entry from the Send FAX Directory screen, enter the new fax number into the FAX Details dialog box, and select or click on Send.

Alternatively, if you have to send a fax to the same number on a regular basis, say a report you have to send to the same fax number each week, use the Edit Entry selection from the Actions pull-down menu, leave the FAX Details intact, change the list of selected files to include this week's report, and send the fax.

To delete an entry from the Send FAX Directory when you have no further use for it, select the entry you want to delete with the arrow keys or with the mouse, and use Delete the Current Entry (F6) from the Actions pull-down menu, or click on Delete on the message bar. Use these options carefully, as they delete the fax entry immediately, without asking for your confirmation first.

CHECKING THE FAX LOG

When you want to check on the status of a fax, you can select the fax log from two different menus:

- Select Check Fax Log from the Actions pull-down menu in the Send FAX Directory screen.

- Select Check the Fax Log directly from the initial Telecommunications submenu.

Either way, you will see the screen shown in Figure 11.10. If there are no entries in the fax queue, you will see the message

Nothing in FAX Queue.

as the only entry on this screen.

This screen is divided into eight columns, as follows:

- To shows the name of the person the fax was sent to. This entry includes an index number listed on the left for each transmission.

- From indicates the name of the person sending the fax.

- Date and Time show the date and time the fax was sent, or if the date and time are in the future, the date and time that the fax will be sent.

- Status shows you the state of each fax transmission. Status can be one of the following:

  Aborted shows that you canceled the transmission.

  Dialing indicates that the number is being dialed now.

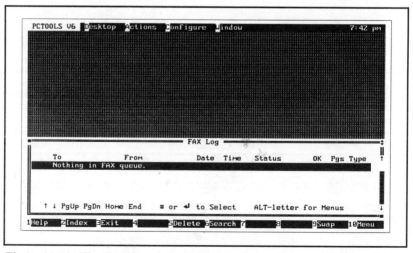

Figure 11.10: The Fax Log screen showing all the fax transmissions in the fax queue

Sending shows that the fax is being sent now.

Sent indicates that the fax has been successfully sent.

Receiving indicates that a fax is being received now.

Received shows that the fax has been successfully received.

An error message shows that the fax card is experiencing problems sending or receiving a fax, or that there are problems with the phone line. Errors include *Non CCP* which indicates that one of the fax cards in the link is not compatible with PC Tools Telecommunications. *Bad Phone, Drop* points to the phone line as the problem.

- OK displays YES if there were no problems with the fax, and NO if problems were encountered.

- Pages tells you how many pages the fax was, including the cover page.

- Type tells you if you are using fax mode or nonfax mode for file transmission.

To delete an entry from the fax log, select Delete the Selected Entry (F5) from the Actions pull-down menu, or click on Delete on the message line. Delete removes the entries without asking for confirmation, so be careful when you use this option.

To search for a Fax Log entry, choose Search (F6) from the Actions pull-down menu, enter the text you want to search for, and select OK. All the fax log entries that meet the search criteria are shown on the screen.

The FAX Drive selection is available both here from the Actions pull-down menu in Check the Fax Log, and from the Configure pull-down menu in Send a Fax.

You can also set the rate at which the fax log is updated with the AutoUpdate option in the Configure pull-down menu. Enter a number in seconds to specify the time period between updates of the fax log.

Send a Fax and Check the Fax Log combined with Modem Telecommunications should meet all your communications needs at home or at the office, all right from your computer.

USING THE UTILITIES

The Utilities selection from the Desktop main menu offers four menu items: Hotkey Selection, ASCII Table, System Menu/ Window Colors, and Unload PC Tools Desktop. This chapter describes only the ASCII Table. See Chapter 12 for a complete discussion of the other menu selections.

LOOKING AT THE ASCII TABLE

For more information on the ASCII character set, see Appendix B.

Desktop contains a complete extended ASCII character set table available from the Utilities menu. Select ASCII Table from the Utilities pull-down menu to see the screen shown in Figure 11.11.

The ASCII characters are displayed on the screen in two columns of 16 characters each. The ASCII character is shown in the center of each column. The hexadecimal code for the character is shown on the left and the decimal code is shown on the right. If you look at the first 32 ASCII characters, this display changes. The left side of the display still shows the hex codes, the characters, and the decimal codes, but the right side now shows the control codes for these characters and their abbreviated names.

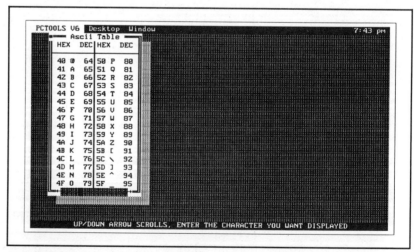

Figure 11.11: A portion of the ASCII table from the Utilities menu

You can move through the table with ↑ and ↓, the PgUp and PgDn keys, and Home or End. You can also click on the scroll bar with the mouse.

To find a character in the table, just type the character from the keyboard and the display will change to include that character. If you type an E, the display changes to include the E character. If you enter a control character such as Ctrl-J, the display moves to the first part of the ASCII table, which includes all the control characters. You can access the extended ASCII character set (that part of the table higher than decimal 128) if you hold down the Alt key and type a number between decimal 128 and decimal 255 from the ten-key pad. This is especially useful when you are working with the PC line-drawing set or other special symbols.

SUMMARY

In this chapter, you learned how to use the Telecommunications module to upload and download files using your modem, and how to send faxes from your PC. You also learned how PCs and Apple Macintoshes can communicate, how to transfer encrypted files, and how to use automatic communications. In addition, the chapter explained how you can accomplish file transfers in background mode.

12

Tailoring
PC Tools
to Your Needs

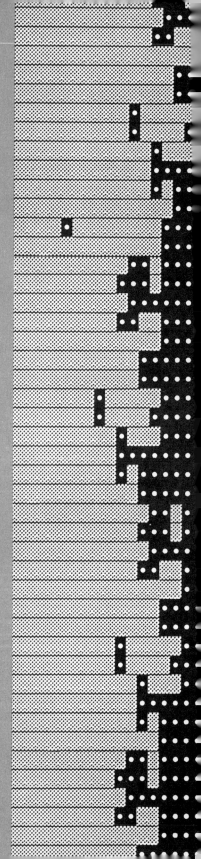

12

You can run the PC Tools Deluxe programs in many different ways. This chapter details some of the settings you can use to tailor PC Shell and Desktop to your individual needs. As there are several significant differences between PC Shell 5.5 and PC Shell 6.0, I will deal with each version separately.

USING PC SHELL 5.5

See Appendix A for a complete list of the optional parameters used in PC Tools Deluxe programs.

You can use many shortcut keys in PC Shell 5.5. The function keys F1 (Help), F2 (Help Index), and F3 (Escape) are the same in all PC Tools programs that use function keys. The other function keys are dedicated to particular uses in each program. In PC Shell, the function keys are used as indicated in Table 12.1.

Table 12.1: Function Keys in PC Shell

FUNCTION KEY	SCREEN ABBREVIATION	MENU SELECTION
F1	Help	No equivalent
F2	Index	No equivalent
F3	Exit	Exit PC Shell
F4	Unsel	Reset selected files
F5	Info	Disk info
F6	Display	File display options
F7	Switch	Active list switch
F8	List	File list filter
F9	Select	File select filter
F10	Menu	No equivalent

Use these function keys to gain access to part of PC Shell quickly. For example, to see information about the current drive, press F5 and the Disk Info window will open over the main PC Shell screen.

There are several additional shortcut keys that you can use:

Alt	Menu selection
Ins	Two-list display
Del	One-list display
Tab	Tree/file list switch
Alt-spacebar	Size/move windows
C	Copy file
M	Move file
t	Delete file
R	Rename file
V	View file
x	Hex edit
i	File search
P	Print file
L	Find file
E	File Edit
U	Undelete
Z	Zoom

You can use these shortcut keys to invoke their menu equivalents without using the menus. If there is no shortcut key for the item you need, you must use the usual menu selection method.

ONE- OR TWO-SCREEN LISTS

If you want to open another set of windows on another drive, just press Ctrl-*n*, where *n* is the letter of the drive you want to read.

PC Shell usually displays one tree and file list at a time and you use the Tab key to move from one to the other. If you use a mouse, you can just click in the other window to make it active. You can also use the Tree/File Switch selection in the Options pull-down menu to do the same thing.

You can make PC Shell display a second set of tree and file lists. Being able to use two lists is especially handy when you are moving or copying files from one directory to another because you can see both directories at the same time. To see the second tree and file list, select Two-List Display from the Options pull-down menu or press the Ins key.

Once two sets of windows are shown on the screen, choose the new directory you want to display or select a different drive letter from the drive command line if you want to work with two different disks. Figure 12.1 shows a two-window display of a root directory and the \PCTOOLS directory on the same hard disk.

You can have several windows open at the same time, but only one window can be the active window. The active window has a double-line border while the other windows have single-line borders. If you are using a two-list display, the Active List Switch selection from the Options pull-down menu allows you to change to the other set of windows. You can also press F7 to switch between windows. If the windows are stacked, the active window is on top.

To save the two-list display settings, select Save Configuration from the Options pull-down menu. To resume using just one window, select One List Display from the Options pull-down menu or press the Del key.

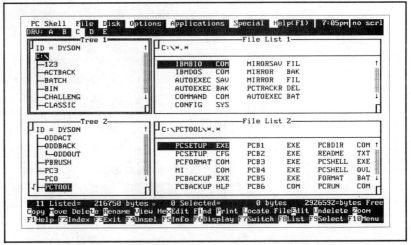

Figure 12.1: Two-window display showing root and \PCTOOLS directories

If you are on a Novell network and view the files on the network server with PC Shell, you will only see files for which you have at least read privileges. This cuts down considerably on the number of files you will see.

The current display options are shown on the right side of the dialog box under Current Options and Current Order.

LISTING FILES   Once you have decided between one- or two-list displays, you can use several of the other items in the Options pull-down menu to specify which files you want to display. Normally, PC Shell lists files in alphabetical order by file name. If you want to change this order or display different information, use the File Display Options selection from the Options pull-down menu or press F6. The Display Options dialog box opens, as shown in Figure 12.2.

Make your choice from the following display options:

- Size displays the file size.

- Date displays the file date.

- Time displays the file creation time.

- Attribute displays the file's attributes: read-only, system, hidden, and archive.

- Number of Clust displays the number of clusters in the file.

Then choose from the list of sort options:

- Name sorts the files by name.

- Ext sorts the files by extension.

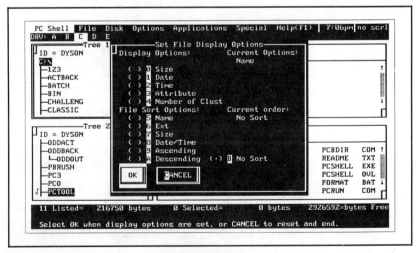

Figure 12.2: The Display Options dialog box

- Size sorts the files by size.
- Date/Time sorts the files according to the date and time.

When you have chosen a sort option, select the type of sort you want from this list:

- Ascending lists the files in ascending order using the options that you have chosen. File names and extensions are listed in alphabetical order, size from small to large, and date/time from oldest to newest first by date and then by time.

- Descending lists the files in descending order using the options that you have chosen. The order described under ascending is reversed.

- No Sort lists the files as they occur. This is the default setting.

I often sort the files on my hard disk according to file name extension in order to group files according to function. This option also sorts by file name within each extension.

Use File List Filter from the Options pull-down menu or press F8 to choose which files are displayed in the File List. The File List Filter dialog box opens, as shown in Figure 12.3.

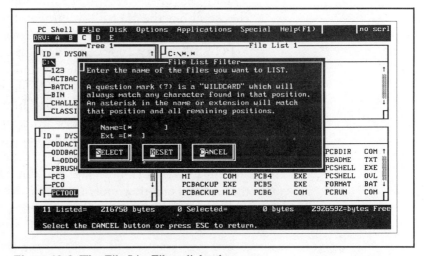

Figure 12.3: The File List Filter dialog box

Enter the file name and extension of the files you wish to list. You can use the DOS wildcard character ? to replace a single character or * to replace all subsequent characters in a file name or extension. For example, *.* lists all the files in the directory and *.EXE lists only those files with the .EXE extension. Choose the SELECT button to show only the file names or extensions that match your criteria in the files list.

Once you have used a filter to screen out certain files, you must remove the filter to look at all the files in that directory. Choose the RESET button to reset the Name and Extension boxes to *.* and thus show all files in the directory.

SELECTING FILES   To select an individual file in PC Shell, position the highlighted bar over the file and press Enter. If you use a mouse, you can click on the file you want. You can also use the File Select Filter to select groups of files that have common names or extensions. The File Select Filter works just like the File List Filter but the files that match the settings in the File Select Filter are selected and appear in bold on the screen. Choose the SELECT button when you have made a choice; you are returned to the main PC Shell display, which shows the files selected by your criteria.

To reset (or unselect) these files after you have selected them, choose either the RESET button in the File Select Filter, Reset Selected Files from the Options pull-down menu, or F4.

PC Shell saves a copy of the directory structure on a disk in a file called PCSHELLn.TRE, where n stands for the letter of the drive. When you change drives in PC Shell, this file is read if it exists on the drive or is created if it does not exist. In this way, just the file is read rather than the whole directory structure. This usually saves time and results in a faster drive changeover. If you know that the directory structure has changed but those changes are not reflected in the current PCSHELL.TRE file, you can use Re-Read the Tree from the Options pull-down menu to force PC Shell to recreate this file.

Table 12.2 lists several file names that are used in special ways in PC Shell.

Table 12.2: Special File Names in PC Shell

FILE NAME	APPLICATION
COMPRESS.CFG	Compress configuration file
COMPRESS.HLP	Compress help file
MIRROR.BAK	Previous version of the Mirror file
MIRROR.FIL	Current copy of a disk's system area made by Mirror
MIRRORSAV.FIL	Mirror data file
PARTNSAV.FIL	Copy of a hard disk's partition table
PCSECURE.CFG	PC Secure configuration file
PCSECURE.HLP	PC Secure help file
PCSHELL.CFG	PC Shell configuration file
PCSHELL.HLP	PC Shell help file
PCSHELL.IMG	Copy of video RAM when PC Shell is run in memory-resident mode
PCSHELL.IMX	Program image when PC Shell is run in shell mode
PCSHELL.THM	Swapped memory area when PC Shell is run in memory-resident mode
PCSHELLn.TRE	Tree list file used when PC Shell is used in shell mode
PCTRACKR.DEL	Delete tracking data file
README.TXT	PC Tools Deluxe information file

SETTING SCREEN COLORS AND SIZING THE WINDOWS

To change the screen colors used by PC Shell, select Screen Colors from the Options pull-down menu. The Color Change dialog box opens, as shown in Figure 12.4.

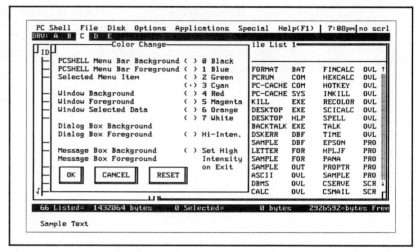

Figure 12.4: The Color Change dialog box

Your choices are as follows:

- PCSHELL Menu Bar Background changes the color of the menu bar you use to select items from the menu.

- PCSHELL Menu Bar Foreground changes the color of the text of the menu item.

- Selected Menu Item changes the color of the highlighted characters used to select menu items.

- Window Background changes the background color of the tree and file lists.

- Window Foreground changes the color of the text in the tree and file lists.

- Window Selected Data changes the color that indicates selected files in the file list window, or of data in the Data Base Viewer.

- Dialog Box Background changes the background color of all dialog boxes.

- Dialog Box Foreground changes the color of the text in all dialog boxes.

- Message Box Background changes the background color of all message boxes.

- Message Box Foreground changes the color of the message text in all message boxes.

- Set High Intensity on Exit. Suppose you hotkey into PC Shell from an application using a high-intensity background on a CGA or EGA monitor. When you leave PC Shell, the characters on your screen may be in blink mode. Use this selection to set the high intensity again when you exit from PC Shell.

For each setting, choose your color from Black, Blue, Green, Cyan, Red, Magenta, Orange, or White. Remember that some color combinations are hard on your eyes. Research has shown that white text on a blue background is easy on your eyes. Use Save Configuration in the Options pull-down menu to save your color settings for use in future PC Shell sessions.

The Size/Move Window selection in the Options pull-down menu allows you to resize or move the tree or file list windows using the arrow keys on the keyboard. First, make the window you want to change the active window. Then choose Size/Move Window from the Options pull-down menu. The Window Control dialog box offers S for size or M for move. Use ↑ and ↓ with ← and → to resize a window. The upper-left corner of the window cannot be moved, so use the arrow keys to reposition the lower-right corner.

If you are using a mouse, click on the size box in the lower-right corner of the active window and then drag the window to resize it. Again, only the lower-right corner moves; the upper-left corner remains anchored.

When you move a window, its position changes but its size stays the same. Use the arrow keys to move the window and press the Enter key when you have positioned the window in the correct place. If you're using a mouse, position it on the top bar of the window border (but not on the close box), hold down the mouse button, and drag the window to its new location.

You can also use the Zoom selection from the Options menu to expand the window to fill the screen in a single operation. With a mouse, just click on Zoom. If you select Zoom a second time, the window returns to its original size.

RUNNING APPLICATIONS
PROGRAMS FROM INSIDE PC SHELL

With PC Shell in shell mode, you can run certain applications programs from the Applications pull-down menu. If you used PC Setup to install PC Tools, several programs will already be shown in the list. Figure 12.5 shows the Applications menu on my computer.

The PC Tools programs—Compress Disk, PCBACKUP, Mirror, PC Format, and PC Secure—are already installed in the menu, as is the WordStar word processor. If you have Lotus or dBASE on your system, PC Setup will also install them automatically.

To run one of the programs in the Applications pull-down menu, select the name of the program you want to run and press Enter. If you use a mouse, just click on the name and the program will run. When you have finished using the program, you return directly to PC Shell.

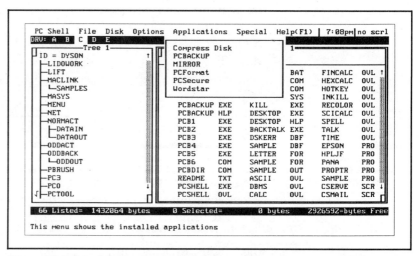

Figure 12.5: My Applications pull-down menu

MODIFYING THE APPLICATIONS LIST

To add a program to the Applications menu, select Modify Applications List from the Options pull-down menu. You will see the screen shown in Figure 12.6.

Select NEW to create a new entry. The other selections on the screen are

- NEXT displays information on the next program in the list.

- PREV displays information on the previous program in the list.

- EDIT allows you to edit the information shown on the current Modify Applications List screen.

- DEL allows you to delete the current program from the applications list.

- SAVE saves your applications list.

- EXIT returns you to the main PC Shell display.

Now that you have chosen NEW, you can enter the information on the program into the Modify Applications List screen as follows:

- Title: Enter the text you want to appear in the Applications pull-down menu. To highlight a character in the name, use

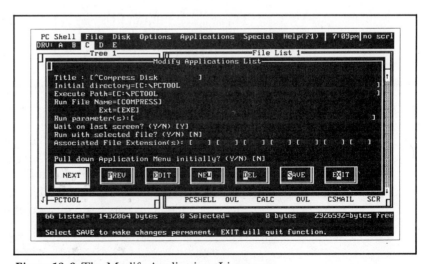

Figure 12.6: The Modify Applications List screen

the ^ character before the letter. You can then use this letter to start the program. Very often this title will be different from the name of the file used to start the program. For example, you can enter WordPerfect into this box as the title of the program, but you must enter WP into the Run File Name box and EXE into the Ext box, because the name of the file used to start WordPerfect is WP.EXE.

- Initial directory: Enter the path for the program and its associated overlay and data files.

- Execute Path: Enter the path for the program.

- Run File Name: Enter the exact file name used to start the program.

- Ext: Enter the file name extension of the file used to start the program.

- Run parameter(s): Enter any additional run-time parameters you want to use with the program.

- Wait on last screen? (Y/N): Pauses the computer screen before returning you to PC Shell if you enter Y for yes.

- Run with selected file? (Y/N): Answer yes (Y) to this question if you want the program to run using a file you previously selected in the main PC Shell screen. For example, if you are using WordPerfect and you set this option to yes, selecting a file in the main PC Shell display causes Word-Perfect to open the file so that you can start working with it immediately.

- Associated File Extension(s): Enter any file extensions always associated with the program. For example, imagine that you have Lotus 1-2-3 installed in the applications list and you enter the file name extensions of .WK1 or .WKS into these Associated File Extension boxes. When you select a file with one of these extensions from the main PC Shell display, Lotus 1-2-3 is loaded automatically and the file you selected is opened as the data file. This can save you a great deal of time.

- Pull down Application Menu initially? (Y/N): If you set this option to yes (Y), the Applications menu stays pulled down all the time. If you set it to no (N), the menu works like all other PC Shell pull-down menus. This is a global setting and applies to all programs in the applications list.

Select the OK button to accept your entries or the CANCEL button to return to the main PC Shell screen. The new program appears in the Applications pull-down menu and is ready for use at any time.

Finally, use Save Configuration from the Options pull-down menu to save your new application settings and any other changes you have made to windows or screen colors. All this information is kept in a file called PCSHELL.CFG. If you delete this configuration file, the settings in PC Shell revert to their original default states.

RUNNING A PROGRAM FROM INSIDE PC SHELL

If you want to run a program from inside PC Shell, you can use the Run selection from the File pull-down menu. PC Shell must be running in shell rather than memory-resident mode.

When you select Run from the File pull-down menu, a dialog box asks you for the name of the file to run. You can enter any command-line arguments required into the Run Parameter(s) box. When you have entered everything, select the RUN button to run the program. When you exit from the application program, you automatically return to PC Shell.

The default setting for Quick Run is on.

There is also a selection in the Options pull-down menu called Quick Run. If Quick Run is on, a check mark appears next to its name in the menu. Quick Run is not available if PC Shell is in memory-resident mode. If Quick Run is on, PC Shell does not free up memory before running an application program or the second DOS command-line processor. Memory is only made available when you exit PC Shell. If Quick Run is off (no check mark), memory is freed up before you run the application on the second DOS command-line processor. However, since there is a short pause while information is saved, this option is slower.

PC Shell uses about 200K in shell mode, so if your programs can run in the remaining amount of memory, set Quick Run on to get the maximum speed advantage. However, if you need more memory for an especially large application program or if you want to load a large data file, set Quick Run off to recover more memory. Be prepared for things to run a bit more slowly, however.

Use Run for the occasional application program; it is far better to install your commonly used programs in PC Shell and run them from the Applications pull-down menu.

INVOKING DOS FROM INSIDE PC SHELL

If you use PC Shell in memory-resident mode, the word "unavailable" appears next to the DOS selection in the File pull-down menu.

When you run PC Shell in shell mode, you can use the DOS option in the File pull-down menu to invoke a second DOS command-line processor from inside PC Shell. To do so, choose DOS from the File pull-down menu, or press Shift-F9. You can then execute DOS commands or run other applications programs. When you are ready to return to PC Shell, enter

EXIT

at the DOS prompt.

Do not load any memory-resident programs from this second DOS command-line processor.

If you are using PC Shell in shell mode, the extra selection, Quick Run, appears in the Options pull-down menu. When Quick Run is on, PC Shell does not free any extra memory before running the DOS command-line processor. This allows the DOS command-line processor to load rapidly. However, if you need to free up as much memory as possible, turn off Quick Run in the Options pull-down menu. Now when you choose the DOS option from the File pull-down menu, you will notice a short pause as memory is swapped out before the second command-line processor is run.

USING PC SHELL 6.0

There are several important improvements to the PC Shell user interface in PC Tools 6.0, including configurable user levels and user-defined function keys.

CHOOSING YOUR USER LEVEL

You can choose your user level in PC Shell to be either Beginner, Intermediate, or Advanced user mode. Select the Options pull-down menu, and choose Setup Configuration. This option displays another menu beginning with Change User Level, as shown in Figure 12.7.

When you select this option, the Change User Level dialog box opens, asking you to select your user level. Choose Beginner to have access to basic DOS-type commands for finding and copying files; choose Intermediate if you want more complex functions like deleting and editing files, and sorting directories; and choose Advanced to have access to the entire range of PC Shell's capabilities. The selections available in the File, Disk, and Special pull-down menus change as you change your user level. Applications and Options pull-down menu selections do not change.

DEFINING FUNCTION KEYS AND SHORTCUT KEYS

You can make the function keys perform the commands you use most often in PC Shell 6.0. F1 Help, F3 Exit, and F10 Menu always stay the same; however, you can assign your favorite functions to the other keys. Select Define Function Keys from the Setup Configuration menu, and you will see the Define Function Keys dialog box as shown in Figure 12.8.

Figure 12.7: The Change User Level menu from the Setup Configuration submenu

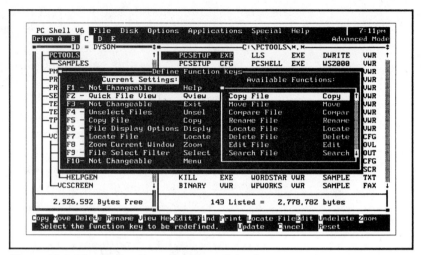

Figure 12.8: The Define Function Keys dialog box

Use ↑ and ↓ to locate the function key you want to use, then press Enter to select it. Use Tab to move to the other side of the display where the available functions are listed, then use the arrow keys or PgUp or PgDn to select the PC Shell command you want to have associated with that key. Press Enter to confirm your choice. When you have made all your selections, press U for Update (shown on the message line at the bottom of the screen) to save your selection and close the dialog box.

The shortcut keys contain commonly used commands from the menus, and they are displayed just above the line of function keys at the bottom of the screen in Advanced user mode. The shortcut keys are:

C	Copy File
M	Move File
t	Delete File
R	Rename File
V	View File
x	Hex Edit
i	Text Search

P   Print File

L   Locate File

E   File Edit

U   Undelete

Z   Zoom

The shortcut keys are turned off in Beginner and Intermediate user modes. When you use PCSETUP to install PC Tools 6.0, the program looks for a PCSHELL.CFG file from PC Tools 5.5. If it finds the file, PCSETUP installs PC Shell 6.0 with the shortcut keys turned on so that it looks like and works like Version 5.5. If you are in Advanced user mode you can turn the shortcut keys on or off with the shortcut keys ON/OFF selection in the Setup Configuration submenu.

ONE- OR TWO-SCREEN LISTS

PC Shell usually displays one tree and one file list at a time, and you use the Tab key or the mouse to move from one to the other. If you need to see a second set of tree and file lists, use Modify Display from the Options pull-down menu, and select Two-List Display. You will see the same result if you press the Insert key on the keyboard.

If you are using a two-list display to copy files from one directory or disk to another, you can use the Active List Switch selection from this same menu to move between the different sets of windows. Remember, the active window always has a double-line border, while the other windows have single-line borders.

You can turn the tree list or the file list parts of the display off completely by using two selections from the Options pull-down menu; click on or select Tree List Window once to turn the tree list off. Choose it again to turn it back on again. You can do the same thing with the File List Window. The status of both these entries is shown at the end of the menu selection line by the word ON or OFF.

You can also turn on the File View window from the Options pull-down menu by clicking on or selecting View Window. If you turn the

View Window on, the tree and file windows are moved over and the File Viewer takes over the left side of the screen.

By using the Default Viewer command in the Setup Configuration menu, you can choose between the Binary File or the Text Viewer. By using the Viewer Cfg. selection in the same menu, you can select between a horizontal or vertical display for the File Viewer.

LISTING FILES Once you have decided the number of tree and file list windows you want to have open, you can use several of the commands from the Options pull-down menu to specify which files you want to display. File Display Options allows you to choose what information is displayed for each file, and File List Filter allows you to choose the actual files themselves. These commands work as I described for PC Tools 5.5 above.

SELECTING FILES Selecting files works just the same in PC Tools 6.0 as it did in 5.5, both when you use the mouse and when you use the keyboard. The File Select Filter is in the Modify Display menu from the Options pull-down menu. To reset your selected files, use the Unselect Files command from this same menu or F4. This command unselects all your selected files.

SETTING SCREEN COLORS
AND SIZING THE WINDOWS

Choose Screen Colors from the Setup Configuration menu from the Options pull-down menu when you want to change the colors PC Shell uses. As well as the selections described above for PC Tools 5.5, there is a new selection in 6.0 for your laptop computer's liquid crystal display. You can also specify a black and white display if you prefer.

Similarly, to change the position or size of one of the windows use the Size/Move Window selection from the Options pull-down menu as described for PC Tools 5.5.

Finally, when you are happy with all your changes and selections in PC Shell, don't forget to use Save Configuration File in the Options pull-down menu so that they will be saved and used the next time you use PC Shell.

RUNNING APPLICATIONS PROGRAMS FROM INSIDE PC SHELL

As PCSETUP installed PC Tools 6.0, the program looked for common applications programs on your system. These programs are installed as selections in the Applications pull-down menu. The PC Tools programs—Compress Disk, PCBACKUP, MIRROR, PCFormat, and PCSecure—are all in the list.

To run one of the programs in the Applications pull-down menu, select the name of the program you want to run and press Enter. If you use a mouse, just click on the name and the program will run. When you have finished using the program, you are returned to PC Shell.

MODIFYING THE APPLICATIONS LIST I described how to modify the applications list in PC Shell 5.5 earlier in this chapter, but the process is slightly different in PC Shell 6.0.

To add an applications program to the Applications menu, select the Applications pull-down menu, and choose or click on Add (F4) on the message line. Note that some of the other function keys now have special functions; Edit (F5), Delete (F6), and Move (F7) are all specific to the Applications menu.

Next, choose the place in the Applications Menu where you want your new entry to appear. You can maintain the alphabetical order of the original list, or you can reorganize the list, placing those applications you use most often at the top of the list so that you can select them quickly. Press Enter when you have decided on the location, and the Applications Editor opens as shown in Figure 12.9.

- Application. Enter the name you want to see in the Applications Menu. Use the ^ character before the letter you want highlighted on the menu. For example, type Word^Star to highlight the letter S. You can start the application by typing S when the Applications Menu is on the screen.

- Initial Directory. Enter the drive and directory where the data files for the program are stored.

- Execute Path. Enter the drive and directory where the program file is stored. You don't need to specify the Execute

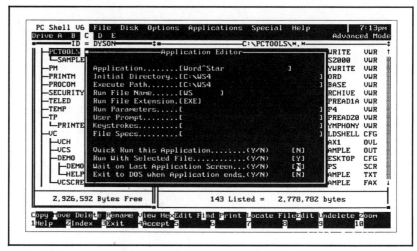

Figure 12.9: Applications Editor in PC Shell 6.0

Path if the program is in the current directory or in a directory specified in the PATH command in your AUTO-EXEC.BAT file.

- Run File Name. Enter the name of the file you execute to run the program, WP for WordPerfect, WS for WordStar, and so on.

- Run File Extension. Enter the file name extension for the program, usually .EXE for an executable file or .BAT for a batch file.

- Run Parameters. Enter any command line arguments you want to use each time the program is started.

- User Prompt. You can use this entry to pause the application program just before it starts, and display the message you entered as the User Prompt. You might use this as a reminder of some sort.

- Keystrokes. You can use this entry to start the program running in a particular way. One popular way to put this to work is to use it to make the program display the File Load menu selections. There are three ways of entering keystrokes:

Type a key and the key appears in the Keystrokes display.

Type a sequence of letters contained within angle brackets, like <esc>. The Applications Editor interprets this as Escape rather than e, followed by s, followed by c.

Press or click on F8 on the message bar to see a list of keywords displayed on the screen. Use the arrow keys to make your selection, and then press Enter. The dialog box closes and the keyword you selected is shown in the Keystrokes box. This way you can choose from the options shown in Table 12.3.

Table 12.3: Keyword Selections

KEYWORD	EXPLANATION
<Path>	Full path and file name of the file.
<Drive>	Drive letter associated with the file.
<Dir>	Path of the file without drive information.
<Dir\>	Path of the file without drive information but including the \ character.
<File>	Full file name with extension.
<Filename>	File name without extension.
<Ext>	Extension only.
<Delay*N*>	Delay passing the characters in Keystrokes to the application program. Replace *N* with the length of the delay in seconds, or tenths of seconds. <Delay3> indicates a delay of three seconds. <Delay.3> indicates a delay of $3/10$ second.
<Typein>	Stops passing characters to the application program, and waits for you to type something in from the keyboard.

- File Specs. Enter information about the files associated with the application program. For example, when using Microsoft Word, enter *.DOC to use files with this extension. You can use the DOS wildcard characters * and ? in this entry.

- Quick Run this Application. Answer yes here if you want to run the application program without first freeing up the memory used by PC Shell. Your answer here will be determined by the size of your application program and the data file you want to load.

- Run with Selected File. Answer yes if you want to pass the currently selected file name to the application program as a command line parameter. For example, when using WordStar you can include a file name on the DOS command line when you start the program, as in

     WS MYFILE

- Wait on Last Application Screen. Answer yes here if you want to pause the application program before returning to PC Shell. Use this if you want to read the program's output on the screen, before the screen is cleared by PC Shell.

- Exit to DOS when Application ends. Answer yes if you want to go back to DOS when the application program ends rather than returning to PC Shell.

When you have completed your choices from the Application Editor, press Enter, and you will see the new program listed in the Applications pull-down menu. You can use the other function key choices to Edit (F5), Delete (F6), or Move (F7) entries in the Applications pull-down menu.

RUNNING TELECOMMUNICATIONS   If you asked PCSETUP to install the modem or fax Telecommunications options, you can invoke them from inside PC Shell from the Applications pull-down menu. For example, if PCSETUP installed the fax options, you will see the selection Send Desktop FAX listed in the PC Shell Applications pull-down menu. If you choose this selection, you go directly to the FAX part of Desktop Telecommunications, and when you have sent your fax and you exit from Desktop, you return to PC Shell again.

For LapLink to work, the two computers must be connected by a null-modem cable. This is a short cable that connects the two computers together via their serial ports.

You can install LLQC in your AUTOEXEC.BAT file to save time.

RUNNING LAPLINK LapLink Quick Connect (LLQC) is a new feature for PC Tools 6.0. Imagine you are leaving on a business trip, and you want to load your important files onto your laptop computer so you can take it with you, and at the end of your trip you will want to load all the changed files back onto your regular computer again. If the two computers use different sized disks this can be a real problem. LapLink allows you to use PC Shell to access the disk drives on both machines, so you can copy files from one machine to the other.

LapLink is really a pair of programs; one is a memory-resident program running in your main computer, the other is a stand-alone program running on your laptop computer. Once the two programs are running, run PC Shell on your regular computer, and your laptop computer's disk drives appear on PC Shell's drive line as networked drives. You can now copy files from one drive to another, just as you would if they were in the same computer. There are functions that you cannot use; you cannot format a disk on the laptop.

To run LapLink, first connect the two computers with the null-modem cable. Run LLS on your laptop computer, and run LLQC on your regular computer. Now start PC Shell and choose the LapLink/QC selection from the Special pull-down menu.

The disk drives of the laptop computer appear in the drive line inside PC Shell running on your regular computer. To copy a file to the laptop, first select the directory and file on your regular computer, and then use Copy File from the File pull-down menu to copy the file to the correct destination disk on your laptop computer.

When you have finished copying your files, choose the LapLink/QC selection from the Special pull-down menu once again to break the connection.

To remove LLQC, type

    KILL

but remember, this command also removes PC Shell, Desktop, and Backtalk if they are loaded as memory-resident programs.

INVOKING DOS FROM INSIDE PC SHELL

You can turn on a single line at the bottom of the screen to allow you access to the DOS command prompt, while keeping the rest of the PC Shell display on the screen. This way you can have the best of both worlds—all the convenience of PC Shell, and DOS commands too. Another selection from the Options pull-down menu, Wait on DOS Screen, can be toggled on or off. When this selection is on, the display pauses before returning to PC Shell to give you time to read the screen, and then adds the reminder

Press any key or a mouse button to re-enter PC Shell

You can use the Tree List Window or the File List Window commands from the Options pull-down menu to turn these two windows on or off. If you turn the windows off, you will see the background mat displayed on the screen where the list used to be if you chose Background Mat ON. Otherwise you will see old DOS information if you chose Background Mat OFF.

Finally, you can turn all the windows off with the Hide Windows command from the Options pull-down menu. To bring the windows back, use Alt-O and select Show Windows.

RUNNING PC SHELL IN MEMORY-RESIDENT OR SHELL MODE

You can run PC Shell in memory-resident mode so that it is available to you at all times. You can also run it in shell mode, just like any other DOS program.

RUNNING IN MEMORY-RESIDENT MODE

There are several important advantages to running PC Shell in memory-resident rather than shell mode:

- You can hotkey into PC Shell from inside another application program. If you want to format a disk quickly or move some files, you won't have to leave your application to do so. When you exit from PC Shell, you return to the same place in your application program.

- You can use optional parameters to configure the amount of memory PC Shell uses.

- You can use expanded memory with PC Shell.

To run PC Shell in memory-resident mode, enter

PCSHELL /R

at the DOS prompt. You can also include this command in your AUTOEXEC.BAT file so that PC Shell is loaded automatically each time you start your computer.

PC Shell's default hotkey is Ctrl-Esc. Press Ctrl-Esc again to return to your original application program. You can change this hotkey combination either in your AUTOEXEC.BAT file or at the DOS prompt. Specify the new hotkey when you first load PC Shell, as follows:

PCSHELL /R /F*n*

where *n* represents the number of a function key, F1 through F10. This changes the hotkey combination from Ctrl-Esc to Ctrl plus the function key you specify. Remember, you can only use this device when PC Shell is in memory-resident mode.

RUNNING IN SHELL MODE

To run PC Shell in shell mode, simply enter

PCSHELL

at the DOS prompt and the program will start just like any other DOS program. When you exit PC Shell, you return to the DOS prompt. There are several optional parameters you can use, including

PCSHELL /BW

which starts PC Shell in monochrome mode, or

PCSHELL /LE

which swaps the left and right mouse buttons.

REMOVING PC SHELL

If you need to recover the memory that PC Shell uses in memory-resident mode, you can use the Remove PC Shell option in the Special pull-down menu. This selection is only available when PC Shell is run in memory-resident mode, and you must hotkey into PC Shell from the DOS prompt. You cannot remove PC Shell if you hotkeyed into it from inside another application. For this selection to be successful, PC Shell must be the last memory-resident program loaded. When you choose the Remove PC Shell option, a window opens to remind you of these conditions, as shown in Figure 12.10. Choose the REMOVE button to remove PC Shell or EXIT to return to the main program.

You can also remove PC Shell by entering

KILL

at the DOS prompt. You must exit PC Shell first to unload it. KILL also removes Desktop and the background communications program Backtalk when they are run in memory-resident mode.

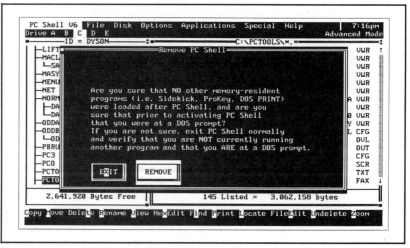

Figure 12.10: Remove PC Shell warning box

DESKTOP

You can get help anywhere in Desktop by pressing F1. In addition, pressing F2 from any application displays the help index.

PC Tools Desktop includes Notepads, Outlines, an Appointment Scheduler, a Database, a Macro Editor, Telecommunications, the Clipboard, four calculators, and a set of utility programs. In addition, if you loaded PC Shell in memory-resident mode before loading Desktop, PC Shell appears in the Desktop main menu and is available at any time from any Desktop application.

You can use shortcut function keys in Desktop. Some are available in all programs and others are used in specific ways in different programs. The F1 (Help), F2 (Help Index), F3 (Escape), and F9 (Swap Active Window) keys are all available in Desktop. The functions assigned to function keys F4 through F10 vary in each Desktop application.

OPENING UP TO 15 WINDOWS AT ONCE

In PC Tools Desktop 6.0, you can only open one copy of the Clipboard, Modem Telecommunications, Fax Telecommunications, the Algebraic, Financial, Scientific, and Programmer's calculators, and the Utilities at once. You can open as many Notepads, Outlines, Databases, Appointment Schedulers, and Macro Editors as you like until you hit the maximum of 15.

In Desktop, you can have up to 15 windows open at once; however, only one of these windows can be the active one. The active window is always the uppermost window and has a double-line border. The other windows have single-line borders. The menu bar at the top of the screen always shows the menu selections for the active window. Figure 12.11 shows three windows open at once: a Notepad, a

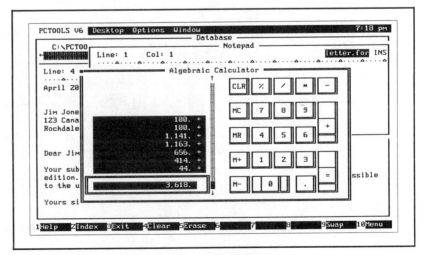

Figure 12.11: Several windows open simultaneously

Database, and the Algebraic calculator as the active window.

The simplest way of changing windows is to use a mouse. Just click somewhere in the window you want to make active. However, if no part of that window is visible or if you want to use the keyboard, select the Switch Active option from the Window pull-down menu or press F9.

If you have only two windows open, they are simply swapped—the inactive window becomes active and the active window, inactive. If you have more than two windows open when you choose Switch Active, a dialog box shows a list of the open windows, the application associated with the window, and the name of the file loaded into the window. Figure 12.12 shows the Switch Active list for the Desktop applications shown in Figure 12.11.

Choose the window you want to make active with ↑ and ↓ and then press the Enter key. If you are using a mouse, you can click on the name of the window you want to make active.

The items in the Switch Active list change depending on which applications you have open.

USING THE FILE LOAD DIALOG BOX

All Desktop applications that load files use the same File Load dialog box for file name entry. Figure 12.13 shows an example from a Notepad.

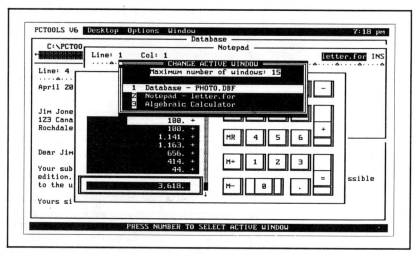

Figure 12.12: The Change Active Window dialog box

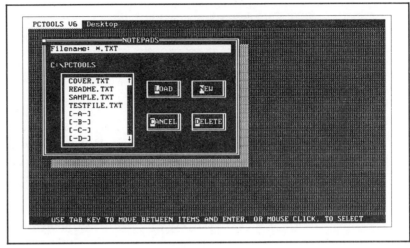

Figure 12.13: The File Load dialog box

When the File Load dialog box opens, all files with the appropriate file name extension are listed on the left of the screen. Notepad files all have an extension of .TXT. Other directories and drives are listed within square brackets.

To change the name of the default directory, enter your choice of directory into the Filename box and press Enter. For example, to use the WordStar directory enter

\WS

The next time you use the File Load dialog box, the WordStar directory name will be shown. This enables you to save different kinds of files in different directories.

Table 12.4 lists several file names used in special ways in Desktop.

Table 12.4: Reserved File Names in Desktop

FILE NAME	APPLICATION
CALC.TMP	Algebraic calculator tape file
DESKTOP.CFG	Desktop configuration file that stores colors, windows, and so on

Table 12.4: Reserved File Names in Desktop (Continued)

FILE NAME	APPLICATION
DESKTOP.HLP	Desktop help file
DESKTOP.IMG	Copy of video RAM when Desktop is used in memory-resident mode
DESKTOP.THM	Copy of swapped memory area when Desktop is used in memory-resident mode
DICT.SPL	Spelling checker dictionary
LEARN.PRO	Macro Editor file created when in learn mode
PHONE.TEL	Telecommunications phone number directory
SCICALC.TMP	Scientific calculator registers file
TALK.CFG	Telecommunications configuration file
TRANSFER.LOG	Captured transmission when using XMODEM on background mode
WORK.TXT	Default file name used if you don't specify one in the File Load dialog box (the extension .TXT is provided by a Notepad)

OPENING A NEW FILE   To create a new file, enter the file name and extension into the Filename box and tab over to the NEW button. If you use a mouse, enter the file name and extension and then click on the NEW button. You can use any legal DOS name, including a different path name if you want the file to be created in another directory.

If you don't want to use an extension with your file name, just end it with a period.

If you don't enter a file name extension, Desktop adds an extension appropriate to the program you are using, as listed in Table 12.5.

LOADING AN EXISTING FILE WITH THE FILE LOAD DIALOG BOX   There are several ways of loading an existing file:

• Enter the desired file name and extension into the Filename box and press Enter.

Table 12.5: Desktop Default File Name Extensions

FILE NAME EXTENSION	APPLICATION
.CFG	Desktop configuration files
.DBF	Database data files
.FOR	Database form files
.LOG	Telecommunications background XMODEM communications dialog file
.OUT	Outlines files
.PRO	Macro Editor files
.REC	Database record files
.SRC	Telecommunications script files
.TEL	Telecommunications phone numbers directory
.TM	Appointment Scheduler
.TXT	Notepad files

- Select the desired file by using ↑ and ↓. You can also use the PgUp, PgDn, Home, or End keys to locate the file. As you select the file, it is highlighted. Press Enter to load it. You can also use the Tab key to move to the LOAD button and then press the Enter key. Finally, you can press Alt-L to load the file automatically.

- With a mouse, click on the file name in the list box and click on the LOAD button to load the file.

- You can save time if you double click on the file name when you use a mouse.

You can use one of the following methods to cancel the File Load dialog box and return to your application at any time:

- Tab to the CANCEL button and press the Enter key.

- Press Alt-C.

- Press the Escape key.

- Press F3, the shortcut function key for Exit.

- Using a mouse, click on the CANCEL button.

- With a mouse, click on the close box in the upper-left corner of the File Load dialog box.

SETTING SCREEN COLORS AND SIZING THE WINDOWS IN DESKTOP

Desktop provides a great deal of flexibility in color selection; you can change many of the colors independently. Although all Desktop applications use windows, some of the windows are fixed in size or location. For example, you cannot move the Financial calculator because its window occupies the whole screen.

The System Menu/Window Colors selection from the Utilities pull-down menu controls the main system color specifications. You make the detailed color selections in the individual applications. Figure 12.14 shows the System Menu/Window Colors screen.

Your choices are as follows:

- Desktop Menu Bar Background changes the color of the menu bar you use to select items from the menu.

- Desktop Menu Bar Foreground changes the color of the menu text.

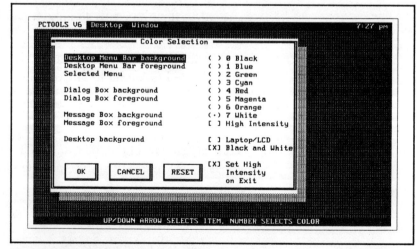

Figure 12.14: The System Menu/Window Colors screen

- Selected Menu changes the color of the highlighted characters used to select menu items.

- Dialog Box Background changes the background color of all dialog boxes.

- Dialog Box Foreground changes the color of the text in all dialog boxes.

- Message Box Background changes the background color of all message boxes.

- Message Box Foreground changes the color of the message text in all message boxes.

- Desktop Background changes the color of the Desktop background.

- Set High Intensity on Exit. If you hotkey into Desktop from an application using a high-intensity background on a CGA or EGA monitor, the characters on your screen may be in blink mode when you leave Desktop. Use this selection to set the high intensity again on exit from Desktop.

Choose Black, Blue, Green, Cyan, Red, Magenta, Orange, or White for each of these settings. Remember that some color combinations are extremely difficult to work with.

CHANGE COLORS   In addition to global color selection, you can use the Change Colors selection from the Window pull-down menu in Notepads, Outlines, Desktop Database, and the Macro Editor. You can make these color selections specific to each file or you can tailor them to the different applications. Figure 12.15 shows the Change Colors screen from the Window pull-down menu in Notepads.

You have the following selections:

- Background changes the color of the window background.

- Window Border changes the color of the window border characters.

- Document Text changes the color of the text in the document.

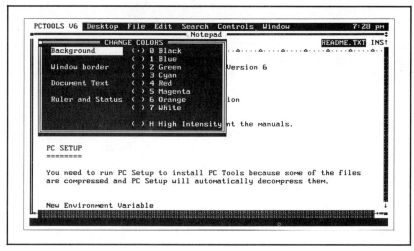

Figure 12.15: Change Colors screen in Notepads

- Ruler and Status changes the color of the ruler and the status line.

Select your colors from Black, Blue, Green, Cyan, Red, Magenta, Orange, or White for each of these settings. As soon as you select a new color, the screen underneath this dialog box changes to show the new color combination, allowing you to preview the new colors. Again, you can set the high intensity on when you leave Desktop.

VIDEO SIZE (VERSION 6.0)   In PC Tools Desktop 6.0, you can select the Video Size. You can choose the current setting, the setting that was in use when you started PC Tools, 25 or 43 lines of display if you have an EGA on your system, or 25 or 50 lines of display if you have a VGA. Remember, running PC Tools Desktop in 43 or 50 line mode limits the number of windows to 7 rather than the usual 15 windows because more memory is needed for each of the windows in 43/ 50 line mode.

RESIZE AND MOVE   Use the Resize option from the Window pull-down menu to change the size of a window, and use the Move option to move a window around on the screen. If your application does not have a Resize option in the Window pull-down menu, you cannot resize the window. Reposition or resize the window using the arrow keys.

ZOOM If you are using Notepads, Outlines, Database, the Macro Editor, or the Clipboard, there is a fast way to enlarge the window to the full size of your screen. Use the Zoom selection from the Window pull-down menu to increase the window to full-screen size. Use Zoom a second time to shrink the window to its original size again.

DESKTOP MEMORY-RESIDENT CONFIGURATION

You can run Desktop in memory-resident mode or in shell mode, just like any other DOS program. If you run PC Tools Desktop in memory-resident mode, Desktop is available from inside your other applications programs, you can cut and paste using the Clipboard, and you can use the alarms in the Appointment Scheduler.

To load Desktop in memory-resident mode, enter

DESKTOP /R

from the DOS prompt. Once Desktop is loaded, you can hotkey into it by pressing Ctrl-spacebar.

If you plan to use Desktop every time you use your computer, you can add a line to your AUTOEXEC.BAT file that will load Desktop in memory-resident mode each time you boot up your computer. Add the line

DESKTOP /R

as the last entry in your AUTOEXEC.BAT file. You can add other letters to this entry to make Desktop open automatically in your most frequently used application, as shown in Table 12.6.

In fact, you can include any of the highlighted letters that Desktop uses for menu selection in this way. For example, to load Desktop and open the Financial Calculator, add

DESKTOP /RCF

to your AUTOEXEC.BAT file.

You do not have to exit all of your Desktop applications to hotkey out of Desktop. If windows are open when you hotkey out, they will still be open when you hotkey back in.

Table 12.6: Abbreviations for Loading Desktop in Memory-Resident Mode

ABBREVIATION	APPLICATION
A	Appointment Scheduler
b	Clipboard
C	Calculators
CA	Calculator, Algebraic
CF	Calculator, Financial
CP	Calculator, Programmer's
CS	Calculator, Scientific
D	Database
N	Notepad
O	Outlines
T	Telecommunications
U	Utilities

To run Desktop in shell mode, enter

DESKTOP

from the DOS prompt along with any optional parameters you want to use.

CHANGING DESKTOP HOTKEYS

If you want to hotkey into PC Tools Desktop from Microsoft Windows, you must change the Desktop hotkey combination to Ctrl-Shift, Ctrl-Alt, or Shift-Alt because Windows reserves the usual hotkey, Ctrl-spacebar, for its own purposes.

If you use Desktop in memory-resident mode, you can hotkey into it using the special hotkey combination. Table 12.7 lists the default hotkeys for Desktop. You can change the defaults by choosing Hotkey Selection from the Utilities pull-down menu.

Use the mouse or ↑ and ↓ to choose the application, and then enter your new hotkey combination. The keys that you press are shown on the screen in angle brackets next to the application name. The new keys are in operation as soon as you leave the hotkey dialog box.

Table 12.7: PC Tools Desktop Hotkeys

HOTKEY	APPLICATION
Ctrl-spacebar	Desktop
Ctrl-Ins	Clipboard—Paste
Ctrl-Del	Clipboard—Cut
Ctrl-O	Screen Autodial

REMOVING DESKTOP

If you are through using Desktop or you want to recover memory space to run a large program, you can remove Desktop from your computer's memory. Choose Unload PCTOOLS Desktop from the Utilities submenu. You will see the warning screen shown in Figure 12.16.

You must hotkey into Desktop from the DOS prompt to remove Desktop. You cannot remove Desktop if you hotkeyed into it from inside an application program. Also, if you are using several memory-resident programs, you must remove them in the opposite

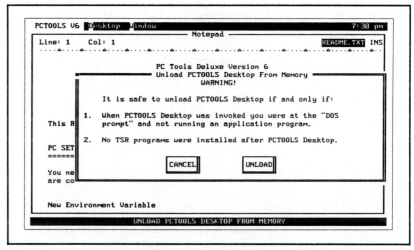

Figure 12.16: The Unload PCTOOLS Desktop warning screen

order from which you loaded them. Otherwise, you may not be able to recover the memory they occupied without rebooting your computer.

You can also remove Desktop by entering

    KILL

at the DOS prompt. Besides removing Desktop, KILL removes PC Shell when it is run in memory-resident mode, the memory-resident portion of LapLink, and the background communications program Backtalk.

SUMMARY

In this chapter, I described how to configure both PC Shell and Desktop to your needs. I explained how to use them in memory-resident or in shell modes, how to change the hotkeys, colors, and window sizes, and how to remove PC Shell and Desktop from memory when you have finished using them.

Complete Command
Reference

In this appendix, I list all the PC Tools programs in alphabetical order. I also detail the parameters that you can use from the DOS command prompt with the programs. You can set many of these optional parameters with PC Setup during the installation of PC Tools Deluxe. Some of the optional parameters can also be extremely useful in batch files.

The descriptions given here are based on the PC Tools Versions 5.5 and 6.0. Anything that applies to only one of these versions is clearly noted.

To make the syntax easier to read, I have used some placeholders for parameters that you can use with a particular program. Two of the most common parameters are

- *drive,* which you should replace with the appropriate drive letter followed by a colon.

- *filespec,* which you should replace with a file's name (and path when necessary).

Also remember that the parameters are optional unless otherwise noted. If you don't use them, the program will start up in the usual way.

COMPRESS

Compress improves your hard-disk performance by unfragmenting your files.

Syntax

To run Compress from the DOS prompt, enter

COMPRESS *drive parameters*

Description

drive   The drive letter of the drive you want to compress. If you don't enter a drive letter, Compress assumes that you want to use the current drive.

/BW   Starts Compress in monochrome mode. This can give a better display if you are using a color card with a monochrome screen.

You can specify your choice of compression selections with the following options:

/CC   Compress performs a full compression and clears all unused sectors.

/CF   Compress performs a full compression.

/CU   Compress unfragments your disk using the minimum compressions option.

You can specify the physical file ordering from the DOS prompt or from a batch file with the following options:

/OD   Compress performs standard DOS ordering—that is, files are kept close to their parent directory.

/OO   Compress performs DOS ordering (subdirectories first)—that is, all files of a given subdirectory will be kept together.

/OP   Compress positions program files (*.EXE and *.COM) at the front of the disk. Program files do not normally grow in size once you have installed them, so placing them at the front of the disk prevents them from becoming fragmented again in the future.

/OS   Compress uses standard ordering; files are placed where it is most convenient for the program. This is the fastest ordering option and is the one you will use most often.

You can select the type of sort from the DOS prompt or from a batch file with the following options:

/SE   Compress sorts by file extension.

/SF   Compress sorts by file name.

/SS   Compress sorts by file size.

/ST   Compress sorts by file creation time.

You can also specify the sort order from the DOS prompt or from a batch file with one of the following parameters:

/NM   Stops Mirror from running automatically when Compress completes the disk optimization. You should always run Mirror once Compress has finished the optimization.

/SA   Compress performs an ascending sort.

/SD   Compress performs a descending sort.

/350   Displays in 350 line resolution with a VGA.

DISKFIX (VERSION 6.0 ONLY)

Diskfix diagnoses and repairs disk and file problems quickly and automatically.

Syntax

To start Diskfix, type

DISKFIX *parameters*

Description

/BW   Starts Diskfix in monochrome mode.

/LCD   Use this parameter if you have a liquid crystal display.

/?   Displays a short help screen.

MI

MI is a memory mapping program that lists the type, size, and location of areas of memory, and the application programs using them.

Syntax

To start MI, type

MI *parameters*

Description

/A	Lists all blocks of memory.
/N	Does not pause a long screen listing.
/Q	Quick summary only.
/V	Lists hooked vectors.

LAPLINK QUICK CONNECT (VERSION 6.0 ONLY)

LapLink allows you to connect your laptop and your regular computer together and move files back and forth using a null-modem cable.

Syntax

To start LapLink on the laptop computer, type

LLS *parameters*

and to start LapLink on the main computer, type

LLQC *parameters*

Description

/B:*nnn*	Sets the baud rate for the transmission. The baud rate can be from 300 to 115200; the default is 115200.
/C:*n*	Selects the communications port; COM1 is the default.
/I:*nn*	When you use COM3 or COM4 you must also select the IRQ (interrupt request) number to use.
/U	Unloads LLQC from memory.
/?	Displays a short help screen.

MIRROR

Mirror saves a copy of the system area of your hard disk for use in recovering files after an accidental erasure or reformatting of the disk.

Syntax

To use Mirror from the DOS prompt, type

MIRROR *drives parameters*

Description

drive	The drive letter for Mirror.
/1	Specifies that Mirror should save only the latest FAT and directory information.
/PARTN	Creates a copy of your hard-disk partition table information.
/T*drive-nnn*	/T stands for enable delete tracking and *drive* is the drive letter to track. The *nnn* parameter is optional and species the maximum number of deleted file entries. The maximum number of entries is 999. If you don't specify a maximum, Mirror makes a file proportional in size to the disk media.

PARK (VERSION 6.0 ONLY)

Park is a stand-alone hard-disk head-parking program. Be sure to run it before you move your computer.

Syntax

To use Park from the DOS command line, type

Park

Description

There are no command line parameters for Park.

PC BACKUP

PC Backup gives you several fast methods of backing up your hard disk to floppy disks or another medium.

Syntax

To start PC Backup, type

PC Backup *drive parameters*

Description

drive   You can specify the drive to be backed up from the command line. This is useful if you are working on a network and want to back up a station hard disk rather than the network server drive. This will also save you time, since the server drive will be large and will contain perhaps hundreds of directories and files.

filename   When you use PC Backup from the DOS command line or in a batch file, you can use a default set of backup options that you have previously saved in a file. Suppose you want to make a backup that will save all WordStar files that have changed since they were last backed up. Use the Options selection in PC Backup to select the method of archive and then use the Save Setup command to save these settings in a file called WORDBACK. Include the line

        PCBACKUP WORDBACK

in your batch file. This will start PC Backup, load the settings you saved in WORDBACK, and ask you to insert a disk. When the backup is complete, you return to the next command in the batch file.

/BW   Starts PC Backup in monochrome mode. This can give a better display if you are using a color card with a monochrome screen.

/DOB	Turns on the automatic detection of the COPY II PC Deluxe Option Board when making a backup to unformatted disks. This change was implemented as a part of the network support.
/LCD	Use this parameter if you have an LCD display. This parameter is new in PC Tools 6.0.
/LE	Switches the functions of the mouse buttons for those who are left-handed.
/NO	Prevents simultaneous hard-disk and floppy-disk DMA (/NO is short for no overlap). If you use this parameter, your backups will be slower but will work on computers that cannot perform these operations simultaneously due to hardware limitations. Try this option if your computer hangs up during the backup or restore process.
/PS2	Use this option if your mouse disappears on a PS/2 computer. This parameter is new in PC Tools 6.0.
/R	With this parameter, you start PC Backup in restore mode and it asks you to insert a backup disk. PC Backup does not read the hard disk's directories and files and starts up much faster.
/?	Displays a short help screen.

PC-CACHE

PC-Cache creates a disk cache in your computer's memory to speed up disk accesses.

Syntax

To run PC-Cache from the DOS prompt, type

PC-CACHE *parameters*

Description

/EXTSTART = *nnn*K	Specifies the start of the cache buffer in extended memory. EXTSTART must be larger than 1 MB (1024K). PC-Cache is compatible with VDISK.SYS.
/FLUSH	Empties the cache.
/Idrive	Specifies the drive or drives that should not be cached.
/INFO	Displays a table showing the size of your drives as well as the size of your cache. It only works before you install PC-Cache. This parameter is new for PC Tools 6.0.
/MAX = *nnnn*K	Specifies the number of sectors that can be saved in the cache from a single read operation.
/MEASURES	Displays the following PC-Cache performance indicators:

Logical transfers: The number of data transfers that have occurred between the cache and the current application.

Physical transfers: The number of data transfers that have occurred between the disk and the current application.

Transfers saved: The number of physical transfers saved by using PC-Cache. This is the difference between the logical and physical transfers.

Percentage saved: The number of saved transfers expressed as a percentage.

/NOBATCH	Reduces the amount of time that the interrupts are disabled between transferring sectors. Sectors are handled one at a time. Used when caching in extended memory.
/PARAM	Displays the current parameters.
/PARAM*	Displays information on your drives and the status of extended memory.
/PAUSE	Acts as a troubleshooting option. Follow the commands on the screen. This parameter is new in PC Tools 6.0.
/QUIET	Disables the startup message for use in batch files. This parameter is new in PC Tools 6.0.
/WRITE	Controls the delay before write operations are sent to disk. This parameter is new in PC Tools 6.0.

You can specify the size of the cache with one of the following parameters. You may use only one SIZE parameter, and you cannot mix standard, expanded, and extended memory.

/SIZE = *nnn*K	Specifies the amount of standard memory for the cache. The default is 64K and the maximum is 512K.
/SIZEXP = *nnn*K	Specifies the amount of expanded memory for the cache.
/SIZEXT = *nnn*K	Specifies the amount of extended memory for the cache. This can only be used with computers using Intel's 80286 or later microprocessors.
/SIZEXT* = *nnn*K	Forces PC-Cache to examine your computer to determine the best method

	of using extended memory. This parameter is new in PC Tools 6.0.
/UNLOAD	Removes the cache.
/X	Use this parameter if you use NEC or WYSE 3.3 DOS and have a single partition of larger than 40MB.
/?	Displays a short help screen.

PC DESKTOP

PC Desktop provides an easy-to-use desktop manager including word processing, database, calculators, an appointment scheduler and a to-do list.

Syntax

To run PC Desktop from the DOS prompt, type

DESKTOP *parameters*

Description

/BW	Starts PC Desktop in monochrome mode. This can give a better display if you are using a color card with a monochrome screen.
/C3 = *nnnn* or /C4 = *nnnn*	Specifies that your modem is on COM3 or COM4 by setting interrupt request, Base Port Address. See your modem manual for details. Not needed if you are using a PS/2, since the hardware automatically assigns a port number and interrupt request to each.
/CS	Clears the screen and displays a pattern when you run PC Desktop in memory-resident mode.
/DQ	Specifies that you will hotkey into PC Desktop from the DOS prompt rather than from inside another application. If you use this selection, the state of the computer memory is not saved

	into a file and PC Desktop consequently starts up much faster.
/IM	Disables the mouse when you are using PC Shell.
/IN	Use this parameter if you have a Hercules InColor card and want to run PC Shell memory resident and in color. Without this parameter, PC Shell will start in monochrome mode.
KILL	After you have run PC Desktop as a memory-resident program, you can remove it from memory with this command. KILL also removes PC Shell (plus Backtalk) from memory if they were the last memory-resident programs loaded.
/LCD	Use this is you have an LCD display. This parameter is new in PC Tools 6.0.
/LE	Swaps the functions of the left and right mouse buttons.
/MM	Allows you to run Desktop without loading any applications that were on the stack last time Desktop was run memory-resident. This parameter is new in PC Tools 6.0.
/O*drive*	Forces PC Desktop to use another drive for building the overlay files. If you use a RAM disk, you will speed up program operation but must have at least 400K of memory. If you want to run both PC Shell and PC Desktop from a RAM disk, you need a minimum of 1000K of memory.
/R	Loads PC Desktop in memory-resident mode.
/RA	Loads PC Desktop in memory-resident mode, starts the program, and the Appointment Scheduler displays today's schedule and to-do list. If you use this parameter in your AUTOEXEC.BAT file, make sure that it is the last command in the file. Any subsequent

commands will only run after you exit PC Desktop.

/350   Use this parameter if you have a VGA.

If Desktop is memory-resident and you want to run background communications, use Backtalk /2 for COM2.

PC FORMAT

PC Format is a safe formatting alternative to the DOS FORMAT command.

Syntax

To run PC Format from the DOS prompt, type

PCFORMAT *drive parameters*

Description

drive	Specifies the letter of the drive you want to format.
/1	Specifies the single-sided format.
/4	Formats a floppy disk as a 360K disk in a high-capacity drive. This means that you can format a low-capacity floppy disk (360K) by using a high-capacity (1.2MB) disk drive. If you format 360K floppy disks in a high-capacity floppy-disk drive, you may not be able to read them with a 360K floppy-disk drive.
/8	Formats a disk with 8 sectors per track, for use with versions of DOS before DOS 2.0.
/DESTROY	Formats the disk and erases all data on the disk.
/F	Specifies a full format.

/F:*nnn*K	Selects the size of the floppy disk. Valid entries are 160, 180, 320, 360, 720, 1200, or 1400.
/N:*xx*	Specifies the number of sectors per track for the format. Valid entries are 8, 9, 15, or 18.
/P	Copies the information from PC Format to the device connected to LPT1.
/Q	Specifies a quick format. This erases the data in the FAT and the root directory.
/R	PC Format reformats every track on the disk. FAT, root directory, and data on the disk remain intact.
/S	Copies the operating system files to the floppy disk to make it a bootable disk.
/TEST	Simulates the format without actually writing to the disk.
/T:*xx*	Specifies the number of tracks for the format. Valid entries are 40 or 80.
/V	Causes PC Format to ask you to input a volume label for the disk when the format is complete.
/?	Displays a short help screen.

When you run PC Format on a hard disk, the following options are available in addition to the /Q, /P, and /TEST parameters just explained:

drive	Indicates the drive letter of the hard disk that you want to format.
/S	Copies the operating system files to the hard disk to make it a bootable disk. First boot your system with the version of DOS that you want installed on your hard disk.
/V	Allows you to add a volume label.

PC SECURE

PC Secure compresses, encrypts, and hides your files.

Syntax

To run PC Secure from the DOS command line, type

PCSECURE *parameters*

Description

filespec	File name of the file for encryption or decryption. You can use the DOS wildcard characters.
/BW	Starts PC Secure in monochrome mode. This can give a better display if you arc using a color card with a monochrome screen.
/C	Turns compression off when decrypting a file.
/D	Decrypts the file specified in *filespec*.
/F	Performs a full encryption on the specified file.
/G	Specifies full Department of Defense procedures. The file is encrypted and the original file is overwritten seven times and verified for complete erasure.
/K*xxxx*	Specifies that the characters defined by *xxxx* are used as the key for encryption/decryption.
/P	In PC Tools 5.5, this parameter prompts you to enter a key to be used in the encryption. In PC Tools 6.0, this parameter allows you to enter a new password after pressing the Escape key.
/Q	Performs a quick encryption on the file specified in *filespec*.
/350	Use this parameter if you have a VGA.

PC SHELL

PC Shell is a DOS shell program that provides disk, file, and applications support.

Syntax

To run PC Shell from the DOS command line, type

PCSHELL *parameters*

Description

/A*nnn*	Specifies the amount of memory PC Shell uses when it is active in memory-resident mode and after you have hotkeyed into it. The default size is 235K. The largest amount of memory you can specify is approximately 200K less than the total memory in your computer.
/BW	Starts PC Shell in monochrome mode. This can give a better display if you are using a color card with a monochrome screen.
/DQ	Specifies that you will hotkey into PC Shell from the DOS prompt rather than from inside another application. If you use this selection, the state of the computer memory is not saved into a file and PC Shell consequently starts up much faster.
/FF	Disables the snow suppression on CGA monitors. If you have a CGA and don't mind the snow, use this parameter when you start PC Shell.
/F*n*	Changes the default hotkey from Ctrl-Escape to Ctrl and a function key, where *n* is the number of the function key, from F1 to F10.
/LCD	Use this if you have an LCD display. This parameter is new in PC Tools 6.0.
/LE	Swaps the functions of the left and right mouse buttons.
/IM	Disables the mouse when you are using PC Shell.
/IN	Use this parameter if you have a Hercules InColor card and want to run PC Shell memory-resident and in color. Without this parameter, PC Shell will start in monochrome mode.

/O*drive*   Forces PC Shell to use another drive for building
             the overlay files. If you use a RAM disk, speeds up
             program operation.

/PS2   Use this if your mouse disappears on a PS/2
             computer. This parameter is new in PC Tools 6.0.

/R   Specifies the amount of resident memory that PC
             Shell uses when it is not active. This parameter
             takes the form shown in Table A.1.

/TR*n*   Specifies that PC Shell do a tree rebuild every *n*
             days. The default setting is 1, which indicates a
             daily tree rebuild.

/350   Use this parameter if you have a VGA.

Table A.1: Resident Memory Used by PC Shell When It Is Not Active

PARAMETER	PC TOOLS 5.5	PC TOOLS 6.0
/R or /RTINY or /RT	9K of memory	10K of memory
/RS or /RSMALL	70K of memory	117K of memory
/RM or /RMEDIUM	90K of memory	155K of memory
/RL or /RLARGE	170K of memory	235K of memory

REBUILD

You can use Rebuild to recover files and directories from an accidentally formatted hard disk.

Syntax

To use Rebuild from the DOS prompt, type

    REBUILD *parameters*

Description

drive	Specifies the drive for Rebuild.
/J	Compares two Mirror files, giving you the option of choosing which should be used for the rebuild. You can escape without doing anything to your system after looking at the files.
/L	Lists on the screen all files and subdirectories found by Rebuild.
/P	Prints the information listed by the /L parameter. I recommend using these parameters together to collect the maximum amount of information about the rebuild. Type

REBUILD *drive***/L/P**

to combine these two parameters.

/PARTN	Restores the partition table information saved by **MIRROR /PARTN** to floppy disk. If you see the DOS message ''Invalid drive specification,'' the partition table may be corrupted.
/PARTN/L	Displays the current drive's partition table.
/PARTN/L/P	Prints a copy of the chosen drive's partition table.
/TEST	Simulates the rebuild process, showing what will happen without writing anything to the disk.
/?	Displays a short help screen.

UNDELETE (VERSION 6.0 ONLY)

Undelete is the command line equivalent of the Undelete utility found inside PC Shell.

Syntax

To start Undelete, type

UNDELETE *drive filespec parameters*

Description

drive	The drive letter of the drive containing the deleted files. If you don't specify a drive, Undelete assumes the current drive.
filespec	File name and path name where the deleted files are found. If you don't specify a path, the current path will be used.
/ALL	Specifies automatic recovery of all the specified files. Undelete will use different characters in a file name if there is a change that it will create duplicate filenames when files are recovered.
/DOS	Uses the DOS method for recovering files.
/DT	Uses information from the delete tracking file to help reconstruct the original file name.
/HELP	Displays a help screen.
/LIST	Lists all the deleted files available for recovery.
/?	Displays a help screen.

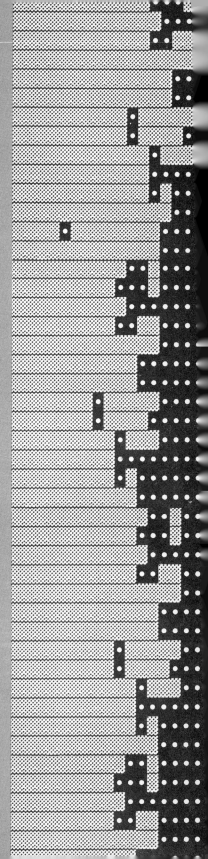

File Types
and Computer
Numbering Schemes

Throughout this book, I have referred to ASCII and program files. As you can work with both types of files when you run PC Tools, acquiring a better understanding of what these file types are and the numbering systems they rely on will enable you to enhance your productivity. As you may know, ASCII files are often called text or non-document files (this last term comes from word processors). Program files are actually binary files.

BINARY FILES

Binary files contain instructions and data (encoded as numbers) that your system's processor can decode and act on. Such files are specific to the microprocessor or microprocessor family they will execute on. For instance, a binary file prepared for an Intel microprocessor will not run on a Motorola microprocessor, and vice versa, without special software.

You cannot read or edit binary files with a word processor. Programmers initially write programs in human-readable computer languages, which are then *compiled, interpreted,* or *assembled* by the computer into binary files.

ASCII FILES

ASCII files are text files. ASCII (pronounced "as-key") stands for the American Standard Code for Information Interchange. ASCII codes represent letters, punctuation symbols, numbers, mathematical symbols, and so on. When you type a character, what the computer actually "reads" is the ASCII code for that character. You can also employ ASCII codes to control devices (such as monitors and printers).

The standard ASCII codes use 7 of the 8 bits in a byte.

In ASCII, each character is represented by a unique integer value, which is commonly referred to as a *decimal value.* The values 0 to 31 are used for control codes, and the range of 32 to 127 is used to represent the letters of the alphabet and common punctuation symbols. The entire set of 0–127 is called *standard* ASCII. All computers that use ASCII characters can understand the standard ASCII set, although not all can work with the *extended character set,* which are the values 128 to 255. These values encode uncommon symbols and punctuation marks, for example, Greek letters. (We'll examine this set shortly.)

ASCII CONTROL CHARACTERS

The *control code* characters (0 to 31) are reserved for special purposes that usually have to do with controlling devices or communications.

Codes 1 to 4—which stand for SOH, STX, ETX, and EOT—are used in communications to indicate the start and end of both the transmission (codes 1 and 4) and its text (codes 2 and 3). Other codes are used to control the flow of transmitted data; for example, ACK (acknowledge) and NAK (negative acknowledge) indicate whether the data was received successfully, and ENQ (enquire), SYN (synchronize), ETB (end-of-transmission block), and CAN (cancel) are also used to control the flow. Additional codes punctuate the flow of information; FS (file separator), GS (group separator), RS (record separator), and US (unit separator) all fall into this category.

Several codes are used to control peripheral devices, particularly printers. The CR (carriage return), LF (line feed), FF (form feed, which is sometimes referred to as new page), HT (horizontal tab), BS (backspace), and VT (vertical tab) sequences all find uses in device control. For a complete listing of the control codes, see Table B.1.

Codes 1 to 4 are generally not used in modern microcomputer communications.

The VT sequence is rarely used to control devices.

Table B.1: The ASCII Control Codes

DECIMAL VALUE	HEX VALUE	KEYS TO PRESS	NAME
000	00	Ctrl-@	NUL (null character)
001	01	Ctrl-A	SOH (start of header)
002	02	Ctrl-B	STX (start of text)
003	03	Ctrl-C	ETX (end of text)
004	04	Ctrl-D	EOT (end of transmission)

Table B.1: The ASCII Control Codes (Continued)

DECIMAL VALUE	HEX VALUE	KEYS TO PRESS	NAME
005	05	Ctrl-E	ENQ (enquire)
006	06	Ctrl-F	ACK (acknowledge)
007	07	Ctrl-G	BEL (bell)
008	08	Ctrl-H	BS (backspace)
009	09	Ctrl-I	HT (horizontal tab)
010	0A	Ctrl-J	LF (line feed)
011	0B	Ctrl-K	VT (vertical tab)
012	0C	Ctrl-L	FF (form feed or new page)
013	0D	Ctrl-M	CR (carriage return)
014	0E	Ctrl-N	SO (shift out)
015	0F	Ctrl-O	SI (shift in)
016	10	Ctrl-P	DLE (data link escape)
017	11	Ctrl-Q	DC1 (X-ON)
018	12	Ctrl-R	DC2 (tape)
019	13	Ctrl-S	DC3 (X-OFF)
020	14	Ctrl-T	DC4 (no tape)
021	15	Ctrl-U	NAK (negative acknowledge)
022	16	Ctrl-V	SYN (synchronize)
023	17	Ctrl-W	ETB (end of transmission block)
024	18	Ctrl-X	CAN (cancel)
025	19	Ctrl-Y	EM (end of medium)
026	1A	Ctrl-Z	SUB (substitute)

Table B.1: The ASCII Control Codes (Continued)

DECIMAL VALUE	HEX VALUE	KEYS TO PRESS	NAME
027	1B	Ctrl-[	ESC (escape)
028	1C	Ctrl-/	FS (file separator)
029	1D	Ctrl-]	GS (group separator)
030	1E	Ctrl-^	RS (record separator)
031	1F	Ctrl-_	US (unit separator)

Ctrl-S is often called X-OFF, and Ctrl-Q is often called X-ON.

Ctrl-S and Ctrl-Q are often used as pause and restart commands, and Ctrl-[produces the Esc character. An escape sequence, comprising the Esc character followed by one or more other characters in a set order, is a common way of controlling complex devices such as terminals and printers that have more capabilities than can be controlled by the individual ASCII control characters alone. See your printer manual for more details.

THE EXTENDED CHARACTER SET

255 is the largest decimal value that can be represented by using all 8 of the bits in one 8-bit byte.

The IBM extended character set starts where the standard ASCII set leaves off. The next available decimal code is 128, and the extended set runs from 128 to 255. Its characters—which include the PC line-drawing set, mathematical symbols, and graphics characters—are not standard on computers that are not compatible with IBM's microcomputers. Word processing programs have different ways of allowing you to use the characters in the extended ASCII set. In WordStar, for example, you can display these characters by simultaneously pressing the Alt key and typing the decimal value of the appropriate character on the numeric keypad (you cannot use the regular number keys for this purpose). Printers vary in their ability to print these characters.

Because different languages (for example, Norwegian and Portuguese) use different characters and keyboard layouts, there are a number of language-specific ASCII tables. These tables use decimal codes 128–255 for necessary characters that are not provided by the standard ASCII set. Each of these tables is called a *code page*.

Table B.2 lists the standard and IBM extended ASCII characters and their decimal and hexadecimal values.

Table B.2: The Standard and Extended ASCII Sets

CHARACTER	DECIMAL VALUE	HEX VALUE	CHARACTER	DECIMAL VALUE	HEX VALUE
	000	00	♫	014	0E
☺	001	01	☼	015	0F
☻	002	02	►	016	10
♥	003	03	◄	017	11
♦	004	04	↕	018	12
♣	005	05	‼	019	13
♠	006	06	¶	020	14
•	007	07	§	021	15
◘	008	08	▬	022	16
○	009	09	↨	023	17
◙	010	0A	↑	024	18
♂	011	0B	↓	025	19
♀	012	0C	→	026	1A
♪	013	0D	←	027	1B

Table B.2: The Standard and Extended ASCII Sets (Continued)

CHARACTER	DECIMAL VALUE	HEX VALUE	CHARACTER	DECIMAL VALUE	HEX VALUE
└	028	1C	.	046	2E
↔	029	1D	/	047	2F
▲	030	1E	0	048	30
▼	031	1F	1	049	31
	032	20	2	050	32
!	033	21	3	051	33
"	034	22	4	052	34
#	035	23	5	053	35
$	036	24	6	054	36
%	037	25	7	055	37
&	038	26	8	056	38
'	039	27	9	057	39
(	040	28	:	058	3A
)	041	29	;	059	3B
*	042	2A	<	060	3C
+	043	2B	=	061	3D
,	044	2C	>	062	3E
−	045	2D	?	063	3F

Table B.2: The Standard and Extended ASCII Sets (Continued)

Character	Decimal Value	Hex Value	Character	Decimal Value	Hex Value
@	064	40	R	082	52
A	065	41	S	083	53
B	066	42	T	084	54
C	067	43	U	085	55
D	068	44	V	086	56
E	069	45	W	087	57
F	070	46	X	088	58
G	071	47	Y	089	59
H	072	48	Z	090	5A
I	073	49	[	091	5B
J	074	4A	\	092	5C
K	075	4B	]	093	5D
L	076	4C	^	094	5E
M	077	4D	_	095	5F
N	078	4E	`	096	60
O	079	4F	a	097	61
P	080	50	b	098	62
Q	081	51	c	099	63

Table B.2: The Standard and Extended ASCII Sets (Continued)

CHARACTER	DECIMAL VALUE	HEX VALUE	CHARACTER	DECIMAL VALUE	HEX VALUE
d	100	64	∪	118	76
e	101	65	н	119	77
f	102	66	x	120	78
g	103	67	y	121	79
h	104	68	z	122	7A
i	105	69	{	123	7B
j	106	6A	¦	124	7C
k	107	6B	}	125	7D
l	108	6C	~	126	7E
m	109	6D	△	127	7F
n	110	6E	Ç	128	80
o	111	6F	ü	129	81
p	112	70	é	130	82
q	113	71	â	131	83
r	114	72	ä	132	84
s	115	73	à	133	85
t	116	74	å	134	86
u	117	75	ç	135	87

Table B.2: The Standard and Extended ASCII Sets (Continued)

CHARACTER	DECIMAL VALUE	HEX VALUE	CHARACTER	DECIMAL VALUE	HEX VALUE
ê	136	88	ü	154	9A
ë	137	89	¢	155	9B
è	138	8A	£	156	9C
ï	139	8B	¥	157	9D
î	140	8C	₨	158	9E
ì	141	8D	ƒ	159	9F
Ä	142	8E	á	160	A0
Å	143	8F	í	161	A1
É	144	90	ó	162	A2
æ	145	91	ú	163	A3
Æ	146	92	ñ	164	A4
ô	147	93	Ñ	165	A5
ö	148	94	ª	166	A6
ò	149	95	º	167	A7
û	150	96	¿	168	A8
ù	151	97	⌐	169	A9
ÿ	152	98	¬	170	AA
ö	153	99	½	171	AB

Table B.2: The Standard and Extended ASCII Sets (Continued)

CHARACTER	DECIMAL VALUE	HEX VALUE	CHARACTER	DECIMAL VALUE	HEX VALUE
¼	172	AC	╛	190	BE
¡	173	AD	┐	191	BF
«	174	AE	└	192	C0
»	175	AF	┴	193	C1
░	176	B0	┬	194	C2
▓	177	B1	├	195	C3
▒	178	B2	─	196	C4
│	179	B3	┼	197	C5
┤	180	B4	╞	198	C6
╡	181	B5	╟	199	C7
╢	182	B6	╚	200	C8
╖	183	B7	╔	201	C9
╕	184	B8	╩	202	CA
╣	185	B9	╦	203	CB
║	186	BA	╠	204	CC
╗	187	BB	═	205	CD
╝	188	BC	╬	206	CE
╜	189	BD	╧	207	CF

Table B.2: The Standard and Extended ASCII Sets (Continued)

Character	Decimal Value	Hex Value	Character	Decimal Value	Hex Value
⊔	208	D0	Γ	226	E2
⊤	209	D1	π	227	E3
π	210	D2	Σ	228	E4
⊔	211	D3	σ	229	E5
⊢	212	D4	μ	230	E6
╠	213	D5	τ	231	E7
π	214	D6	Φ	232	E8
╫	215	D7	θ	233	E9
╪	216	D8	Ω	234	EA
┘	217	D9	δ	235	EB
┌	218	DA	∞	236	EC
■	219	DB	∅	237	ED
▬	220	DC	∈	238	EE
▌	221	DD	∩	239	EF
▐	222	DE	≡	240	F0
▄	223	DF	±	241	F1
α	224	E0	≥	242	F2
β	225	E1	≤	243	F3

Table B.2: The Standard and Extended ASCII Sets (Continued)

CHARACTER	DECIMAL VALUE	HEX VALUE	CHARACTER	DECIMAL VALUE	HEX VALUE
⌠	244	F4	·	250	FA
⌡	245	F5	√	251	FB
÷	246	F6	ⁿ	252	FC
≈	247	F7	²	253	FD
°	248	F8	■	254	FE
•	249	F9		255	FF

A NOTE ON DIFFERENT NUMBERING SCHEMES

As you have seen in the previous section, a computer relies on various numbering systems. Understanding these systems will make it easier to work with your computer—you'll have a better grasp of what is happening and why. The main thing to remember about these different systems is that they are all methods of representing the same thing.

DECIMAL

The *decimal* system is the system people are most familiar with, as it is the first numbering system taught in school. It counts in base 10 using ten digits—0, 1, 2, 3, 4, 5, 6, 7, 8, and 9—to represent numbers.

The position of each digit contributes to the value of the number. The right-hand digit is the ones place, the second position (moving to the left) is the tens place, the third is the hundreds place, and so on. To determine a decimal number's value, you can multiply each digit by its position and then add the individual sums together. For example, the decimal number 1234 equals

$$(1 \times 4) \quad + \quad (10 \times 3) \quad + \quad (100 \times 2) \quad + \quad (1000 \times 1)$$
$$= \quad 4 \quad + \quad 30 \quad + \quad 200 \quad + \quad 1000$$

BINARY

The *binary* system uses only two digits, 0 and 1, which represent the only possible states of a bit—off or on. Counting in binary is relatively straightforward, although it is rather different from the traditional decimal-numbering scheme.

In the binary system, the weight of each position doubles each time you move a position to the left, instead of increasing by a factor of ten as in the decimal system. To convert the binary number 1011 into decimal, for example, you would perform the following calculation:

$$(1 \times 2^0) + (1 \times 2^1) + (0 \times 2^2) + (1 \times 2^3)$$
$$= \quad 1 \quad + \quad 2 \quad + \quad 0 \quad + \quad 8$$
$$= 11$$

Table B.3 shows the place values of the first eight places in the binary system in its top row. The bottom row shows the binary equivalent of decimal 11.

The binary system represents the exact state of the bits in a byte well, but it is inconvenient when all you want to know is the value of the byte and don't care about the status of its individual bits. In cases like this, it is often easier to work with the hexadecimal (or sometimes octal) system.

HEXADECIMAL

The third major numbering scheme used when working with computers is the *hexadecimal* system. This is often abbreviated to hex or the single letter H. Sometimes even the H is omitted, and you have to guess from the context that the number is expressed in hexadecimal.

The hexadecimal digits A–F are always uppercased.

The hexadecimal system counts in base 16, using the digits 0 to 9 and A to F in the sequence 0, 1, 2, 3, 4, 5, 6, 7, 8, 9, A, B, C, D, E, and F. The decimal and binary equivalents for this sequence are shown in Table B.4. In a hexadecimal number, each digit's value is 16 times greater than the digit immediately to its right.

For example, to convert the hex number FF to decimal, remembering that F in hex is equivalent to 15 in the decimal system, perform the following calculation:

$$(15 \times 16^0) + (15 \times 16^1)$$
$$= \quad 15 \quad + \quad 240$$
$$= \quad 255$$

Hexadecimal notation is a convenient way to express byte values because a single hexadecimal digit is equivalent to four binary digits. Since there are eight binary digits in a byte, the value of a byte can be expressed as two hex digits.

Table B.3: Decimal 11 in the Binary System

PLACE VALUES	128	64	32	16	8	4	2	1
BINARY DIGITS	0	0	0	0	1	0	1	1

Table B.4: A Comparison of Decimal, Binary, and Hexadecimal Numbers

DECIMAL	BINARY	HEXADECIMAL	DECIMAL	BINARY	HEXADECIMAL
0	0	0	8	1000	8
1	1	1	9	1001	9
2	10	2	10	1010	A
3	11	3	11	1011	B
4	100	4	12	1100	C
5	101	5	13	1101	D
6	110	6	14	1110	E
7	111	7	15	1111	F

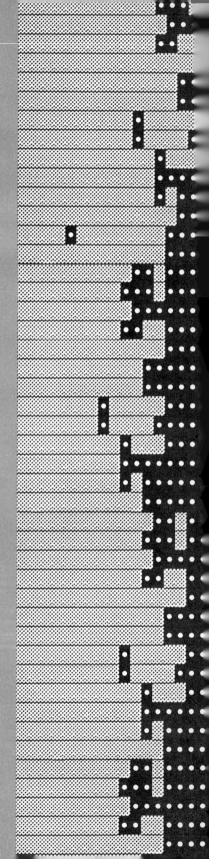

C

A Note
on Data
Communications

 **C**

In this appendix, I explain the reasons for using a communications protocol for file exchange between computers. Then I describe the basic theory behind the XMODEM protocol, and conclude with a short description of fax machines.

COMPUTER-TO-COMPUTER COMMUNICATIONS

Eventually, you will want to move a file from one computer to another or download a file from a dial-up service such as a bulletin board. You must pay special attention to many aspects of hardware and software to get two computers to communicate successfully.

HARDWARE

Before your PC can communicate with another computer, both computers must have certain pieces of hardware. With computers in close proximity, you can establish a direct hardware link by using an RS-232 cable or a data-line facility built into your office phone system. If the computers are a long way apart, however, connecting them with a cable is obviously impossible.

The most common way of linking two computers that are far apart is by means of a standard telephone line and a modem. The modem may be internal (you install it in one of the spare slots inside your computer) or external (the unit must be connected to your computer by an RS-232 cable). Either type of modem is connected to the phone system by a modular telephone jack. You can either unplug your phone or find a voice/data switch that allows you to plug two jacks into the same line.

Modems vary in their speed. Currently, most modems used in PCs are either 1200 or 2400 bits per second (bps), although 9600 bps modems are coming on to the market. Large mainframe computer installations use communications speeds far higher than these rates. The Hayes company has pioneered the use of a standard set of modem commands known as the AT set (see the next section).

Versions of DOS up to 3.2 can address up to two serial ports called COM1 and COM2. DOS 3.3 can address up to four serial ports and

OS/2 can address up to eight. You usually set the port address by setting a hardware or software switch to configure the board as COM1 or COM2. Internal modems may have switches or jumpers to set the port address. External modems use the port address of the serial port to which they are attached.

Each device attached to your computer uses an interrupt request (IRQ) to tell the microprocessor when it needs attention. For example, IRQ1 is assigned to the keyboard, IRQ6 to the floppy disks, and IRQ7 to the printer. By default, COM1 uses IRQ4 and COM2 uses IRQ3. On 286 and 386 machines that conform to the AT architecture, you can use IRQ9 as a serial port if the other two are in use. On PS/2 computers, you can have up to eight serial ports and the hardware automatically assigns a port number and IRQ to each.

FORMATTING THE DATA

The data format you use to send the data must also be used by the receiving computer to receive the data. Otherwise, you will receive garbage. The data format consists of

- Start bit
- Data word length
- Type of parity
- Number of stop bits

The start bit tells the receiving modem that what follows is data. There is always 1 start bit so you don't have to set it.

After the start bit come 7 or 8 data bits, depending on the word length in use. Since 7 bits can represent all ASCII values from 0 to 127 decimal, only 7 data bits are required to transmit text data. However, much of the data in computer-to-computer communications is in binary form and needs all 8 bits. Program files are transmitted using 8 data bits.

The data bits are followed by the parity bit. Parity is a simple form of error checking and may be set to ODD or EVEN. When ODD parity is used, a 1 is placed in the parity bit if the sum of the data bits is even and a 0 if the sum of the data bits is odd. When EVEN parity is used, a 1 is placed in the parity bit if the value of the data bits is odd. Otherwise, a 0 is placed in the parity bit.

No parity is used with 8 data bits, and you indicate this by setting parity to NONE. You can also use NONE with 7 data bits. The sending computer sets the parity, and the receiving computer checks that the parity bit shows the correct relationship to all the other bits. If it does not, something went wrong during the transmission.

The end of the transmitted byte is defined by 1 or 2 stop bits. You use 1 stop bit with 8 or 7 data bits and parity other than NONE. With 7 data bits and NO parity, use 2 stop bits.

COMMUNICATIONS PARAMETERS

In addition to the data format, you must match several other settings before communications can begin. You must set transmission speed, whether your computer is the originator or the answerer, and the direction of communication.

The most common communications error is mismatched transmission speed between sending and receiving computers.

The transmission speed is measured in bits per second (bps). As mentioned, modern modems allow transmission speeds of 300, 1200, or 2400 bps, and some can transmit at 9600 bps. You must match transmission speed at both ends or you will receive garbage. Use the highest speed modem setting both computers can handle. The higher the rate at which you can transmit and receive data, the lower your unit cost.

When two computers communicate, one is always considered the originator and the other the answering computer. The originator initiates the communications. When you log onto a bulletin board, set your computer to originate since the bulletin board computer will always be set to answer.

Communications between computers can be *simplex* (one direction only), *half duplex* (both directions but at different times), or *full duplex* (both directions at the same time). Most communications between microcomputers are in full duplex mode.

Communications protocols are methods of detecting transmission errors during the transmission. They usually divide the data into blocks, send the block, and then check that the block was received correctly. The sending and receiving computers must both use the same protocol.

THE XMODEM PROTOCOL

XMODEM is one of the most popular communications protocols. It is included in most microcomputer communications packages and is used by almost all DOS-based bulletin boards.

XMODEM divides data into blocks. Each block consists of the start-of-header character 01h, a 1-byte block number, the one's complement of the block number, 128 bytes of data, and a 1-byte checksum, as you can see in Table C.1.

Table C.1: XMODEM Protocol Block Format

LOCATION	CONTENTS
0	SOH (start-of-header character, ASCII 01)
1	Block number (starts at 1 and goes to 0 after FFh)
2	One's complement of the block number (255 − block number)
3 to 130	128 bytes of data
131	Checksum. Add all data bytes and ignore any carry

The block number starts at 1 and is computed modulo 256. In other words, after 255 (FFh) it goes back to zero. You determine the one's complement by complementing all bits in the number (changing the zeros to ones and the ones to zeros) or by subtracting the block number from 255. You calculate the single-byte checksum by adding the ASCII values for all 128 data bytes and ignoring any overflow.

XMODEM offers two types or error checking: a checksum and a CRC (cyclical redundancy check).

The 1-byte checksum does not always detect all errors. For this reason, an extension to XMODEM incorporates a 2-byte figure called a *cyclical redundancy check* (CRC-16). The CRC detects at least 99.99 percent of all errors. Table C.2 shows the CRC-16 format.

There are many other communications protocols. YMODEM, YMODEM batch, and WXMODEM are variations of XMODEM. Kermit, developed at Columbia University, is often used between PCs and mainframe computers. Many communications software packages such as Crosstalk or SmartCom include excellent proprietary protocols of their own. Just remember that both computers involved in the transfer of a file must use the same protocol.

Table C.2: XMODEM Protocol Block Format with CRC-16

LOCATION	CONTENTS
0	SOH (start-of-header character, ASCII 01)
1	Block number (starts at 1 and goes to 0 after FFh)
2	One's complement of the block number (255 − block number)
3 to 130	128 bytes of data
131	High byte of CRC
132	Low byte of CRC

HAYES COMPATIBILITY

You often hear the phrase ''Hayes compatible,'' but there is no absolute modem standard. Even different models of Hayes modems are not entirely compatible with each other. This is why communications programs have separate options for the Smartmodem 300, 1200, and 1200B and for the 2400 and 2400B. More modern modems have codes that older software will not recognize, but this is not usually a problem. Your main concern is whether the modem will work with your communications software. Table C.3 lists the most frequently used AT commands for Hayes modems.

Table C.3: Summary of the AT Command Set Used by Hayes Modems

COMMAND	EXPLANATION
AT	Command prefix
A/	Repeat last command
ATB	Use CCITT V.22
ATC	Assume carrier signal is always present
ATD	Dial: go into originate mode, dial number that follows, go to on-line state

Table C.3: Summary of the AT Command Set Used by Hayes Modems
(Continued)

COMMAND	EXPLANATION
ATDT	Tone Dial: go into originate mode, dial number that follows, go to on-line state
ATDP	Pulse Dial: go into originate mode, dial number that follows, go to on-line state
ATDR	Reverse Mode: go into originate mode, dial number that follows, go to on-line state
ATE	Controls character echo
ATH	Controls modem hang-up
ATI	Requests modem ID information
ATL	Controls speaker volume
ATM	Controls speaker response
ATO	Go to on-line state
ATQ	Controls result-codes
ATS	Sets modem S registers
ATV	Displays result-codes
ATX	Controls features respresented by result-codes
ATY	Disables long space disconnect
ATZ	Modem hang-up, restores all default settings
AT&C	Controls modem based on DCD (data carrier detect)
AT&D	Controls modem based on DTR (data terminal ready)
AT&F	Restores factory settings as active configuration
AT&G	No guard tone
AT&J	RJ-aa/RJ-41S/RJ-45S jack
AT&P	Pulse dial make and break ratio = 39/61
AT&Q	Operates in asynchronous mode

Table C.3: Summary of the AT Command Set Used by Hayes Modems
(Continued)

COMMAND	EXPLANATION
AT&R	Tracks CTS (clear to send) according to RTS (ready to send)
AT&S	Assumes presence of DSR (data set ready) signal
AT&T	Terminates presence of DSR signal
AT&V	Views current configuration
AT&Zn = x	Stores phone number x in location n

FACSIMILE TRANSMISSIONS

Facsimile transmission has been available over telephone lines for a long time. Fax standards were first established in the 1960s, by the European-based CCITT (International Consultative Committee on Telephone and Telegraph), and machines based on the group 1 standard took about 6 minutes to transmit one page. Group 2 fax machines cut this transmission time in half by the mid 1970s.

Modern fax machines are known as group 3 fax machines, and follow a standard introduced in the early 1980s. Group 3 machines use a 9600 bit-per-second half duplex modem to transfer data over standard telephone lines, and they use a data compression technique to make the transfer as fast as possible. Transmission times vary a great deal, but a typical page of text might take from 30 to 60 seconds. On poor phone lines the fax machine's modem will drop back to 7200 bps at first, then down to 4800 bps, and finally down to 2400 bps in an attempt to get the fax through.

As well as increases in speed, there have also been improvements in readability. Group 1 and group 2 fax machines had a resolution of about 100 dots per inch (dpi). Group 3 machines have a resolution of either 100 by 200 dpi in normal resolution or 200 by 200 dpi in fine resolution mode.

There is a group 4 fax standard, and these machines can send a page in 5 to 10 seconds at a resolution of up to 400 dpi. However, they require an all-digital telephone system, not expected to be commonly available until after the end of this century.

PC Tools Telecommunications offers the additional feature of sending binary files in nonfax mode to another computer using a similar fax card. This is done by using the 9600 bps modem (usually reserved for the fax transmission) as a regular modem. As there are no standards for 9600 bps modem transmissions, each manufacturer uses its own file-transfer protocol. This is why you have to have the same manufacturer's board at both ends of the link.

All the fax examples in this book were made using Intel Corporation's Connection CoProcessor fax card. The heart of this full-length card is a 10 MHz 80186 processor that allows true background fax transmission via the 9600 bps fax modem. The board also contains 256K of RAM so it doesn't need to use as much of the computer's main memory.

D

Memory-Resident
Programs

D

In this Appendix, I describe terminate and stay-resident (TSR) programs and memory-resident programs. I will detail the problems that they can cause and include some possible solutions.

WHAT IS A MEMORY-RESIDENT PROGRAM?

One of the major problems of MS-DOS is that it does not support more than one program running at a time. DOS is a single-user single-tasking operating system. In contrast to this, OS/2 is a single-user multi-tasking, and UNIX is a multiuser multi-tasking operating system. The terminate and stay-resident program is an ingenious method that at least partially overcomes this limitation in DOS.

A TSR program loads itself into memory and returns control to DOS, but waits in the background. When you press a certain key combination from the keyboard (the *hotkey*), the TSR interrupts the application you were running and gives instant access to its services. When you are finished with the TSR program, you return to your application program. You can run PC Shell, Desktop, or both programs in this TSR mode.

Other memory-resident programs in the PC Tools package work in a slightly different way. They attach themselves to the operating system and remain in memory, working constantly in the background, much like the DOS PRINT utility. Indeed, PRINT is often cited as the first real memory-resident program. PC-Cache is a program in this category, as is the small portion of the Mirror program that performs delete tracking. These programs work all the time, unlike PC Shell or Desktop, which are activated only when you press their hotkey.

You derive several major benefits to using TSR programs rather than programs loaded from the DOS command prompt (often called *transient applications*).

- Speed. You can access Notepads or Outlines to make a note to yourself, or use the calculators without leaving your main application. If you are using a large and complex application, you can save a significant amount of time.

- Configuration. Loading a selected set of utilities allows you to configure your own computing environment exactly as you want it, rather than having to work with several different large foreground applications that may contain features you never use.

- Data Exchange. You can capture data from your foreground application and paste it into the clipboard for later use in a word processor.

- Convenience. You have several programs accessible at virtually the same time.

PROBLEMS WITH TSR PROGRAMS

Microsoft has published preliminary guidelines for writing reliable TSRs, but they have not been universally accepted.

A main advantage of memory-resident programs is that they can be used together. However, these programs are often distributed by different manufacturers and there are no universally adopted standards for writing TSRs. Not surprisingly, conflicts occasionally arise between different TSR programs and between TSR programs and the main application.

COEXISTING WITH OTHER TSRS

If you use several TSRs, problems may arise because they do not coexist properly, sharing the same hardware and operating system. One delinquent TSR can disable your whole system, even causing you to lose data. Ideally, TSRs should be loaded into memory in sequence and should form an unbroken structure in which control is passed from program to program with no one being bypassed.

If you install a new TSR and one of your other TSRs stops working, the second program is probably interfering with the first. Loading order is often critical for certain TSR programs.

The recommended loading order for PC Tools is as follows:

- DOS internal commands (PROMPT, PATH, and so on)
- DOS external commands (MODE, PRINT, and so on)
- Mouse commands
- Print spoolers

- Mirror
- PC-Cache
- PC Shell
- PC Desktop
- Menu/Shell programs (1DIRplus, Direct Access, and so on)

To determine where programs are located in your computer's memory, use the Memory Map option in the Special menu of PC Shell. This lists the memory areas in use, the number of bytes (or kilobytes) in use by a program, and the name of the program using the memory.

Most TSRs are automatically loaded with the AUTOEXEC.BAT file. Some TSR installation programs change the contents of this file without telling you, which can sometimes lead to unexpected results. If you experience conflicts between programs after adding a new TSR to your system, you can start tracking down the culprit by executing the commands in your AUTOEXEC.BAT file one at a time from the DOS prompt. To isolate the problem, make sure that you don't load any TSR programs at all. You can do this by booting your computer from a DOS floppy disk that does not contain an AUTOEXEC.BAT file, and then making drive C the current drive. Enter the statements from your AUTOEXEC.BAT file that load your first TSR program. After loading the TSR, run it to test it. When it performs as desired, type in the next entry from your AUTOEXEC.BAT file to load the next TSR. Test this program and also test the TSR you loaded previously. Continue this process until you have loaded and tested all of your TSR programs. This method should help you find out which program is causing the problem.

You can also have hotkey conflict, where two programs are looking for the same key combination at the same time. The result is that the first program responds to the hotkey every time and the second program never sees the hotkey and therefore never runs. In both PC Shell and Desktop, you can change the hotkey specification to avoid this kind of conflict.

Memory space is always at a premium, and well-designed TSR programs should allow you to decide how much memory to allot to a particular application. Some TSR programs require that large areas of memory be permanently allocated for their use, but PC Tools uses only a small area of memory while dormant. When you use the hotkey, PC Tools saves the contents of your computer's memory into a temporary disk file. In this way, PC Tools occupies the smallest amount of space in memory when it is dormant, and can use all the memory needed when you activate it with the hotkey.

If you have expanded memory installed in your computer, PC Desktop uses it to store the image of the foreground application. This memory is cleared when you hotkey out of Desktop. With the optional parameters available for PC Tools programs, you can configure the PC Tools memory allocations to be optimum for your system.

Finally, well-designed TSR programs should check for double installation, and refuse to install themselves if they are already installed. This way, you avoid having multiple copies of a program in memory.

CONFLICTS WITH THE MAIN FOREGROUND APPLICATION

The main areas of conflict between TSR programs and foreground applications programs are the same as those between TSR programs themselves. Key conflicts can arise with your foreground application too. Some programs use esoteric key combinations to perform various functions, and sometimes these key combinations can interfere with or prevent the proper working of your TSR programs. For example, in WordStar you use the Ctrl key in combination with many other keys to perform text-manipulation commands. Your TSR program may require that same key combination for correct operation. Again, a well-designed TSR program that lets you choose the hotkey has the advantage here.

Memory can continue to be a problem, and you may find that you cannot load a particular application and its data file if you have too many TSR programs installed in your system. You may have to uninstall a TSR so that you can load your application and its data. You can always use the DOS CHKDSK command to check if you have sufficient memory available.

Restoring the correct video mode as you exit from the TSR can be a problem. The screen may fill with garbage characters. There can also be conflicts between programs running in text mode and in graphics mode returning the screen correctly.

REMOVING TSR PROGRAMS

Well-organized TSR programs can remove themselves from memory or uninstall themselves. In PC Tools, you can use a program called KILL to uninstall Desktop, PC Shell, and Backtalk, as long as they were the last memory-resident programs you loaded.

You can also remove a TSR program from your computer by removing from your AUTOEXEC.BAT file the commands that load the program and then rebooting your computer. This is a brutal approach, but with programs that don't have a removal mechanism, it is the only way to stop them from being loaded.

Another approach for releasing memory used by TSR programs is to use one of the TSR management utility programs, such as MARK or RELEASE, available as shareware from TurboPower Software. These programs manage multiple TSR programs (even programs from different vendors), and will release them from memory in the correct order.

Index

SYBEX®

TO JOIN THE SYBEX MAILING LIST OR ORDER BOOKS
PLEASE COMPLETE THIS FORM

NAME _____ COMPANY _____

STREET _____ CITY _____

STATE _____ ZIP _____

☐ PLEASE MAIL ME MORE INFORMATION ABOUT **SYBEX** TITLES

ORDER FORM (There is no obligation to order)

PLEASE SEND ME THE FOLLOWING:

TITLE	QTY	PRICE
_____	____	____
_____	____	____
_____	____	____
_____	____	____

TOTAL BOOK ORDER ____ $____

CUSTOMER SIGNATURE _____

SHIPPING AND HANDLING PLEASE ADD $2.00 PER BOOK VIA UPS _____

FOR OVERSEAS SURFACE ADD $5.25 PER BOOK PLUS $4.40 REGISTRATION FEE _____

FOR OVERSEAS AIRMAIL ADD $18.25 PER BOOK PLUS $4.40 REGISTRATION FEE _____

CALIFORNIA RESIDENTS PLEASE ADD APPLICABLE SALES TAX _____

TOTAL AMOUNT PAYABLE _____

☐ CHECK ENCLOSED   ☐ VISA
☐ MASTERCARD   ☐ AMERICAN EXPRESS

ACCOUNT NUMBER _____

EXPIR. DATE _____ DAYTIME PHONE _____

CHECK AREA OF COMPUTER INTEREST:

☐ BUSINESS SOFTWARE

☐ TECHNICAL PROGRAMMING

☐ OTHER: _____

THE FACTOR THAT WAS MOST IMPORTANT IN YOUR SELECTION:

☐ THE SYBEX NAME

☐ QUALITY

☐ PRICE

☐ EXTRA FEATURES

☐ COMPREHENSIVENESS

☐ CLEAR WRITING

☐ OTHER _____

OTHER COMPUTER TITLES YOU WOULD LIKE TO SEE IN PRINT:

_____

_____

OCCUPATION

☐ PROGRAMMER   ☐ TEACHER

☐ SENIOR EXECUTIVE   ☐ HOMEMAKER

☐ COMPUTER CONSULTANT   ☐ RETIRED

☐ SUPERVISOR   ☐ STUDENT

☐ MIDDLE MANAGEMENT   ☐ OTHER:

☐ ENGINEER/TECHNICAL   _____

☐ CLERICAL/SERVICE

☐ BUSINESS OWNER/SELF EMPLOYED

CHECK YOUR LEVEL OF COMPUTER USE

☐ NEW TO COMPUTERS

☐ INFREQUENT COMPUTER USER

☐ FREQUENT USER OF ONE SOFTWARE
   PACKAGE:
   NAME _____

☐ FREQUENT USER OF MANY SOFTWARE
   PACKAGES

☐ PROFESSIONAL PROGRAMMER

OTHER COMMENTS:

_____
_____
_____
_____
_____
_____
_____

PLEASE FOLD, SEAL, AND MAIL TO SYBEX

SYBEX, INC.
2021 CHALLENGER DR. #100
ALAMEDA, CALIFORNIA USA
                        94501

MENU COMMANDS AND KEYBOARD SHORTCUTS

COMMANDS	KEYBOARD SHORTCUTS	COMMANDS	KEYBOARD SHORTCUTS	COMMANDS	KEYBOARD SHORTCUTS
PC DESKTOP (cont.)		PC DESKTOP (cont.)		PC DESKTOP (cont.)	
†Check the FAX Log		†Video size		Financial registers	F5
Actions		Switch Active		Data registers	F6
Delete the Selected		Move		Window	
Entry		Resize		Change colors	
Search		Zoom		†Video size	
Configure		Clipboard		Switch active	
FAX Drive		File		Move	
AutoUpdate		Print		Programmer's (hex)	
Window		Copy/Paste		calculator	
Change colors		Paste from Clipboard		*HEX	
Video size		Copy to Clipboard		*OCTAL	
Switch Active		†Set Playback Delay		*BINARY	
Move		Edit		*DECIMAL	
Resize		Erase block		†RegisterDisplay	
Zoom		Mark block		Stack registers	
Macro Editor		Unmark block		Data registers	
File		Delete all text		Window	
Load	F4	Insert file		Change colors	
Save	F5	Goto		†Video size	
Autosave		Search		Switch active	
Macro activation	F8	Find	F6	Move	
Edit		Replace	F7	Scientific calculator	
Cut to clipboard		Window		Register Display	
Copy to clipboard		Change colors		Stack Registers	F4
Paste from clipboard		†Video size		Data Registers	F6
Mark block		Switch Active		Window	
Unmark block		Move		Change colors	
Delete all text		Resize		†Video size	
Insert file		Zoom		Switch active	
Goto		Calculators		Move	
Search		Algebraic calculator		Utilities	
Find	F6	Options		Hotkey selection	
Replace		Clear Display	F4	Window	
Controls		Erase Tape	F5	Change colors	
Erase all macros		Copy to Clipboard		†Video size	
Playback delay		Print tape		Move	
Learn mode		Wide Display		Ascii table	
Save setup		Window		Window	
Window		Change colors		Change colors	
Change colors		†Video size		†Video size	
		Switch active		Move	
		Move		System menu/window	
*Version 5.5 only		Financial calculator		colors	
†Version 6.0 only		RegisterDisplay		Unload PCTOOLS	
		Stack registers	F4	Desktop	